Studies in Perception and Action IV

Ninth International Conference on Perception and Action

July 20-25, 1997

Toronto, Ontario, Canada

Studies in Perception and Action IV

Ninth International Conference on Perception and Action

July 20-25, 1997

Toronto, Ontario, Canada

Edited by

Mark A. Schmuckler
University of Toronto at Scarborough
Scarborough, Ontario, Canada

John M. Kennedy
University of Toronto at Scarborough
Scarborough, Ontario, Canada

LEA LAWRENCE ERLBAUM ASSOCIATES, PUBLISHERS
1997   MAHWAH, NEW JERSEY

Lawrence Erlbaum Associates, Inc., Publishers
10 Industrial Avenue
Mahwah, New Jersey 07430

Library of Congress Cataloging-in-Publication Data

International Conference on Perception and Action (9th : 1997 :
Toronto, Ont.)
    Studies in perception and action IV / Ninth International
Conference on Perception and Action : July 20-25 1997, Toronto,
Ontario, Canada : edited by Mark A. Schmuckler, John M. Kennedy.
        p.   cm.
    Includes bibliographical references and indexes.
    ISBN 0-8058-2872-9 (alk. paper)
    1. Perceptual-motor processes--Congresses. 2. Perception--
Congresses.   I. Schmuckler, Mark A. II. Kennedy, John M. (John
Miller), 1942-   . III. Title.
BF295.I58 1997
152.1--dc21   97-17261
                                                   CIP

Printed in the United States of America

10 9 8 7 6 5 4 3 2 1

Table of Contents

I.C Haptics and Touch

Section II. Perception-Action Coupling

II.A Affordances

Section III: Action

III.A Patterns of Coordination

III.B. Movement and Dynamics

III.C *Posture and Locomotion*

Preface

This book is the fourth volume in the "Studies in Perception and Action" series, and contains a collection of posters presented at the Ninth International Conference on Perception and Action, held in Toronto, Ontario, Canada, July 20th - 25th, 1997. The previous poster books accompanied conferences at Marseille (1995), Vancouver (1993) and Amsterdam (1991). The conference is sponsored by the International Society for Ecological Psychology.

Like its predecessor, *Studies in Perception and Action IV* is a collection of short reports, mostly empirical in nature. The reports are considerably larger than the abstracts presented in the Proceedings of many conferences, and provide the authors with an opportunity to present an argument, method, results and conclusion in a condensed form. In effect, these are miniature articles, as previous editors in this series stressed.

This book follows closely the format established in previous volumes, particularly the structure of the 1995 book edited by B. Bardy, R. J. Bootsma, and Y. Guiard. Thus, there are three sections, beginning with perception, ending with action, and, bridging the two, perception-action coupling. Each of these sections are subdivided. Perception contains sections on vision, audition, and haptics and touch; Perception-Action Coupling contains sections on affordances, visually-guided actions, and intermodal and perceptual-motor coordination; and Action contains sections on patterns of coordination, movement and dynamics, and posture and locomotion. One might think that categorizing papers in such sections would be a straightforward endeavor; in practice, however, the task proved quite difficult. Some research defied classification into our categories; others spanned multiple categories, producing numerous areas of overlap between sections. Accordingly, our classifications are rough, and may reflect our own (occasionally limited) knowledge of the topic under study. To aid readers, we have included an index of keywords for these papers. We hope that this index provides additional help in finding related research.

Putting together a book such as this is daunting. The logistics of coordinating a large collection of papers is the stuff of which editors' nightmares are made. This volume contains 86 reports, generally in keeping with the number of papers appearing in previous volumes. We have edited these papers sparingly. Because this series depends on submissions made in January for a midsummer conference, we have had no more than two months for editing and preparation of camera-ready pages if the volume was to be available at the conference. Maintaining high standards in the content and style of these poster books depends on the authors presenting coherent, polished, and carefully-worded text. We are impressed with the quality of the submissions, and believe this volume is a worthy continuation of the series. We also note the extent to which the reports complement each other. They suggest a scientific discipline that, although far-ranging, is integrated and making significant progress, with precision of thought, apt procedures and clear measurements. In our lives as busy teachers and scholars, we do not often have the chance to sample widely from the table of scientific inquiry; we urge those of you receiving this book to take advantage of the opportunities this volume affords.

We appreciated aid and support from William Mace, from the International Society for Ecological Psychology. We benefited a great deal from colleagues at the University of Toronto at Scarborough, with website maintenance by William Barek, registration procedures managed by Jack Martin, work on graphics by Diane Gradowski, moral support from Colin MacLeod, the Chair of Life Sciences, and encouragement and financial support from Principal Paul Thompson.

Mark A Schmuckler
John M. Kennedy
Toronto, Ontario, Canada
March 31, 1997

Contributors

Karen E. Adolph, Department of Psychology, Carnegie Mellon University, Pittsburgh, PA 15213-3890, U.S.A. (adolph@andrew.cmu.edu)

Martha Wagner Alibali, Department of Psychology, Carnegie Mellon University, Pittsburgh, PA 15213-3890, U.S.A.

Thomas R. Alley, Department of Psychology, 418 Brackett Hall, Clemson University, Clemson, SC 29634-1511, U.S.A. (alley@clemson.edu)

Eric L. Amazeen, Faculty of Human Movement Sciences, Vrije Universiteit, Amsterdam, The Netherlands (e_amazeen@fbw.vu.nl)

Polemnia G. Amazeen, Faculty of Human Movement Sciences, Vrije Universiteit, Amsterdam, The Netherlands (p_amazeen@fbw.vu.nl)

Krista L. Anderson, CESPA, Department of Psychology, University of Connecticut, U-20, 406 Babbidge Road, Storrs, CT 06269-1020, U.S.A. (KLA95004@UconnVM.uconn.edu)

Jeffrey T. Andre, Whitely Psychology Laboratories, Franklin & Marshall College, Lancaster PA 17604-3003, U.S.A. (j_andre@acad.fandm.edu)

Anthony M. Avolio, Department of Psychology, Carnegie Mellon University, Pittsburgh, PA 15213-3890, U.S.A.

Edward Baines, School of Cognitive and Computing Sciences, University of Sussex, Brighton, BN1 9QH, U.K. (edb@cogs.susx.ac.uk)

Frank C. Bakker, Institute for Fundamental and Clinical Human Movement Sciences, Faculty of Human Movement Sciences, Vrije Universiteit, Van de Boechorststraat 9, 1081 BT, Amsterdam, The Netherlands (F_C_Bakker@FBW.VU.NL)

Benoît G. Bardy, Mouvement et Perception, University of the Mediterranean, Faculty of Sport Sciences, 163 Avenue de Luminy, 13288 Marseille cedex 09, France

Peter J. Beek, Faculty of Human Movement Sciences, Vrije Universiteit, Van der Boechorststraat 9, 1081 BT Amsterdam, The Netherlands (P_J_Beek@fbw.vu.nl)

Angela Belden, Department of Psychology, University of Arkansas at Little Rock, 2801 South University, Little Rock, AR 72204-1099, U.S.A.

Simon Bennett, Department of Exercise and Sport Science, Manchester Metropolitan University, Alsager, U.K. (S.J.Bennett@mmu.ac.uk)

Cathi T. Best, Wesleyan University and Haskins Laboratories, U.S.A.

Geoffrey Bingham, Department of Psychology, Indiana University, Bloomington, IN 47405, U.S.A. (gbingham@indiana.edu)

Alana Blumental, Department of Psychology, Miami University, Oxford, OH 45056, U.S.A.

Mireille Bonnard, Mouvement et Perception, CNRS, Université de la Méditerranée, Faculté des Sciences du Sport, Marseille, France

Reinoud J. Bootsma, Mouvement & Perception, University of the Mediterranean, Faculty of Sport Sciences, 163 Avenue de Luminy, 13288 Marseille cedex 09, France

Mark F. Bradshaw, Department of Psychology, University of Surrey, Guildford, GU2 5XH, U.K. (m.bradshaw@currey.ac.uk)

Lawrence Brancazio, University of Connecticut, Department of Psychology, Box U-20, 406, Babbidge Rd., Storrs, CT 06268, U.S.A. (lab93006@uconnvm.uconn.edu)

Michael Broderick, Université de Poiters and Department of Kinesiology, Pennsylvania State University, 109 White Building, University Park, PA 16802 U.S.A. (mpb3@psu.edu)

Frank Brown, Department of Psychology, University of Arkansas at Little Rock, 2801 South University, Little Rock, AR 72204-1099, U.S.A.

Kotoe Bruce, Department of Psychology, East Carolina University, Greenville, NC 27858, U.S.A.

Megan M. Burke, CESPA, Department of Psychology, University of Connecticut, Box U-20, 406, Babbidge Rd., Storrs, CT 06268, U.S.A.

Catherine M. Burns, Cognitive Engineering Laboratory, Department of Mechanical and Industrial Engineering, University of Toronto, Toronto, ON, Canada

Chris Button, Department of Exercise and Sport Science, Manchester Metropolitan University, Alsager, U.K.

Matthew Butwill, CESPA, Department of Psychology, University of Connecticut, U-20, 406 Babbidge Road, Storrs, CT 06269-1020, U.S.A. (MTB95001@UconnVM.uconn.edu)

Claudia Carello, CESPA, Department of Psychology, University of Connecticut, Box U-20, 406 Babbidge Road, Storrs, CT 06269-1020, U.S.A. (cespa1@uconnvm.uconn.edu)

Carly Cenedella, Department of Psychology, Carnegie Mellon University, Pittsburgh, PA 15213-3890, U.S.A.

Paola Cesari, Department of Kinesiology, Pennsylvania State University, State College, PA 16802, U.S.A.

Avi Chaudhuri, Department of Psychology, McGill University, 1205 Dr. Penfield Avenue, Montreal, Quebec H3A 1B1 Canada (chang@ego.psych.mcgill.ca)

Yann Coello, Laboratoire de Psychologie Cognitive, Départment de Psychologie, Université Lille-3, BP 149, 59653 Villeneuce d'Ascq, France (coello@univ-lille3.fr)

David R. Collins, CESPA, Department of Psychology, University of Connecticut, U-20, 406 Babbidge Road, Storrs, CT 06268, U.S.A. (drc93001@uconnvm.uconn.edu)

Alan Costall, Department of Psychology, King Henry Building, University of Portsmouth, Portsmouth PO1 2DY, U.K. (costalla@psyc.port.ac.uk)

Cathy M. Craig, Department of Psychology, University of Edinburgh, EH8 9JZ, Scotland

Sarah H. Creem, Department of Psychology, University of Virginia, Charlottesville, VA, U.S.A.

Marvin J. Dainoff, Department of Psychology, Miami University, Oxford, OH, U.S.A.

Frédéric Danion, Mouvement et Perception, CNRS, Université de la Méditerranée, Faculté des Sciences du Sport, Marseille, France

Keith Davids, Department of Exercise and Sport Science, Manchester Metropolitan University, Alsager, U.K.

Alyson M. Davis, University of Surrey, Department of Psychology, Guildford, Surrey GU2 5XH, U.K. (adavis@surrey.ac.uk)

Bart De Bruyn, Department of Psychology, University of Surrey, Guildford, GU2 5XH, U.K.

M. Della-Grasta, Mouvement et Perception, CNRS and University of the Mediterranean, Faculty of Sport Sciences, 163 Avenue de Luminy, 13009 Marseille, France.

Cathy Dent-Read, Center for the Study of Women, University of California, Los Angeles, CA, U.S.A. (cdent@ucla.edu)

D. Michael Deron, Psychology Department, Northeast Louisiana University, Monroe, LA 71209, U.S.A.

Kerri G. Donahue, Department of Psychology, 418 Brackett Hall, Clemson University, Clemson, SC 29634-1511, U.S.A.

Andrew P. Duchon, Department of Cognitive and Linguistic Science, Brown University, Providence, RI 02906-1978, U.S.A. (duchon@cog.brown.edu)

Heather Edkins, Department of Psychology, Miami University, Oxford, OH 45056 U.S.A.

Marion Eppler, Department of Psychology, East Carolina University, Greenville, NC 27858, U.S.A.

Molly Erdahl, University of Minnesota, Institute of Child Development, 51 East River Road, Minneapolis, MN 55455, U.S.A.

Brett R. Fajen, CESPA, Department of Psychology, University of Connecticut, Box U-20, Storrs, CT 06269-1020, U.S.A. (brf93003@uconnvm.uconn.edu)

M. Farell, Movement et Perception, CNRS and University of the Mediterranean, Faculty of Sport Sciences, 163 Avenue de Luminy, 13009 Marseille, France.

Paula Fitzpatrick, Department of Psychology, Assumption College, Worcester, MA 01615, U.S.A.

Ittai Flascher, Department of Psychology, Indiana University, Bloomington, IN 47405, U.S.A.

Steven B. Flynn, Psychology Department, Northeast Louisiana University, Monroe, LA 71209, U.S.A. (psflynn@alpha.nlu.edu)

Florent Fouque, Mouvement et Perception, University of the Mediterranean, Faculty of Sport Sciences, Box 910, 163 Avenue de Luminy, 13009 Marseille, France

Carol A. Fowler, Department of Psychology, University of Connecticut, Box U-20, 406, Babbidge Rd., Storrs, CT 06268, U.S.A.

Douglas L. Gardner, Department of Psychology, Miami University, Oxford, OH 45056 U.S.A.

Piper Goodspeed, Department of Psychology, University of Arkansas at Little Rock, 2801 South University, Little Rock, AR 72204-1099, U.S.A.

Kathleen M. Gorday, Department of Psychology, University of Cincinnati, Cincinnati, OH 45221-0376, U.S.A.

Joanna K. Graham, University of Surrey, Department of Psychology, Guildford, Surrey GU2 5XH, U.K.

Kelly Grandt, Department of Psychology, Miami University, Oxford, OH 45056, U.S.A.

Christopher D. Green, Department of Psychology, York University, North York, ON M3J 1P3, Canada (christo@yorku.ca)

Richard P. Grutzmacher, Whitely Psychology Laboratories, Franklin & Marshall College, Lancaster, PA 17604-3003, U.S.A.

Jennifer L. Hankins, Department of Psychology, Illinois State University, Normal, IL 61790-4620, U.S.A.

Dorothy Heffernan, Department of Psychology, University of Strathclyde, Glasgow, Scotland (chhp15@pop-hub.strath.ac.uk)

Timothy Hirons, Department of Psychology, Miami University, Oxford, OH 45056, U.S.A.

Rainer Hoeger, Department of Psychology, Ruhr-University Bochum, F.R.G. (hoegerbq@rz.ruhr-uni-bochum.de)

Floris Holsheimer, Institute for Fundamental and Clinical Human Movement Sciences, Faculty of Human Movement Sciences, Vrije Universiteit, Van de Boechorststraat 9, 1081 BT, Amsterdam, The Netherlands

Barry Hughes, Department of Psychology, University of Auckland, Private Bag 92019, Auckland, New Zealand (b.hughes@auckland.ac.nz)

Gil Hupert-Graff, Research Center for Work Safety and Human Engineering, Technion - IIT, 32000 Haifa, Israel

Kiyohide Ito, Institute of Special Education, University of Tsukuba, 2-1 Tennoudai, Tsukuba, Ibaraki 305, Japan (SGK01206@niftyserve.or.jp)

Jason Jordan, Department of Psychology, University of Arkansas at Little Rock, 2801 South University, Little Rock, AR 72204-1099, U.S.A.

Peter Juslin, Department of Psychology, Uppsala University, Box 1225, S-75142 Uppsala, Sweden (Peter.Juslin@psyk.uu.se)

Astrid M. L. Kappers, Helmholtz Instituut, Princetonplein 5, 3584 CC Utrecht, The Netherlands (a.m.l.kappers@fys.ruu.nl)

Bruce A. Kay, Department of Cognitive & Linguistic Sciences, Box 1978, Brown University, Providence, RI 02912-1978 U.S.A.

J. A. Scott Kelso, Center for Complex Systems, Florida Atlantic University, Boca Raton, FL 33431, U.S.A. (kelso@walt.ccs.fau.edu)

John M. Kennedy, Department of Psychology, University of Toronto at Scarborough, Scarborough, ON M1C 1A4, Canada (kennedy@banks.scar.utoronto.ca)

Nam-Gyoon Kim, CESPA, Department of Psychology, Box U-20, University of Connecticut, Storrs, CT 06269-1020, U.S.A.

Jan J. Koenderink, Helmholtz Instituut, Princetonplein 5, 3584 CC Utrecht, The Netherlands (j.j.koenderink@fys.ruu.nl)

Alissa J. Kramen, Department of Psychology, Illinois State University, Normal, IL 61790-4620, U.S.A.

Itsuo Kumazawa, Department of Computer Science, Tokyo Institute of Technology, Meguro-ku, Tokyo 152 Japan

M. Laurent, Movement et Perception, CNRS and University of the Mediterranean, Faculty of Sport Sciences, 163 Avenue de Luminy, 13009 Marseille, France.

David N. Lee, Department of Psychology, University of Edinburgh, Scotland (d.n.lee@ed.ac.uk)

François-Xavier Li, University of Birmingham, School of Sport and Exercise Sciences, Edgbaston, Birmingham B15 2TT, U.K. (lifx@sportex.bham.ac.uk)

Li Li, Department of Cognitive & Linguistic Sciences, Box 1978, Brown University, Providence, RI 02912 (lili@cog.brown.edu)

Chang Hong Liu, Department of Psychology, McGill University, 1205 Dr. Penfield Avenue, Montreal, Quebec H3A 1B1, Canada, (chang@ego.psych.mcgill.ca)

Pierre Magne, Laboratoire de Psychologie Cognitive, Départment de Psychologie, Université Lille-3, BP 149, 59653 Villeneuce d'Ascq, France

Ludovic Marin, Mouvement et Perception, University of the Mediterranean, Faculty of Sport Sciences, 163 Avenue de Luminy, 13288 Marseille cedex 09, France

Leonard Mark, Department of Psychology, Miami University, Oxford, OH 45056, U.S.A. (lm24psyf@miamiu.acs.muohio.edu)

Daniel S. McConnell, Department of Psychology, Perception-Action Laboratory, Indiana University, Bloomington, IN 47405, U.S.A. (dsmcconn@ucs.indiana.edu)

Keith McGregor, Department of Psychology, Box 176A, 1 College St., College of the Holy Cross, Worcester, MA 01610-2395, U.S.A.

Joachim Meyer, Department of Industrial Engineering and Management, Ben Gurion, University of the Negev, P.O. Box 653, Beer Sheva 84105, Israel (joachim@bgumail.bgu.ac.il)

Claire F. Michaels, Faculty of Human Movement Sciences, Vrije Universiteit, van der Boechorststraat 9, 1081 BT, Amsterdam, The Netherlands (j_f_stins@fbw.vu.nl)

Giuseppe Mirabella, Department of Psychology, University of Toronto at Scarborough, Scarborough, ON M1C 1A4, Canada

Suvobrata Mitra, CESPA, Department of Psychology, U-20, University of Connecticut, 406 Babbidge Road, Storrs, CT 06269 U.S.A. (riley@indra.psy.uconn.edu)

Masami Miyazaki, Lab. Applied Environmental Physiology, Department of Health Sciences, School of Human Sciences, Waseda University, 2-579-15, Mikajima, Tokorozawa, Saitama 359, Japan. URL<http://alpha564.human.waseda.ac.jp>

Michael M. Muchisky, Perception-Action Laboratory, Department of Psychology, Indiana University, Bloomington, IN 47405, U.S.A.

Karl Newell, Department of Kinesiology, Pennsylvania State University, 109 White Building, University Park, PA 16802 U.S.A.

Henrik Olsson, Department of Psychology, Uppsala University, Box 1225, S-75142 Uppsala, Sweden (Henrik.Olsson@psyk.uu.se)

Amanda M. Olson, Department of Psychology, 418 Brackett Hall, Clemson University, Clemson, SC 29634-1511, U.S.A.

D. Alfred Owens, Whitely Psychology Laboratories, Franklin & Marshall College, Lancaster PA 17604-3003, U.S.A. (j_andre@acad.fandm.edu)

Janina Paasche, Department of Psychology, Miami University, Oxford, OH 45056 U.S.A.

Christopher C. Pagano, Department of Psychology, Clemson University, Clemson, SC 29634-1511, U.S.A. (cpagano@clemson.edu)

Randy J. Pagulayan, Department of Psychology, University of Cincinnati, Cincinnati, OH 45221-0376, U.S.A.

Jean Pailhous, Mouvement et Perception, CNRS, Université de la Méditerranée, Faculté des Sciences du Sport, Marseille, France

Hyeongsaeng Park, CESPA, University of Connecticut, Box U-20, 406 Babbidge Road, Storrs, CT 06269-1020, U.S.A.

Bernard Pavis, Cognitive and Behavioral Neuroscience Group, Université de Poiters, 4 Allée Jean Monnet, 86000 Poiters, France (pavis@zeus.univ-poitiers.fr)

Melanie A. Pearson, Department of Psychology, Clemson University, Clemson, SC 29634-1511, U.S.A.

Andrew J. Peck, CESPA, University of Connecticut, U-20, 406 Babbidge Road, Storrs, CT 06269-1020, U.S.A.

C. (Lieke) E. Peper, Faculty of Human Movement Sciences, Vrije Universiteit, Van der Boechorststraat 9, 1081 BT Amsterdam, The Netherlands (C_E_Peper@fbw.vu.nl)

Gert-Jan Pepping, University of Birmingham, School of Sport and Exercise Sciences, Edgbaston, Birmingham B15 2TT, U.K. (g.j.pepping@bham.ac.uk)

J.R. (Rob) Pijpers, Institute for Fundamental and Clinical Human Movement Sciences, Faculty of Human Movement Sciences, Vrije Universiteit, Van de Boechorststraat 9, 1081 BT, Amsterdam, The Netherlands (J_R_Pijpers@FBW.VU.NL)

John Pittenger, Department of Psychology, University of Arkansas at Little
  Rock, 2801 South University, Little Rock, AR 72204-1099, U.S.A
  (jbpittenger@ualr.edu)

Tjasa Planinsek, Faculty of Education, University of Ljubljana, Slovenia

Sylvia C. Pont, Helmholtz Instituut, Princetonplein 5, 3584 CC Utrecht, The
  Netherlands (S.Pont@fys.ruu.nl)

Auke Post, Institute for Fundamental and Clinical Human Movement Sciences,
  Faculty of Human Movement Sciences, Vrije Universiteit, Van der
  Boechorststraat 9, NL - 1081 BT Amsterdam (a_a_post@fbw.vu.nl)

Dennis R. Proffitt, Department of Psychology, University of Virginia,
  Charlottesville, VA 22906-2477, U.S.A.

Gordon M. Redding, Department of Psychology, Illinois State University,
  Campus Box 4620, Normal, IL 61790-4620, U.S.A.
  (gredding@rs6000.cmp.ilstu.edu)

Michael A. Riley, CESPA, Department of Psychology, University of
  Connecticut, U-20, 406 Babbidge Road, Storrs, CT 06269, U.S.A.
  (riley@indra.psy.uconn.edu)

Rocco Ross, University of Minnesota, Institute of Child Development, 51 East
  River Road, Minneapolis, MN 55455, U.S.A.

Amy Rouse, Department of Psychology, Miami University, Oxford, OH 45056,
  U.S.A.

Sverker Runeson, Department of Psychology, Uppsala University, Box 1225,
  S-75142 Uppsala, Sweden (Sverker.Runeson@psyk.uu.se)

Heather F. Russell, Psychology Department, Northeast Louisiana University,
  Monroe, LA 71209, U.S.A.

Michael K. Russell, CESPA, Department of Psychology, University of
  Connecticut, Box U-20, 406 Babbidge Road, Storrs, CT 06269, U.S.A.
  (mrussell@uconnvm.uconn.edu)

Julie C. Rutkowska, School of Cognitive and Computing Sciences, University
  of Sussex, Brighton, BN1 9QH, U.K.

Marie-Vee Santana, CESPA, Department of Psychology, University of
  Connecticut, 406 Babbidge Road, Box U-20, Storrs, CT 06269-1020,
  U.S.A. (mas94008@uconnvm.uconn.edu)

Takeshi Sato, Lab. Applied Environmental Physiology, Department of Health
  Sciences, School of Human Sciences, Waseda University, 2-579-15,
  Mikajima, Tokorozawa, Saitama 359, Japan (sato@human.waseda.ac.jp)
  URL<http://alpha564.human.waseda.ac.jp>

Tammy Satterwhite, Department of Psychology, East Carolina University, Greenville, NC 27858, U.S.A.

Geert Savelsbergh, Faculty of Human Movement Sciences, Free University, Amsterdam, and Research Institute for Fundamental and Clinical Human Movement Sciences, Amsterdam/Nijmegen, The Netherlands (g_j_p_savelsbergh@fbw.vu.nl)

R. C. Schmidt, Department of Psychology, Box 176A, 1 College St., College of the Holy Cross, Worcester, MA 01610-2395, U.S.A.

Mark A. Schmuckler, Division of Life Sciences, University of Toronto at Scarborough, Scarborough, ON M1C 1A4, Canada (marksch@banks.scar.utoronto.ca)

Lisa Sconzo, Department of Psychology, 127 Hofstra University, Hempstead, NY 11550 U.S.A.

Yang-Yi Sheng, Department of Psychology, University of Cincinnati, Cincinnati, OH 45221-0376, U.S.A.

Takako Shiratori, Department of Kinesiology, Pennsylvania State University, State College, PA 16802, U.S.A. (txs192@email.psu.edu)

Marty Sobel, Department of Psychology, 127 Hofstra University, Hempstead, NY 11550, U.S.A.

L. J. Smart, Department of Psychology, University of Cincinnati, Cincinnati, OH 45221-0376, U.S.A.

Catherine S. Stergiou, Department of Psychology, Carnegie Mellon University, Pittsburgh, PA 15213-3890, U.S.A.

Jennifer A. Stevens, Department of Psychology, Emory University, Atlanta, GA, U.S.A. (jstev02@curly.cc.emory.edu)

John F. Stins, Faculty of Human Movement Sciences, Vrije Universiteit, van der Boechorststraat 9, 1081 BT, Amsterdam, The Netherlands (j_f_stins@fbw.vu.nl)

Thomas A. Stoffregen, Department of Psychology, University of Cincinnati, Cincinnati, OH 45221-0376, U.S.A. (stoffrta@email.uc.edu)

Matthew Stroop, CESPA, Department of Psychology, University of Connecticut, 406 Babbidge Road, Box U-20, Storrs, CT 06269-1020, U.S.A. (mas94007@uconnvm.uconn.edu)

Kei Suzuki, Department of Computer Science, Tokyo Institute of Technology, Meguro-ku, Tokyo 152, Japan

Agnes Szokolszky, Department of Psychology, Attila József University, 2000 Szentendre, Levendula u.15., Szeged, Hungary (szokol@izabell.elte.hu)

J. Jacques Temprado, Mouvement et Perception, CNRS and University of the Mediterranean, Faculty of Sport Sciences, 163 Avenue de Luminy, 13009 Marseille, France.

James A. Thomson, Department of Psychology, University of Strathclyde, Glasgow, Scotland.

Paul J. Treffner, Deptartment of Psychology, University of Southern Queensland, Toowoomba, Australia (treffner@usq.edu.au)

Hannah Y. Tsang, Division of Life Sciences, University of Toronto at Scarborough, Scarborough, ON M1C 1A4, Canada

Richard A. Tyrrell, Department of Psychology, Clemson University, Clemson, SC 29634-1511, U.S.A. (Tyrrell@Clemson.edu)

S. Stavros Valenti, Department of Psychology, 127 Hofstra University, Hempstead, NY 11550 U.S.A. (psyssv@vaxc.hofstra.edu)

John van der Kamp, Faculty of Human Movement Sciences, Free University, Van der Boechorststraat 9, 1081 BT, Amsterdam, and Research Institute for Fundamental and Clinical Human Movement Sciences, Amsterdam/Nijmegen, The Netherlands (J_van_der_Kamp@fbw.vu.nl)

Richard E. A. van Emmerik, Department of Exercise Science, University of Massachusetts, 160 Totman building, Amherst, MA 01003, U.S.A (rvanemmerik@excsci.umass.edu)

Erwin E. H. van Wegen, Department of Exercise Science, University of Massachusetts, 160 Totman building, Amherst, MA 01003, U.S.A

Ingrid M. L. C. Vogels, Helmholtz Instituut, Princetonplein 5, 3584 CC Utrecht, The Netherlands (i.m.c.vogels@fys.ruu.nl)

Robert C. Wagenaar, Department of Physical Therapy, Vrije Universiteit Hospital, Amsterdam, The Netherlands

Ken K. Wagner, Department of Psychology, 127 Hofstra University, Hempstead, NY 11550, U.S.A.

William H. Warren, Department of Cognitive & Linguistic Sciences, Box 1978, Brown University, Providence, RI 02912-1978, U.S.A. (Bill_Warren@brown.edu)

Jeff Wendt, Department of Psychology, East Carolina University, Greenville, NC 27858, U.S.A. (grwendt@ecuvm.cis.ecu.edu)

Emily A. Wickelgren, Department of Psychology, Perception-Action Laboratory, Indiana University, Bloomington, IN 47405, U.S.A. (ewickelg@othello.ucs.indiana.edu)

Maryjane Wraga, Department of Psychology, University of Virginia, Charlottesville, VA 22903-2477, U.S.A. (mjw4f@faraday.clas.virginia.edu)

Albert Yonas, University of Minnesota, Institute of Child Development, 51 East River Road, Minneapolis, MN 55455, U.S.A. (yonas@turtle.psych.umn.edu)

Frank T. J. M. Zaal, Department of Psychology, Indiana University, Bloomington, IN 47405, U.S.A.

Patricia Zukow-Goldring, Center for the Study of Women, 276 Kinsey Hall, 405 Hilgard Avenue, University of California, Los Angeles, CA 90095-1504, U.S.A. (zukow@ucla.edu)

Section I: *Perception*

I.A: *Vision*

Studies in Perception and Action IV
M. A. Schmuckler & J. M. Kennedy (Eds.)
© 1997 Lawrence Erlbaum Associates, Inc.

Perception Of Lifted Weight In Photographs And Stick-Figure Displays

S. Stavros Valenti[1], Lisa Sconzo[1], & Alan Costall[2]

[1] Department of Psychology, Hofstra University, Hempstead, NY, U.S.A.
[2] Department of Psychology, University of Portsmouth, Portsmouth, U.K.

Numerous investigations have shown that the perception of dynamics can be supported by kinematic (movement) patterns alone (e.g., Valenti & Costall, 1997). The success of experiments on the *kinematic specification of dynamics* in animate and nonanimate events have led some writers, perhaps unintentionally, to underestimate the informativeness of static configurations of the human form. In the domain of art, however, writers have long maintained that static images convey dynamics (e.g., Arnheim, 1988). The key problem for painters and sculptors is how best to bring an awareness of animacy in the viewer.

Two opposing approaches to movement depiction in art have been discussed by artists and philosophers. One is to deliberately blend postures of the subject, so as to show "attitudes unstably suspended between a before and after" (Merleau-Ponty, 1961/1964, p. 184). This approach was favored by Rodin who argued that the path of the observer's gaze would reveal, over time, the progression of action in the depicted event, such as the striding *Saint John the Baptist*. As Gsell described in his conversations with Rodin, "the science of the sculptor has consisted precisely in imposing all of these facts (about the depicted action, e.g., the walking of Saint John) upon the spectator in the order in which I have stated them, so that their succession will give the impression of movement" (Rodin, 1957/1983, p. 33). While we know of no empirical investigations on the effectiveness of blending of postures in static depictions of action, this may be an interesting avenue of research for students of the psychology of visual arts.

The other approach is to capture the true, exact postures or "attitudes" of the human or beast, as can be seen in some of the paintings of Degas, Eakins, or Remington following the development of instantaneous photography. Although it is clear that many painters of human or animal motion employed instantaneous photographs soon after Muybridge promoted his photographic technique in the 1880's, the use of photographically literal depictions ("Muybridgism") was most often regarded by painters and photographers as unaesthetic and ineffective in the depiction of action (Scharf, 1974). Nonetheless, our own research on instantaneous photographs has shown impressive levels of visual weight discrimination based on static views of certain phases of the activity of lifting and carrying, these levels approximating that obtained with videotapes of the entire lifting-carrying event (Valenti & Costall, 1997). Some photographically "frozen" samples of the optic array, it appears, are sufficiently rich in structure to specify the original event dynamics, although it is not yet clear which aspects of structure support the perception of dynamics in these static displays.

The purpose of the current study was to determine if posture alone, in the absence of facial expressions or muscular strains, would support the perception of the dynamics of a lifting-carrying event.

Method

Sixteen observers on three separate sessions viewed 40 photographs and 40 stick figures of an actor lifting and walking with a weighted box, and provided estimates of lifted weight in pounds. Sets of displays, randomized and arranged in small photo albums, yielded factorial combinations of four variables: Actor (2 levels) X phase of action (lift, walk) X box weight (1, 8, 16, 24, 31 kg) X repetitions (4 levels). Observers viewed displays from one actor on Sessions 1 and 2, and a transfer set from the second actor on Session 3. Half of the observers received feedback on Session 2 whenever their judgments were within 10 pounds of the actual weight.

The photographs, generated from still frames of a videotape of the original lifting-carrying event, were taken from two distinct action phases: lift and walk. Stick figures were traced from the still video frames through the use of a computer drawing program and a video-RGB mixer.

Results

Figure 1 presents boxplots of correlations of perceived and actual box weight, the principal measure of weight discrimination accuracy as a function of action phase and display type. Although photographs yielded better performance than the minimal displays of posture in the stick figures, the pattern of performance across action phases is the same and is consistent with

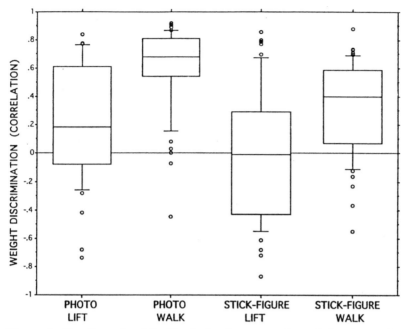

Figure 1. Boxplots of weight discrimination scores (correlations) as a function of display type and action phase.

previous studies from our laboratory: Displays of lifting yielded lower performance than did displays of walking. Analysis of variance revealed reliable effects only for display type, $F(1,14) = 55.40$, $p < .001$, and for phase of action, $F(1,14) = 18.29$, $p < .001$. The effects of feedback condition, session, and their interactions were not reliable.

Discussion

The minimal stick-figure displays of a person carrying a box yielded modest group performance, with correlation coefficients averaging about .40. Inspection of individual data showed about 50% of the observers reliably discriminated box weight in the stick-figure displays of walking, and about 20% reliably discriminated box weight in stick figures of lifting. For some observers, therefore, minimal displays of momentary postures supported the perception of the dynamics of the original event.

We should note that, for a small number of observers, performance was high and roughly equal across photographs and stick figures. A preliminary examination of the postural changes associated with various weighted boxes suggested that, across action phases, the heaviest boxes were always kept close to the body and above the feet (necessary for keeping the center of mass above the body support), and the lightest boxes where almost always lifted or carried away from the body (not necessary for postural stability). These regularities in posture, some biomechanically lawful, can indeed support the perception of dynamics in this simple lifting-carrying action.

References

Arnheim, R. (1988). Visual dynamics. *American Scientist, 76,* 585-591.

Merleau-Ponty, M. (1964). Eye and mind (C. Dallery, Trans.). In J. M. Edie (Ed.) *Maurice Merleau-Ponty: The primacy of perception, and other essays on phenomenological psychology, the philosophy of art, history and politics* (Chapter 5, pp. 159-190). Evanston, IL: Northwestern University Press. (Original work published 1961)

Rodin, A. (1983). *Rodin on art and artists.* New York: Dover. (Original work published 1957)

Scharf, A. (1974). *Art and photography.* Middlesex: Penguin Books Ltd. (Original work published 1968)

Valenti, S. S., & Costall, A. (1997). Visual perception of lifted weight from kinematic and static (photographic) displays. *Journal of Experimental Psychology: Human Perception and Performance, 23,* 181-198.

Studies in Perception and Action IV
M. A. Schmuckler & J. M. Kennedy (Eds.)
© 1997 Lawrence Erlbaum Associates, Inc.

Stimulus Complexity Determined By Fractal Geometry

Rainer Hoeger

Department of Psychology, Ruhr-University Bochum, F.R.G.

The classical way to determine the complexity of a visual stimulus proceeds in counting the number of turning points within the graphical representation of the stimulus (Attneave, 1957). This procedure fails if the stimulus is a photograph or a realistic drawing of a natural object. The different shadings of gray within a photograph do not automatically provide lines and edges which can be used to determine turning points. Therefore a procedure has to be applied to photographs which generates line segments from the original material. One way to do this is the detection of zero-crossings within the luminance gradients of the photograph (cf. Marr, 1982). By marking all detected zero-crossings, an edge-only version of the image results. Within an edge-only image the number of turning points can be counted.

A new concept of complexity is introduced by the theory of dynamic systems. Within this theoretical frame new mathematical tools have been developed. One of these tools is the fractal geometry which describes some properties of trajectories and attractors reflecting the different states of a dynamic system. The most well-known mathematical figure to which the fractal geometry can be applied is the so-called 'apple-man'. If one zooms into the border of this figure, then new structures can be detected until the apple-man itself emerges. Thus the figure is characterizable by two properties: self-similarity and infinite border. A single value to measure these structural properties is given by the fractal dimension (Steeb, 1992). Within applications of the theory of dynamic systems, the fractal dimension is used to measure the complexity of attractors.

In the present study this new measure of complexity was applied to pictures of natural objects and compared with the classical method to determine stimulus complexity.

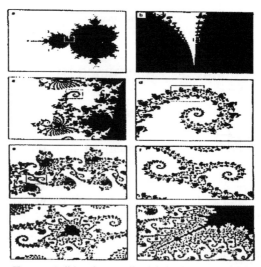

Figure 1: "Apple-man" with its border region.

Method

Subjects. Sixteen students participated in the study for course credit. The subjects consisted of 6 males and 10 females.

Stimuli and Procedure. The stimuli consisted of 20 realistic black and white drawings of natural objects stemming from fauna and flora. The pictures had a size of 10 cm x 10 cm and were each printed on a sheet of paper. All objects had to be judged for their complexity on a five-point rating scale, and drawings were digitized by a flat-bed scanner. High scores represented complex objects. For the objective measurements of complexity all drawings were digitized by a flat-bed scanner.

For all objects first the number of turning points were counted. Therefore an edge-only version of each picture was generated by determining the zero-crossings within the grey-level gradients. In a second step the fractal dimension of each object was estimated using the grating method.

The grating method works as follows: The selected image is first converted into a binary version (only black and white pixels are allowed) and then successively covered by gratings of different mesh-size. For each mesh-size, the number of cells which are hit by the graphical structure is counted. Mesh-size (E) and number of hits (N) are plotted against each other using logarithmic scales. Then a linear regression analysis is applied to the data points. The

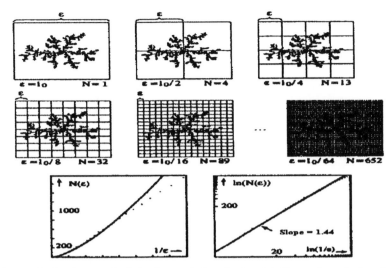

Figure 2. Grating method for determining the fractal dimension of drawings (adapted from Worg, 1993, p. 131).

fractal dimension is given by the slope of the regression line. Figure 2 shows by means of an example the determination of the fractal dimension for a dendrite.

Results

For each of the objects the judgments of all subjects were put together and the mean was calculated. These mean complexity judgments were correlated with the number of turning points and with the fractal dimensions. The following two diagrams depict the relationships between the objective and subjective measures of stimulus complexity. Note that the data points refer to the different objects (n = 20). The product-moment correlation between complexity judgment and number of turning points amounts to $r = .58$ ($p < .01$), that between complexity judgment and fractal dimension to $r = .70$ ($p < .001$).

Discussion

The results show that the stimulus complexity determined by the grating method fits better to the judged complexity than the counted number of turning points. That fractal dimension is a quite potent predictor of complexity judgments is contradictory to the results of Cutting and Garvin (1987). The authors found only a small correlation between the judged complexity and the

Hoeger

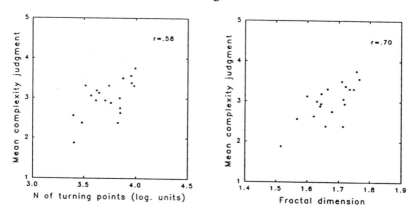

Figure 3. Relationships between objective measures of complexity and subjective judgments of complexity.

fractal dimension of their objects. The reason for this finding presumably has to do with the stimulus material which consisted of synthetically generated geometric forms.

From the point of view of perceptual psychology, one interesting aspect of the grating method is that it operates at different spatial scales. Corresponding to the multi-channel approach (e.g., Ginsburg, 1986) which postulates different perceptual mechanisms at different spatial resolution levels, it can be assumed that stimulus complexity depends on the extent of organization in multi-level information. Probably the fractal dimension reflects the mental expenditure to integrate the information stemming from different spatial scales.

References

Attneave, F. (1957). Physical determinants of the judged complexity of shapes. *Journal of Experimental Psychology, 6,* 183-193.

Cutting, J. E., & Garvin, J. J. (1987). Fractal curves and complexity. *Perception & Psychophysics, 42,* 365-370.

Ginsburg, A. (1986). Spatial filtering and visual form perception. In K. R. Boff, L. Kaufman & J. P. Thomas (Eds.), *Handbook of perception and human performance, Vol. II, Cognitive processes* (pp. 34/1-34/41). New York: Wiley.

Marr, D. (1982). *Vision.* New York: Freeman.

Steeb, W. H. (1992). *Chaos and fractals.* Mannheim: Wissenschaftsverlag.

Worg, R. (1993). *Deterministisches Chaos* [Deterministic Chaos]. Mannheim: Wissenschaftsverlag.

Studies in Perception and Action IV
M. A. Schmuckler & J. M. Kennedy (Eds.)
© 1997 Lawrence Erlbaum Associates, Inc.

The Müller-Lyer Illusion As A Consequence
Of Picture Perception

Gordon M. Redding, Alissa J. Kramen, & Jennifer L. Hankins

Department of Psychology, Illinois State University, Normal, IL, U.S.A.

Gregory's (1963) influential explanation of the Müller-Lyer illusion assumes that retinal images produced by drawings are processed in the same manner as images produced by "real" 3D corners. Such a direct perception account is incomplete in two respects. First, it fails to explain why arrow and fork junctions should be processed as a convex and concave corner, respectively (Haesen, 1974). Second, even if such representation is granted, the theory provides no basis for assuming that the convex corner is closer than the concave corner, as is necessary for differential size scaling to the account for the illusion (Rock, 1975).

The present hypothesis is that the illusion arises because stimuli are processed as 2D drawings of 3D corners (Nicholls & Kennedy, 1993). Such an indirect perception account avoids the above problems. First, junctions can be interpreted as boundary junctions having an interior line where object faces meet to form an edge and boundary lines where an object face obscures other faces (Waltz, 1975). Under this assumption of boundary junctions, interior lines for arrow and fork junctions are constrained to depict convex and concave edges, respectively (Redding & Hawley, 1993). Second, under the assumption of right-angle corners (e.g., Shepard, 1981), Müller-Lyer figures can be interpreted as perspective projections of dihedral angles with implied vanishing points and horizon line from which the drawing station point can be recovered (Rosinski & Farber, 1980).

As illustrated in Figure 1, arrow junction stimuli depict convex corners in front of the picture plane, while fork junction stimuli depict concave corners behind the picture plane. For stimuli with the same interior line, different picture plane distances force the conclusion of a convex corner smaller than the concave corner. This hypothesis was tested with size judgments of stimuli produced by rotation or translation of 3D (virtual) corners. Illusion should be

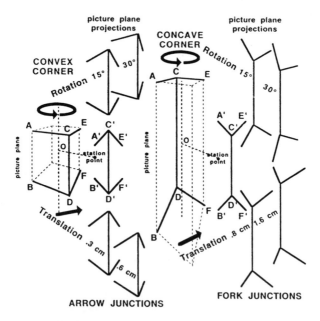

Figure 1. Hypothesized (virtual) convex and concave corners which project to arrow and fork junctions, respectively. Also illustrated are rotation and translation transformations and the resultant picture plane projections used as stimuli.

reduced by rotation because depicted distance from the picture plane is decreased (with corresponding corner size changes to project a constant size), but illusion should not be reduced by translation which does not change depicted picture plane distance or corner size.

Method

Untransformed stimuli with junctions on 3.3 cm interior lines were projections of virtual corners located .8 cm from the picture plane with 1.6 cm station point distance. Length of the virtual edge was 1.7 and 4.9 cm for convex and concave corners, respectively. Rotations of 15° and 30° produced stimuli that depicted corners closer to the picture plane (.7 and .6 cm) with corresponding difference in size (1.8 and 1.9 cm for convex corners; 4.8 and

4.7 cm for convex corners)[1]. Additional stimuli were produced by lateral translation of .3 and .6 cm for convex corners and .8 and 1.6 cm for concave corners, with no changes in picture plane distance or corner size.

The two transformations were tested in different experiments (40 participants each). Half the participants in each experiment saw stimuli produced by opposite directions of their transformation. Experimental stimuli were presented with a T junction control in each of 4 random trial blocks. Size was reported by matching length from a comparison series. Stimuli were constructed with a graphics application (Aldus SuperPaint 3.0) and presented by a Macintosh IIx computer running the PsyScope application, version 1.0f10 (Cohen et al., 1993). Participants viewed the monitor in a darkened booth from 73 cm, constrained by a chin-forehead rest.

Results and Conclusions

Data were differences in response between experimental and control stimuli. Figure 2 illustrates combined data for arrow and fork junction stimuli.

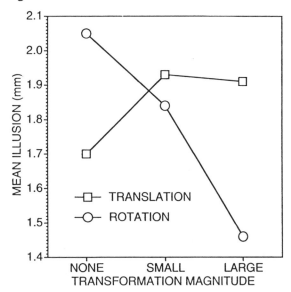

Figure 2. Mean illusion for both arrow and fork junctions as a function of magnitude of rotation and translation transformations.

---

[1] Lateral displacement produced by rotation was removed by translation before projection.

Consistent with prediction, illusion decreased largely under rotation, $F(2,78) =$ 11.56, $p < .001$. In contrast, translation produced a smaller increase in illusion, $F(2,78) = 3.56$, $p < .05$. The fact that the translation experiment produced a smaller illusion for untransformed stimuli suggests a sample difference between experiments that might account for the small effects of translation. Control experiments are underway. The present data support the conclusion that the illusion can be explained, at least in part, by interpretation of the stimuli as perspective drawings of 3D corners.

Acknowledgments. The authors wish to thank Jean Huck, Paula Kern, and Bret Phillips for their contributions to preliminary experiments.

References

Cohen, J., MacWhinney, B., Flatt, H., & Provost, J. (1993). PsyScope: An interactive graphic system for designing and controlling experiments in the psychology laboratory using Macintosh computers. *Behavior Research Method, Instruments, and Computers, 25*, 257-271.

Gregory, R. L. (1963). Distortion of visual space as inappropriate constancy scaling. *Nature, 199*, 678-680.

Haesen, W. (1974). An examination of R.L. Gregory's inappropriate constancy scaling theory of geometrical optical illusions. *Psychologica Belgica, 14*, 239-259.

Nicholls, A. L., & Kennedy, J. M. (1993). Angular subtense effects on perception of polar and parallel projections of cubes. *Perception & Psychophysics, 54*, 763-772.

Redding, G. M., & Hawley, E. A. (1993). Length illusion in fractional Müller-Lyer stimuli: An object-perception approach. *Perception, 22*, 819-828.

Rock, I. (1975). *An introduction to perception.* New York: Macmillan.

Rosinski, R. R., & Farber, J. (1980). Compensation for viewing point in the perception of pictured space. In M. A. Hagen (Ed.), *The perception of pictures: Vol. 1, Alberti's window: The projective model of pictorial information* (pp. 137-176). New York: Academic Press.

Shepard, R. N. (1981). Psychophysical complementarity. In M. Kubovy and J. Pomerantz (Eds.), *Perceptual organization* (pp. 279-341). Hillsdale, NJ: Erlbaum.

Waltz, D. (1975). Understanding line drawings of scenes with shadows. In P. H. Winston (Ed.), *The psychology of computer vision* (pp. 19-92). New York: McGraw-Hill.

Studies in Perception and Action IV
M. A. Schmuckler & J. M. Kennedy (Eds.)
© 1997 Lawrence Erlbaum Associates, Inc.

Inference And Pattern In Perception Theory

John M. Kennedy[1] & Christopher D. Green[2]

[1] Department of Psychology, University of Toronto, Scarborough, ON, Canada
[2] Department of Psychology, York University, North York, ON, Canada

Two rival positions in perception psychology are the inference theory of Helmholtz, and the information theory of Gibson. Helmholtz argued perception behaves as though it were making an inference. For instance, if one receives light from a particular direction, call it d, then one will assume that its source, say a lamp, is in direction d as well. We can represent this inference with the logical formula "if x then y." Helmholtz's key point was that perceptual inferences of this sort are not always justified, e.g., if we receive light from a certain direction, it does not follow that the lamp is in that direction as well, for there may be a mirror intervening, reflecting the light to our eye. Only if the medium of transmission of the light is uniform (let us call this z) is the inference about the direction of the lamp justified. Thus, if z is true, then the proposition "if x then y" is true also. We could write this: If z then (If x then y).

A major alternative to Helmholtz's inference theory is Gibson's theory of perceptual information. Gibson contended that information is found in patterns specific to their sources. Consider the example of the direction of a lamp. There is optical information for the medium of transmission of light being uniform, and optical information for the media being non-uniform, e.g., optical information for water surfaces, glass surfaces and the wavering columns of heated air that disturb the uniform transmission of light above a fire. Hence, optical information co-exists for, one, the direction of light sources and, two, the direction of travel of the light being uniform through the medium. Notice that these two conditions are identical to two of the propositions in the analysis of Helmholtzian theory above:

x = "one receives light from direction d," and
z = "the medium of transmission is uniform."

The co-existence can be described by "x and z" and only if this is satisfied will proposition y ("the lamp is in direction d") be true as well. Thus the whole Gibsonian claim can be represented by "If (x and z) then y". That is, if x (light is coming from a certain direction) and z (the medium for transmission of light is uniform), then y (the light source is in the direction from which the light comes).

There is clearly a parallel between "If (x and z) then y", the Gibson claim, and the Helmholtzian one "If z then (if x then y)", though one uses the "and" logical connective and the other only uses "if ... then" logical connectives. Is there any difference in their logical consequences? If not, then both have the same implications or "truth tables". Let us see what their truth-tables are, in fact.

We will represent the "If... then..." form with the symbol $\rightarrow$ (e.g., $x \rightarrow y$ represents "If x then y"). We will also represent "and" with the symbol & (e.g., x & y means "x and y").

The truth table for $x \rightarrow y$ can be written as follows:

$$x \rightarrow y$$
$$T\ T\ T$$
$$T\ F\ F$$
$$F\ T\ T$$
$$F\ T\ F$$

In this truth-table, T means true, F means false. The first line under $x \rightarrow y$ means x is true (T is under x), and y is true (T is under y) and the claim with the connective is true (since x is true and y is true, it is also true that "if x then y" is true). The other rows can be read in this same fashion. Note in particular that $x \rightarrow y$ is true any time x is false, regardless of whether y is true or not. Some may find this odd, but we need not go into the intriguing debates on this issue here.

The truth table for "If z then (If x then y)" can be written in a similar fashion. The symbolic representation is $z \rightarrow (x \rightarrow y)$. In the truth table, the overall proposition being evaluated is shown by T or F under the connective following z, i.e., $z \rightarrow (...$. The truth table for If z then (If x then y) is:

$$z \rightarrow (x \rightarrow y)$$

```
T T  T T T
F T  T T T
T T  F T T
F T  F T T
T F  T F F
F T  T F F
T T  F T F
F T  F T F
```

The truth table to be compared with that for the Helmholtzian claim z →(x →y) is that for the Gibsonian claim (x & z) → y. The key connective summarizing the status of the overall claim is the one prior to y, i.e., ... → y. Here is the truth table:

$$(x \ \& \ z) \rightarrow y$$

```
T TT T T
F FT T T
T FF T T
F FF T T
T TT F F
F FT T F
T FF T F
F FF T F
```

The line of Ts and Fs under the connective in z → (... and the line under the connective in ... → y are identical in the two truth-tables.

Evidently, the two propositions, one derived from Helmholtz and the other from Gibson, have the exact same set of conditions satisfying them. They are only false when x is true, y is false, and z is true. Under all other truth conditions, they are both true.

In plainer English, there is no logical difference between Helmholtz's and Gibson's claims. Gibson writes about information in light, in complex patterns. Helmholtz writes about packets of light that can be used to make valid inferences if certain conditions obtain. If those conditions obtain, and there is perceptible information to indicate this, Helmholtz's argument is Gibson's. (Hence, differences in the predictions of the two theories can only arise when there is no perceptible information to indicate what conditions are relevant.)

Studies in Perception and Action IV
M. A. Schmuckler & J. M. Kennedy (Eds.)
© 1997 Lawrence Erlbaum Associates, Inc.

"Body-Image" Distortion And Accuracy Of Size Perception For Inanimate Objects

Thomas R. Alley & Amanda M. Olson

Department of Psychology, Clemson University, Clemson, SC, U.S.A.

Women so often feel overweight that worry about weight and dieting can be considered a normative phenomenon (Rodin, Silberstein, & Striegel-Moore, 1985). Many go beyond just worrying and dieting and succumb to eating disorders. It is commonly believed that eating disorders are accompanied by body-image distortion, a belief reflected in the research literature and in the inclusion of body-image disturbance in diagnostic criteria of the DSM-IV (cf. Schlundt & Johnson, 1990). Some evidence indicates that those who distort their body-image have poor visuospatial abilities, but others have found little to no relationship between visuospatial ability and levels of body distortion (e.g., Strauss & Ryan, 1988; Thompson & Spana, 1991).

Unfortunately, many of the techniques for assessing body-image distortion have questionable validity and reliability (Brodie, Slade, & Rose, 1989). A major flaw in many of these is that the perceiver's body shape may not lie anywhere on the series or continuum of body shapes. More accurate responses are likely to be obtained from techniques that ask perceivers to judge the exact size of specific body parts. Our study uses a new and precise measure of perceived size to measure body-image distortion and explore whether a visuospatial deficit contributes to this distortion. Our method also allows us to compare accuracy in these size judgments with signs of eating disorders.

Method

Materials. One helium neon gas laser was mounted on a swivel base and aimed at a thin vertical line on a large white marker board. A 50 cm long rod was attached to the top of the laser to provide a handle and enhance user control. This apparatus provides a perceiver-controlled means to precisely indicate perceived linear dimensions by aiming the beam to a spot a selected distance from a reference line or point (Alley, 1997).

Three objects were placed to the side of the testing room. The largest of these was a 77.4 cm wide black metal cabinet. The other two objects were a cylindrical tapered trash can and a curved-back chair with specific locations marked with a rubber band: 37.1 cm wide on the chair back and 29.8 cm wide on the can.

Procedure. To measure the accuracy of perceived size, university students were asked to stand behind the laser apparatus, about 3 m from the projection surface. Each was shown how to use the laser apparatus and told that "width" refers to the linear distance. An outline drawing of a human body was used to help communicate the exact location of the three body areas (shoulders, waist, and hips) to be judged.

All 25 male and 41 female students first moved the light beam to reproduce the exact width of their shoulders or hips at the widest point, or their waist at the narrowest point (requested in varying random orders). Next, visuospatial ability was assessed by asking participants to reproduce the width of the three objects described above, again requested in random order. These objects were placed so that participants were unable to see them and the laser beam simultaneously.

After making all size judgments, participants completed a one-page survey form containing the Eating Attitudes Test (EAT-26; Garner et al., 1982), a survey designed to detect symptoms of eating disorders. The form also contained additional questions about eating behavior, exercise, weight preferences, age, height, weight, and sex. Finally, the height and weight of each participant were recorded, and the exact widths of the shoulders, waist and hips were measured using anthropometric calipers.

Results & Discussion

Scores on the EAT-26 were converted into a total EAT-26 score and scores on the three subscales of Dieting, Bulimia and Food Preoccupation, and Oral Control (Garner et al., 1982). As expected, females scored significantly higher on this 26-item scale ($t(62.4) = 6.92$; $p < .001$), and on two (Bulimia and Dieting) of the three subscales ($p < .001$). No males but 11 females were above the clinical cut-off of 20 on the EAT-26.

The mean of the absolute value of the percentile error scores for size judgments of the three objects and three body parts served as our indices of accuracy for, respectively, object and body size judgment. A simple mean of the percentile error scores was computed to indicate systematic bias in body perception.

The self-reports of weight and height by our participants were not significantly inaccurate ($p > .68$). In contrast, participants tended to overestimate the size of the three test objects (combined) as well as all three body locations ($p < .001$). The overestimation of body size is consistent with the results of some earlier studies that used a variety of different assessment techniques (Brodie, Slade, & Rose, 1989). The fact that people also tend to overestimate the size of inanimate objects suggests that overestimation of body size may be a normal aspect of size judgment rather than a clinical symptom.

The correlation matrix for the object, body parts, weight and height error scores are shown in Table 1. None of these measures were significantly correlated ($r < .19$; $p > .12$), except for the two alternative measures of accuracy of body size perception ($r = .87$; $p < .001$). The same pattern of correlation was found when these data were examined separately for each sex. There were no sex differences in the accuracy of judgments for objects or body parts, the overall bias in body part estimates, or the accuracy of self-reported height ($p > .63$).

There were no significant correlations between error in judgments of the size of objects or body parts, considered either separately or together, and any of six measures of eating disorder: two different total scores on the EAT-26 (using raw scores or Garner's conversions) total score, scores on the three subscales, and answers to a question about bingeing. Thus, we found no

Table 1
Intercorrelations of Size Accuracy Measures

	Mean |Error| For 3 Objects	Mean |Error| For 3 Body Parts	Body Size Bias	Reported Weight Error	Reported Weight Error
Object |Error|	1.00	.134	.127	-.136	-.085
Body Parts |Error|		1.00	.873*	-.011	-0.93
Body Size Bias			1.00	.088	-0.46
Reported Weight				1.00	1.88

Note: * $p < .001$

support for the hypothesis that eating disorders are due to deficits in the ability to accurately assess the size of objects or body parts.

References

Alley, T. R. (1997). *A new laser-based technique for measuring accuracy and distortion in judgments of linear dimensions.* Unpublished manuscript .

Brodie, D. A., Slade, P. D., & Rose, H. (1989). Reliability measures in distorting body-image. *Perceptual and Motor Skills, 69,* 723-732.

Garner, D. M., Olmsted, M. P., Bohr, Y., & Garfinkle, P. E. (1982). The Eating Attitudes Test: Psychometric features and clinical correlates. *Psychological Medicine, 12,* 871-878.

Rodin, J., Silberstein, L. R., & Striegel-Moore, R. H. (1985). Women and weight: A normative discontent. In T. B. Sonderegger (Ed.), *Nebraska symposium on motivation: Psychology and gender* (pp. 267-307). Lincoln: University of Nebraska.

Schlundt, D. G. & Johnson, W. G. (1990). *Eating disorders: Assessment and treatment.* Boston: Allyn and Bacon.

Strauss, J., & Ryan, R. M. (1988). Cognitive dysfunction in eating disorders. *International Journal of Eating Disorders, 7,* 19-28.

Thompson, J. K. & Spana, R. E. (1991). Visuospatial ability, accuracy of size estimation, and bulimic disturbance in a noneating-disordered college sample: A neuropsychological analysis. *Perceptual and Motor Skills, 73,* 335-338.

Studies in Perception and Action IV
M. A. Schmuckler & J. M. Kennedy (Eds.)
© *1997 Lawrence Erlbaum Associates, Inc.*

Blur Selectively Affects The Bases For Alignment: Position And Orientation

Itsuo Kumazawa[1], John M. Kennedy[2], & Kei Suzuki[1]

[1] Department of Computer Science, Tokyo Institute of Technology, Meguro-ku, Tokyo, Japan
[2] Division of Life Sciences, University of Toronto, Toronto, Canada

In Figure 1, line segments can be grouped as a line, using the positions and orientations of the segments. Finding such groupings in the presence of different kinds of distractors can be affected by blur, and selective effects of blur may indicate whether position functions differently than orientation.

In our tests, several four-line segment items are radially positioned, like a clock with several hands, the axes of the items converging at the center of the display. One of the items is the target. It is the item with segments consistent

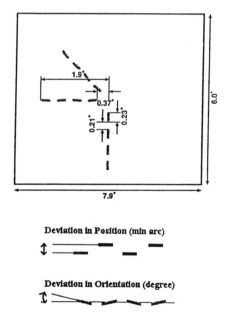

Deviation in Position (min arc)

Deviation in Orientation (degree)

Figure 1. Detailed constitution of the stimuli.

in position and orientation. The other items have segments inconsistent in their positions or orientations and are called distractors. The displays were presented to subjects briefly. The displays were blurred to different degrees, and the resulting error rates in the search trials were recorded.

In Experiment 1, the four line segments in each distractor were aligned in position (measuring from the centers of the line segments) but their orientations were inconsistent. In Experiment 2, the four line segments in each distractor were parallel, but their centers were offset.

Method

The two subjects, KS and TW, have corrected eye sight. Each subject participated in three sets of trials--one for each level of blur. The stimuli were generated using a personal computer and displayed on a 1024 by 726 monitor of 17 inch size. Details of the configuration of the display are shown in Figure 1. The distractor's line segments deviated from perfect alignment in position or orientation, measured as shown in Figure 1. The position deviation is measured by an angular subtense at the observer's viewpoint at a distance of about 2.2 meters. The edges of line segments were blurred to three different degrees. In Experiment 1 and Experiment 2, a set of trials consisted of 480 trials. During each set of trials, the number of items and the degree of deviation varied randomly. Each trial started when the subject pressed a button of the computer "mouse". A blank display appeared for between 1000 msec and 1500 msec (with duration varied randomly) with no fixation point. Then the stimulus display appeared for 130 msec, followed by the masking stimuli (eight circles). In a forced-choice task, subjects indicated the target's location by selecting one of the eight circles of the mask.

Results

Figure 2 shows the results of Experiment 1. Each circle, triangle or square shows the error rate for 32 search trials performed for each deviation value (circles for trials with one distractor, triangles for two distractors and squares for three). The solid line shows the result for the non-blurred case. Short-segment lines show the weakly-blurred case. Long-segment lines show the strongly blurred case. Accuracy was greater as orientation deviation of the distractors increased. Generally, the stimuli with more blur showed greater error rates. Figure 3 uses the same code as Figure 2, and shows the results of Experiment 2. Greater accuracy was obtained as the position deviation of the

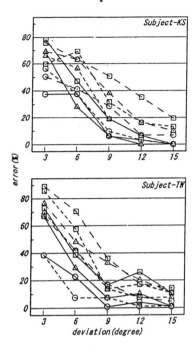

Figure 2. Results of Experiment 1 (inconsistent orientation).

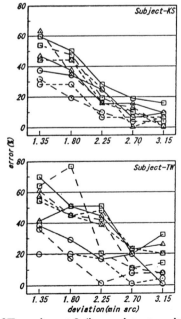

Figure 3. Results of Experiment 2 (inconsistent position).

distractors increased. However, generally the stimuli with more blur showed lower error rates.

Conclusion

Blur hampers search for a target with alignment when distractors have inconsistent orientation, but aids the search when the distractors have inconsistent positions.

Acknowledgments. Steven L. Funk provided useful comments.

Studies in Perception and Action IV
M. A. Schmuckler & J. M. Kennedy (Eds.)
© 1997 Lawrence Erlbaum Associates, Inc.

Learning Faces Through Bi-quantised Pictures

Chang Hong Liu & Avi Chaudhuri

Department of Psychology, McGill University, Montreal, Quebec, Canada

Unlike a multi-tone picture, a bi-quantised picture has only two tones (Figure 1). As a result, much of the detail is lost in a bi-quantised picture compared to its multi-tone counterpart. Despite this, studies have shown that familiar faces are readily recognized in bi-quantised pictures (Hayes, 1988; Bruce et al., 1992; Bruce & Humphreys, 1994). This may be because bi-quantised pictures preserve low spatial frequencies that are important in face recognition (Hayes, 1988).

Since the faces used in prior studies were mainly celebrities, they were most likely learned through a rich set of cues that is contained in published media. These pictures usually contain broadband high and low spatial frequencies, colors, etc. Hence prior to recognizing the celebrities in bi-quantised pictures, subjects would already have rich information about the faces in their memory.

In this study, we examined the opposite case—subjects were asked to learn faces through bi-quantised pictures and later identify the faces in full-color pictures. The results were compared to another subject group in which faces were learned through the usual full-color pictures and tested with bi-quantised versions. We reasoned that because of loss of tonal information, the memory of the facial information learned through bi-quantised pictures would be a degraded replica of that learned through full-color pictures. If face recognition depends on detailed information at the time of learning, faces learned through full-color pictures should produce better recognition performance. However, if face recognition is based on overlapping information between the learned and tested faces, no difference should be expected between the two conditions because the amount of overlap in both cases is exactly the same.

Figure 1. An example of a face in a bi-quantised picture.

Method

Subjects. Forty undergraduate and graduate students from McGill University participated in the study. The mean age was 23.5 (*SD* = 5.1). All had normal or correct-to-normal vision. Subjects were randomly assigned to two groups, with 20 in each.

Materials. Digitized pictures were downloaded from University of Essex face database and transformed into a binary (bi-quantised) version using Adobe Photoshop 3.0. The pictures were transformed in two steps—RGB to 8 bit (256) gray-level pictures and then to binary (1 bit). The photographs of 32 faces used in this study (16 male, 16 females) were unknown to the subjects. All pictures were in full-face view. Each face had two versions—full-color and bi-quantised. An example of a bi-quantised face that was used is shown in Figure 1. The size of the pictures was 200 x 180 pixels (7.1 x 6.4 cm). The pictures were displayed in the center of a 17 inch AppleVision monitor and freely viewed at a distance of 60 cm (6.5° x 6.0° of visual angle).

Procedure. Subjects were individually tested on a Power Macintosh computer (Model 7200/120) after reading the instructions. During the learning phase, 16 faces were presented sequentially in random order. Each face was shown for three seconds. After the presentation of the last face, a brief delay (4 s) was given followed by the test session. The test face was accompanied by a dialogue box containing "Yes" and "No" button responses. Subjects were instructed to click on the "Yes" button if the face was seen during the learning phase or the "No" button otherwise. The test face remained on the display until the subject responded. A total of 32 faces were then tested containing 16 previously viewed and 16 new faces. The testing order of the learned faces was the same as the learning session whereas the new faces were randomized and then mixed with the learned faces. The correct Yes/No answers were determined by Fellows sequence (see Fellows, 1967) to avoid undesired response bias.

In one subject group, the bi-quantised pictures were used during learning followed by full-color testing. In the second group, the full-color pictures were used at the learning and the bi-quantised pictures at the testing. The procedure used for the two groups were otherwise identical.

Results

The proportion of false alarms was subtracted from the proportion of hits for each subject. The resulting composite scores were used in statistical analyses. In this scheme, a score of 0 reflects chance performance whereas a value of 1.0 represents perfect performance. In our study, the mean corrected proportion score was .44 (*SD* = .19) for the group in which faces were learned through bi-quantised pictures and .53 (*SD* = .04) for faces in the full-color group. With an alpha level of .05, the difference was not significant, $t(38)$ = 1.57, p = .12.

Discussion

We have found that recognition of faces initially learned through bi-quantised pictures was similar when the converse procedure was employed— i.e., recognition of bi-quantised faces after viewing full-color faces. This suggests that the amount of information present in memory is relatively unimportant. What is more relevant to face recognition seems to be the overlapping features shared by the learned and the test face. In the present study, this would be the low spatial frequency content in both learned and tested faces.

References

Bruce, V., Hanna, E., Dench, N., Healey, P., & Burton, M. (1992). The importance of 'mass' in line drawings of faces. *Applied Cognitive Psychology, 6,* 619-628.

Bruce, V., & Humphreys, G. W. (1994). Recognizing objects and faces. In V. Bruce & G. W. Humphreys (Eds.), *Object and Face Recognition.* Hillsdale: Lawrence Erlbaum Associates Ltd.

Fellows, B. J. (1967). Chance stimulus sequences for discrimination tasks. *Psychological Bulletin, 67,* 87-92.

Hayes, A. (1988). Identification of two-tone images: Some implications for high- and low-spatial-frequency processes in human vision. *Perception, 17,* 429-436.

Studies in Perception and Action IV
M. A. Schmuckler & J. M. Kennedy (Eds.)
© 1997 Lawrence Erlbaum Associates, Inc.

Can Temporal Direction Affect Memory
For Pictures Of Events?

Thomas R. Alley

Department of Psychology, Clemson University, Clemson, SC, U.S.A.

We are mobile creatures normally situated in a dynamic environment in which objects may undergo a variety of irreversible changes such as ripening, growing, and falling. Human memory might reflect the temporal asymmetry inherent in these events by being more prone to 'distortion' that is consistent with the physical (e.g., gravity; momentum) and biological (e.g., growth; aging) processes that create temporal asymmetry in the world. Freyd (1992) has developed the theory that perceptual representations are dynamic, noting that representations of the world that emphasize the future are a better guide for adaptive behavior than those that represent the past.

Studies of "representational momentum" (Freyd & Finke, 1984) or, more generally, "representational displacement", provide good evidence for this sort of predictable 'distortion' in memory. These studies show that human memory is subject to shifts in the direction of perceived or expected change. These changes may reflect a number of physical forces in addition to momentum (Hubbard, 1995) or other transformations such as changes in pitch (Freyd, Kelly, & DeKay, 1990). They typically present the to-be-remembered object or scene as a pair or ordered series of static images undergoing transformation involving movement, and use error rates as the dependent variable. Some research indicates that memory shifts may occur even when perceivers have not observed any actual change (Alley, 1993; Freyd & Pantzer, 1995). These studies, however, have presented a limited variety of transformations and transformation intervals. Moreover, we know that some static images do not induce representational displacement (Futterweit & Beilin, 1994). Hence, there is suggestive, but not convincing, evidence for the general claim that single static displays which imply change are sufficient to produce representational displacement.

To test the hypothesis that single static views of objects undergoing a variety of unidirectional changes can create representational displacement, adults were shown series of photographs and later given an unexpected memory test. More false alarms were expected for changing objects when the test photo was more recent than the original photo than vice versa.

Method

All participants viewed two sets of 37 slides, each containing one member from 10 pairs of "*Changing*" photos of the same object or scene. The lighting, camera angle, exposure, focal length, etc. were kept constant within each pair. The scenes or objects in these pairs represent a variety of forms of change and time intervals, although cyclical events where past and future could be confused (e.g., sunset/sunrise) were avoided (see Table 1).

The "earlier" and "later" photos were separately grouped with 27 additional photos. These included 9 photos that were identical in both sets, and for which an "old" response in the test phase would be correct. All 27 additional photos depicted objects that were (e.g., people walking), or could be (plants), undergoing change. In addition to the 9 duplicated photos, there were 18 photos selected to form pairs of similar but easily distinguished photos (e.g., a pair of photos of flowering azalea bushes).

University students were tested in 18 groups, with 75 students shown the Early Set of Changing photos first and tested on the Later Set, and 78 students shown the Later Set first. The same 9 random orders of the 37 slides were used in "Earlier" and "Later" test groups. The slides were projected to a size of 77.5 cm x 120.7 cm and viewed from two rows of seats at distances of approximately 4 to 5.5 m.

During the first presentation of slides, participants were given instructions indicating the experiment concerned evaluation of photographs; they were not told about the forthcoming memory test. The slides were presented for 4.5 s each, with an inter-slide interval of 5.5 sec. As each slide was presented, participants were to rate it on two 5-point scales according to how "interesting" and "pleasant" it was to look at. After completing an unrelated task, participants were asked to recall rating photographs about 10 minutes earlier and told that they would be shown more photographs which they were to denote as "old" only if it was "one of the **exact same** photos" they saw earlier.

Table 1.
Objects, Events and Intervals Depicted in the Changing Photograph Pairs.

Object	Type(s) of Change	Temporal Interval
(hand with) ball	dropping	approximately 0.1 seconds
succulent plant	flowering/color	121 hours
banana	ripening	21 hours
candle	burning/shrinking	5 minutes
box	burning	approximately 10 seconds
camelia	flowering	45 hours
cake	size	(not applicable)
tigress	walking	0.119 seconds
tomato plant	aging/ripening	5 days
mountainside	tree growth/erosion	98 years

Results & Discussion

All responses were converted to hits, misses, false alarms, and correct rejections, then analyzed separately for the three categories of test slides: repeated (**same**), **changed** (the "critical" photos), and **new**. (See Table 2.) There was no difference in memory for the changing slides between the group which viewed those slides in the temporally forward direction and the group that viewed them in reverse order. Surprisingly, these two groups displayed significantly different performance on all other measures of memory.

There are at least three reasons why temporal asymmetry in memory for the changing photos did not occur. First, despite a large sample size, it appears that the group viewing the slides in the backwards direction was better at memory for photos. This group out-performed the forward memory group on every measure for every set of photos in which there were significant group differences (see Table 2). Second, the performance on the Changing photos was poor for both groups, over 72% of responses being incorrect (false alarms). Hence, a floor effect may have prevented the appearance of representational displacement. Third, the nature of the events depicted in the changing photos may not support representational displacement. One previous study (Futterweit & Beilin, 1994; Experiment 2) found that still photographs lacking implied motion did not induce representational displacement. Closer examination of the performance across the different events depicted may shed light on this possibility.

Table 2

Mean Memory Performance for Viewers in Forward/Backward Conditions

	Test Photos		
	Same	New	Changing
Hits	7.61/8.13 **		
Misses	1.39/.86 *		
False Alarms		2.92/1.45 **	7.24/7.32
Correct Rejections		15.05/16.55 **	2.56/2.68

Note. * p < .005; ** p < .001;

References

Alley, T. R. (1993). Recognizing faces following natural or reverse growth. In S. S. Valenti & J. B. Pittenger (Eds.), *Studies in Perception and Action II* (pp. 57-60). Hillsdale, NJ: Erlbaum Associates.

Freyd, J. J. (1992). Dynamic representations guiding adaptive behavior. In F. Macar, V. Pouthas, & W. J. Friedman (Eds.), *Time, action and cognition: Towards bridging the gap* (pp. 309-323). Dordrecht: Kluwer.

Freyd, J. J., & Finke, R. A. (1984). Representational momentum. *Journal of Experimental Psychology: Learning, Memory, and Cognition, 10*, 126-132.

Freyd, J. J., Kelly, M. H., & DeKay, M. L. (1990). Representational momentum in memory for pitch. *Journal of Experimental Psychology: Learning, Memory, and Cognition, 16*, 1107-1117.

Freyd, J. J., & Pantzer, T. M. (1995). Static patterns moving in the mind. In S. M. Smith, T. B. Ward, & R. A. Finke (Eds.), *The creative cognition approach* (pp. 181-204). Cambridge, MA: MIT.

Futterweit, L. R., & Beilin, H. (1994). Recognition memory for movement in photographs: A developmental study. *Journal of Experimental Child Psychology, 57*, 163-179.

Hubbard, T. L. (1995). Environmental invariants in the representation of motion: Implied dynamics and representational momentum, gravity, friction, and centripetal force. *Psychonomic Bulletin and Review, 2*, 322-338.

Studies in Perception and Action IV
M. A. Schmuckler & J. M. Kennedy (Eds.)
© *1997 Lawrence Erlbaum Associates, Inc.*

The Relevance Of Imagined Self-Rotations

Sarah H. Creem, Maryjane Wraga, & Dennis R. Proffitt

Department of Psychology, University of Virginia,
Charlottesville, VA, U.S.A.

Most studies on the mental rotation of objects have focused on peoples' ability to imagine an object rotating around its central axis (Shepard & Metzler, 1971). Some researchers even suggest that this type of object-centered rotation is more readily accessible than a viewer-centered rotation around the object (Shepard & Hurwitz, 1985). However, Gibson's (1979) ecological approach argues for the primacy of observation via movement through the environment. We conducted two studies to explore this issue. In the first, subjects performed imagined rotations involving an array of objects; in the second, a single object was used.

Experiment 1

The first study was a replication of Presson (1982). He found that imagined rotations of a miniature array were faster than imagined rotations of the viewer when the task involved rotating a named object to a position in the array. However, this task was biased with regard to the starting referent: in the Array condition, subjects only needed to update the spatial position of one object, whereas in the Viewer condition they updated the entire array. Performance in a second, more neutral condition was faster in Viewer compared to Array. We replicated this experiment, using a life-sized array.

Method

Subjects (N = 24) stood facing a 75 cm^2 diamond-shaped array of 4 objects: snake, car, hammer, and phone. Each subject participated in two conditions. For each, the array was configured differently. Subjects memorized the positions of the objects in terms of top, bottom, left, and right relative to themselves. They were then blindfolded. In the Viewer condition, subjects imagined themselves rotating around the outside of the array while facing inward; in the Array condition, the imagined rotation was of the array itself. The degrees of rotation were 0, 90, 180, and 270. For each trial, subjects received the degree of rotation followed by a position in the array, e.g., "180, what is on the right?" They responded by naming one of the objects. Reaction times and responses were recorded.

Results

Figure 1 shows mean reaction times of correct responses. In general, subjects were faster in the Viewer condition than the Array condition. A 2 (sex) x 2 (rotation direction) x 2 (task order) x 2 (condition) x 4 (degree) mixed-design ANOVA on the scores yielded a main effect of condition, $F(1,16) = 30.08$, $p < .0001$, degree, $F(3,48) = 26.57$, $p < .0001$, and a significant task x degree interaction, $F(3,48) = 18.01$, $p < .0001$. In the Array condition, the 270 rotation took significantly longer than 90 or 180, whereas in Viewer it did not.

Discussion

As expected, subjects found it easier to imagine rotating themselves around the array compared to rotating the array around themselves. These findings contradict the notion that imagined object-relative transformations are more accessible than viewer-relative ones. Despite the fact that the Viewer condition

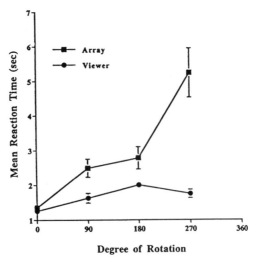

Figure 1. Mean response latencies, Experiment 1.

involved updating the relationship between viewer and the environment in addition to the required rotation, subjects responded more quickly than in Array.

An alternative explanation is that the difficulty of the Array condition resulted from the number of units rotated. Indeed, the four objects could be considered an environment, and people have very little experience with the world in motion. Experiment 2 was designed to control for this possibility.

Experiment 2

Method

Subjects (N = 24) stood facing a toy car. They participated in two rotation conditions: Viewer and Object. Subjects memorized the positions of the car parts (hood, trunk, driver-side, passenger-side) in terms of top, bottom, right, left relative to themselves. For each trial, they either imagined the car rotating around its own axis (Object), or themselves rotating around the car (Viewer). The same rotation degrees and questions were used as in Experiment 1. Reaction times and responses were recorded.

Results

Figure 2 shows mean reaction times of correct responses. Subjects were faster in the Viewer condition than the Object condition. A 2 (sex) x 2 (direction of rotation) x 2 (task order) x 2 (condition) x 4 (degree) mixed-design ANOVA performed on the scores yielded a main effect of condition, $F(1,16) = 13.16$, $p < .002$, degree, $F(3,48) = 13.78$, $p < .0001$, and a significant task x degree interaction, $F(3, 48) = 10.50$, $p < .0001$. In the Object condition, the 270 rotation took significantly longer than 90 or 180, whereas in Viewer it did not.

Discussion

Despite the fact that the array was reduced to one object, subjects were still faster in the Viewer condition. Thus, the Viewer advantage was due to the efficiency of self-movement rather than number of units. This provides stronger evidence that, for certain tasks, imagined movement of the self around an object is more effective than imagined movement of the object itself.

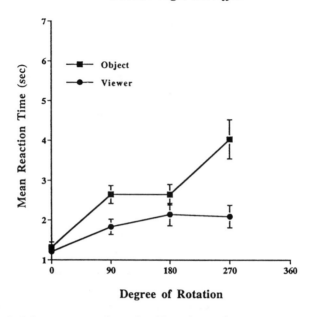

Figure 2. Mean response latencies, Experiment 2.

References

Gibson, J. J. (1979). *The ecological approach to visual perception.* Boston: Houghton-Mifflin.

Presson, C. C. (1982). Strategies in spatial reasoning. *Journal of Experimental Psychology: Learning, Memory, and Cognition, 8,* 243-251.

Shepard, R. N., & Metzler, J. (1971). Mental rotation of three-dimensional objects. *Science, 171,* 701-713.

Shepard, R. N., & Hurwitz, S. (1985). Upward direction, mental rotation, and discrimination of left and right turns in maps. In S. Pinker (Ed.), *Visual Cognition* (pp. 161-193). Cambridge, MA: MIT Press.

Studies in Perception and Action IV
M. A. Schmuckler & J. M. Kennedy (Eds.)
© 1997 Lawrence Erlbaum Associates, Inc.

Predicting Where And When Hidden Moving Objects Reappear

Bart De Bruyn & Mark F. Bradshaw

Department of Psychology, University of Surrey, Guildford, Surrey, U.K.

When we move through a complex structured scene, or objects move within it, parts of the scene/objects will disappear and reappear due to occlusion and/or blending.   A moving object will disappear when it blends with the background (camouflaged, for example, by concurrent motion or color) or when it moves behind an opaque occluder. Reaching and grasping directed towards such moving objects can only be completed accurately if an observer can predict *where* the object will reappear at a fixed point in time (in case of blending) or *when* the object will reappear at a fixed point in space (in case of an occluded motion path).   Therefore, prediction is an extremely important factor in our interaction with the world (e.g. Schmidt, 1971).   What factors affect this ability?   To address this question we investigated spatial and temporal prediction errors (Sharp and Whiting, 1974) for hidden moving objects (due to blending or occlusion) as a function of *(i)* the speed of the object, *(ii)* the spatial and temporal characteristics of the disappearance and *(iii)* the time the object was presented.

Method

Two adjacent Radius 75Hz BW monitors were viewed at 57 cm (well within reaching-distance for all observers) and subtended a visual angle of approximately 80 degrees horizontally and 30 degrees vertically. The displays were controlled by a Apple Power Macintosh 7500.

Figure 1 illustrates the two experimental conditions which simulated the blending and the occlusion of a moving object. In the *where* task (1a), the moving dot (three sequential frames are depicted) blends into the background and the observer is required to predict its position after a fixed temporal interval - indicated by a tone. In the *when* task (1b) the moving dot disappears

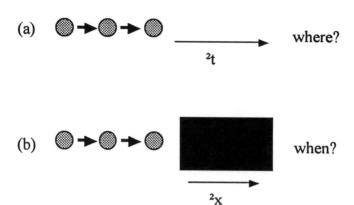

Figure 1. The 'where' and 'when' experimental conditions used to investigate spatial and temporal errors in the prediction of an object-reappearance.

behind a visible occluder (a fixed spatial interval) and the observer is required to predict when it would reappear.

On each trial the dot (dia 0.67 deg) was randomly positioned in the region ± 20 deg. (x and y) in front of the observer for a period of 1.5 secs. Next the dot moved at a constant speed in a rightward direction along a horizontal path. The speed of the dot was selected at random from 5 different speeds: 2.5°/sec, 5°/sec, 7.5°/sec, 10°/sec, and 12.5°/sec. In each block of 40 trials (8/speed) the dot was presented in motion for either 200, 400, or 800 msec. In the where task (1a) performance was measured for objects disappearing for 0, 1, 2 or 4 seconds. The spatial location at which the dot should reappear varied as a function of the presented speed. In the when task (1b) a spatial mask (a white rectangle of 15 deg) occluded the motion path. The time the dot stayed behind the occluder varied between 1 and 6 seconds (correlated with the speed presented). Prediction error was computed as the difference between the actual position/time and the estimated position/time. There was no feedback.

Results and Discussion

A marked increase in spatial prediction errors (the where condition) occurred for all subjects with increases in occlusion time from 1 to 4 seconds. Averaged over presentation time and speed, errors increased by around 200% (to ~ 5 deg).

Figure 2 shows the results for one observer. The left panel shows the effect of stimulus speed on the spatial error (the predicted position), and the right panel shows the effect of stimulus speed on the temporal error (the predicted time).

These results indicate that observers underestimate slow speeds (<7 deg/sec) and over-estimate fast-speeds. As a result, observers predict that the hidden dots moving at slow speeds moved over a lesser extent and so should reappear later and vice versa for fast speeds.

The expected decrease in errors with the increase in presentation time, which may facilitate greater precision in speed estimation was only slightly borne out in the data. To compare performance in both conditions directly the spatial and temporal errors were converted into 'perceived speeds' (the speed of the dot if the observer's, erroneous, judgment was 'correct') and plotted in Figure 3. This indicates that predicting 'where' is more difficult than predicting 'when' and the effect of speed differs between conditions.

Prediction accuracy deteriorates the longer a moving object remains undetectable. We suggest that this results from a decaying memory of the speed signal. It remains to be shown whether or not the 7 deg/sec is an absolute cut-off point, or whether observers are using a 'default average speed' and are enhancing the contrast of the perceived speeds relative to this calibration speed. In future studies we will measure predictive performance for 3D motions and its coupling with preparatory hand and arm movements as recorded by the MACReflex system.

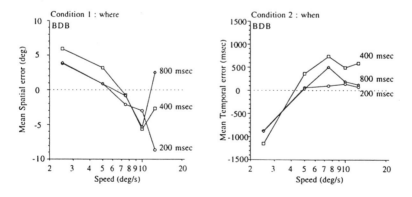

Figure 2. The spatial (left) and temporal prediction errors (ordinate) for each speed (abscissa) separately for the 3 presentation times.

De Bruyn & Bradshaw

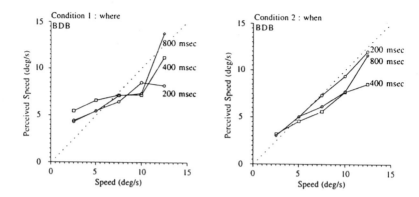

Figure 3. Perceived speed (ordinate) against actual speed (abscissa).

References

Schmidt, R. A. (1971). Proprioception and the timing of motor responses, *Psychological Bulletin, 76*, 383-390.

Sharp, R. H., & Whiting, H. T. (1974). Exposure and occluded duration effects in a ball-catching skill, *Journal of Motor Behavior, 6*, 139- 47.

Studies in Perception and Action IV
M. A. Schmuckler & J. M. Kennedy (Eds.)
© *1997 Lawrence Erlbaum Associates, Inc.*

Trajectory Forms As Visual Information In Bounce Events

Michael M. Muchisky

Perception-Action Laboratory, Indiana University, Bloomington, IN, U.S.A.

Bingham, Rosenblum & Schmidt (1995) proposed that dynamically governed trajectory forms are used in event identification. Trajectory forms refer to variations in velocity along a path of motion. Part of their study investigated observer's (O's) ability to identify patch light displays of bounce style events, one a free-fall and bounce and the other an imitation of the free-fall produced by hand movements. The amplitudes and periods of Free-falling and Hand-moved bounce events were matched to attempt to isolate the trajectory form variations as the source of information for their discrimination. O's were able to identify the bounce events. However, the patch light technique did not allow trajectory forms to be varied parametrically. Thus, the degree of trajectory form variation needed for O's to discriminate events could not be determined.

Using physics modeling software we parametrically controlled trajectory form variations between free-fall and hand-moved bounce events. This also permitted the isolation of trajectory form information in the events. Other potential sources of visual information were either randomized by varying viewing distance (absolute velocities) or fixed between target and standard events (period and amplitude).

The goals of this experiment were threefold. First, how sensitive are O's to trajectory form variations in bounce events? Parametric control of the dynamics generating the bounces (gravitational coefficient for the Free-Fall bounces and stiffnesses & equilibrium points of springs for the Hand-moved bounces) permitted this test. Second, is there a decrement in O's ability to use trajectory form information due to the discontinuity/collision occurring during a bounce? This was tested by switching the dynamics generating the trajectory before versus after the collision. For instance, could O's distinguish a Free-Falling bounce (gravity as the generating dynamic on the descent and ascent portions of the bounce, Gravity-Gravity) versus a composite bounce event (gravity descent but a spring generating the ascent, Gravity-Spring)? Third, is the effect of the discontinuity the same for differences occurring just before versus just after the collision? Do O's better discriminate a Gravity-Gravity bounce from a Spring-Gravity or from a Gravity-Spring bounce? If the effect is not equal for the two composite events then the effect of the discontinuity would appear to be directional in nature.

Method

O's viewed computer simulations (InterActive Physics II8) of a circular object bouncing vertically (3.96 deg to 6.6 deg visual angle of vertical amplitude, 840 msec duration). A 2AFC procedure was used with a standard event (Gravity-Gravity Bounce) and one of three target events (Spring-Spring, Spring-Gravity or Gravity-Spring bounces, see Figure 1). Three levels of trajectory form variation were used for each target type. Pair order (target-standard vs standard-target) was randomized. The O's task was to identify the target event in each pair of displays. Demonstrations of the standard and target events were given prior to testing. Four O's judged 324 pairs of displays for each of the target events. No feedback was given.

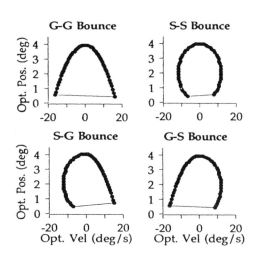

Figure 1. Trajectory forms for the standard (Gravity-Gravity) and the strongest level of form variation for the 3 target bounce events (Spring-Spring, Spring-Gravity, and Gravity-Spring).

Results

Trajectory form variation was defined as the sum of "Curvature Ratios" during the descents and ascents. The Curvature Ratio is the ratio of the maximum to the minimum curvature in a trajectory form. The value of this sum of Curvature Ratios for the Standard bounces (Gravity-Gravity) is 38.23. Each target event's Curvature Ratio is subtracted from this benchmark. Thus the higher the Curvature Ratio value the farther the trajectory form is from the standard bounce event.

The measure of the threshold of trajectory form variation was the average of the 25% and 75% points along the Probit curve (cumulative normal fit to the O's % indicating the first item in a trial is the target). Curvature Ratio thresholds and Pseudo R^2 values (Aldrich & Nelson, 1984) for the target bounce events were as follows: Spring-Spring bounce = 27.58, R^2 = .24; Spring-Gravity bounce = 19.03, R^2 = .20; and Gravity-Spring = 6.81, R^2 = .48. Gravity-Spring bounce events varied the smallest amount from the Gravity-Gravity bounces before reaching threshold, thus O's were most sensitive to this type of trajectory form variation.

Parallelism tests compare the slopes of cumulative normal curves to assess whether the relative sensitivity of O's between two events is equal (see Figure 2). Comparisons of the relative sensitivity between the three bounce events were

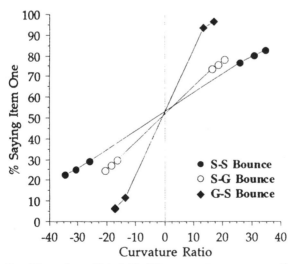

Figure 2. Plot of predicted Probit percentages versus the trajectory form measure "Curvature Ratio." Steeper curves indicate greater sensitivity and lower thresholds.

as follows: Spring-Spring versus Spring-Gravity, $\chi^2(1)$ = 21.62, p < .001; Spring-Spring versus Gravity-Spring, $\chi^2(1)$ = 270.15, p < .001; Spring-Gravity versus Gravity-Spring, $\chi^2(1)$ = 167.14, p < .001.   All of the parallelism tests indicated that none of the three bounce events sensitivities were the same.   O's were most sensitive to trajectory form variations in the Gravity-Spring bounce event, followed by the Spring-Gravity bounce event and the Spring-Spring bounce event.

Discussion

O's were able to discriminate between the Gravity-Gravity standard events and the Spring-Spring target bounce events based on trajectory form variations similar to those in Bingham et al. (1995). The threshold Curvature Ratio value of 27.58 for Spring-Spring bounces indicates that a moderate amount of trajectory form variation is needed before O's can discriminate these two events. However, the presence of the discontinuity in the trajectory form at the point of the collision did not seem to hinder O's from discriminating the Spring-Gravity or Gravity-Spring bounces from the standard Gravity-Gravity bounces. Furthermore, O's were most sensitive to trajectory form variations with the Gravity-Spring bounces. O's seem more sensitive to detecting changes in symmetry in a trajectory form (symmetric standards versus asymmetric targets).   This is consistent with previous findings with asymmetric vs symmetric pendular events (Muchisky, 1995).

References

Aldrich, J. H., & Nelson, F.D. (1984). Linear probability, Logit, and Probit Models. *Quantitative Applications in the Social Sciences*, (45), Sage Publications Inc.

Bingham, G. P., Rosenblum, L. D., & Schmidt, R. C. (1995). Dynamics and the orientation of kinematic forms in visual event recognition. *Journal of Experimental Psychology: Human Perception and Performance, 21*, 1473-1493.

Muchisky, M. M. (1995). Event identification via dynamically governed trajectory forms. In B. G. Bardy, R. J. Bootsma & Y. Guiard (Eds.) *Studies in Perception and Action III* (pp. 359-362). Lawrence Erlbaum Associates Inc.

Studies in Perception and Action IV
M. A. Schmuckler & J. M. Kennedy (Eds.)
© 1997 Lawrence Erlbaum Associates, Inc.

Evidence For The Directness Of Advanced Information Pickup

Sverker Runeson, Peter Juslin, & Henrik Olsson

Deptartment of Psychology, Uppsala University, Uppsala, Sweden

Since the outset, the Gibsonian ecological approach has featured, and is sometimes seen as identical with, the notion of *direct perception*. To support adaptive action, organisms have to perceive meaningful, action-relevant, properties (affordances), and information for these was shown to exist in ambient media, albeit in analytically complex forms. This radical step was complemented, and the contrast with established belief was aggravated, through the claim that such advanced proximal properties could be *picked up directly* -- in a *direct mode of apprehension.*

The primary route to an empirical verification has been to study *performance characteristics* on tasks that require the use of advanced informative properties (e.g., Runeson & Vedeler, 1993). However, the directness aspect is not specifically addressed in this way. Thus it remains a hypothetical possibility that passable performance is achievable only through an indirect, inferential, use of information, with simple cues as the units of perceptual pickup (e.g., Gilden, 1991; Gilden & Proffitt, 1989).

Evidence on the process of apprehension itself is hard to come by. Introspective reports raise tough issues of relevance and validity. However, a distinction between "sensory" and "cognitive" tasks occurs in research on *calibration of confidence* (the relation between people's trust in their judgments and their actual performance). An established finding is that in "knowledge-based" tasks people range from well calibrated to overconfident, whereas underconfidence prevails on sensory tasks. The *sensory sampling model* (Juslin & Olsson, in press) provides a theoretical account for these findings. The model also elucidates the common occurrence of poorer-than-chance results in cognitive tasks and their absence in sensory tasks. Thus confidence judgments may be used for performance-independent assessment of the mode of apprehension deployed in the use of advanced information.

Method

Planar collisions were simulated and displayed by means of an analog-hybrid simulator system (Runeson & Vedeler, 1993). In each trial, Os had the dual task of choosing the heavier of two colliding objects and then rating their confidence in the choice on a 50-100% scale ("pure guess" to "perfectly sure").

The design comprised a 96-trial pretest, a 640-trial training phase with feedback, and a 192-trial posttest. In addition to the application of confidence methodology, a performance-based *critical test* of Gilden & Proffitt's (1989) cue-heuristic model was implemented by including two special sets of collisions in the test blocks. Either of the cues proposed by that model were selectively nulled, leaving the "exit-speed" and the "scatter-angle" cues operative one at a time--in addition to the omnipresent perfect information due to *kinematic specification of dynamics* (Runeson, 1977/1983, 1995). The training phase employed a more representative set of collisions. A total of 15 observers participated.

Results

Pretest results show a mixed picture (Figure 1). In the ExitSpeed-Only condition, average neophyte performance was intermediate between the cue and perfect-invariant predictions. In the ScatterAngle-Only condition, data have no resemblance to the cue prediction, but tend towards the invariant. *After training*, a massive swing to invariant usage has occurred. None of the cues have appreciable explanatory value for the posttest results.

Browsing the individual pretest results, six Os were clearly using ExitSpeed and one used ScatterAngle, while three were already on to a good invariant. In contrast, the posttest revealed most Os were now clearly using a good invariant, with none obviously using any of the cues.

Figure 2 presents the changes in over/underconfidence through the experiment. Figure 3 shows pre- and posttest comparisons of confidence calibration for individual Os and as related to performance. After training, the great majority of Os have either changed from overconfident to underconfident or consolidated their underconfidence. Figure 3 also illustrates the better performance achieved in the posttest. The clear separation of the curves is proof that the plunge in over/underconfidence is not just due to the lower relative difficulty of the task in the posttest.

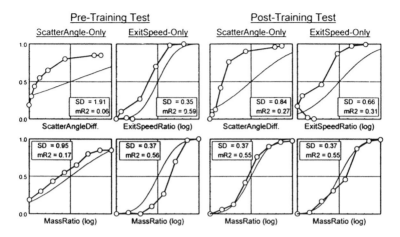

Figure 1. Proportions "Object B heavier" responses obtained in pre- and posttest, separately for the two cue-only conditions. Each dataset is plotted as a function of two candidate kinematic properties: the appropriate cue-heuristic model cue (top panels) and the perfect invariant (m_B/m_A massratio; below). All x-axes are scaled to a ±1 range. Probit-fitted ogives are shown, with associated standard deviations and measures of fit (McFadden's R^2). To support an x-axis candidate, data must form an ogive that passes through the center of the graph (cf. Runeson & Vedeler, 1993).

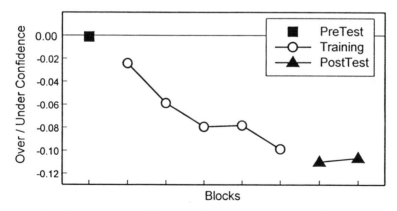

Figure 2. Blockwise confidence-calibration averages. Note progressive emergence of underconfidence as skill increases in the course of training, indicating a transition from a mixed to a direct-perceptual ("sensory") mode of apprehension.

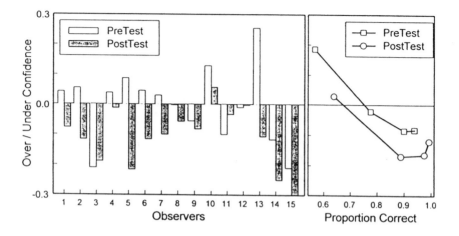

Figure 3. Calibration of confidence in pre- and posttest. Left-hand panel shows results for individual Os. Right-hand panel plots calibration as functions of proportion correct responses. Note displacement of posttest curve to the right, revealing the higher level of skill achieved through training.

Generally, while the pretest pattern of confidence judgments is suggestive of cognitive task data, it agrees closely with typical sensory discrimination results in the posttest. Likewise, a substantial occurrence of poorer-than-chance cases in the pretest has vanished in the posttest.

Discussion

Through the critical design and the confidence methodology, the idea that perception is fundamentally confined to elemental cues has been disproved. Rather, it appears people use cues in lieu of perceptual skill and as pedagogical crutches in exploring a new task. In the course of the minimal experience afforded, most Os discovered better, more advanced, informative properties-- directly apprehendable, as with a *smart perceptual mechanism* (Runeson, 1977).

Acknowledgments. The present study was supported by grants from the *Swedish Council for Research in the Humanities and Social Sciences.*

References

Gilden, D. L., & Proffitt, D. R. (1989). Understanding collision dynamics. *Journal of Experimental Psychology: Human Perception and Performance, 15,* 372-383.

Gilden, D. L. (1991). On the origin of dynamical awareness. *Psychological Review, 98,* 554-568.

Juslin, P., & Olsson, H. (in press). Thurstonian- and Brunswikian origins of uncertainty in judgment: A sampling model of confidence in sensory discrimination. *Psychological Review.*

Runeson, S. (1977). On the possibility of 'smart' perceptual mechanisms. *Scandinavian Journal of Psychology, 18,* 172-179.

Runeson, S. (1983). *On visual perception of dynamic events.* (Acta Universitatis Upsaliensis: Studia Psychologica Upsaliensia, Serial No. 9). (Original work published 1977)

Runeson, S. (1995). Support for the cue-heuristic model is based on suboptimal observer performance: Response to Gilden & Proffitt (1994). *Perception & Psychophysics, 57,* 1262-1273.

Runeson, S., & Vedeler, D. (1993). The indispensability of precollision kinematics in the visual perception of relative mass. *Perception & Psychophysics, 53,* 617-632.

Studies in Perception and Action IV
M. A. Schmuckler & J. M. Kennedy (Eds.)
© 1997 Lawrence Erlbaum Associates, Inc.

Magnitude Production Of Relative Mass:
A Preliminary Study

Steven B. Flynn, Heather F. Russell, & D. Michael Deron

Psychology Department, Northeast Louisiana University,
Monroe, LA, U.S.A.

Can people accurately judge the relative mass of colliding objects? In recent years, this question has engendered considerable controversy (Flynn, 1994, 1995; Gilden & Proffitt, 1989; Gilden, 1991; Runeson & Vedeler, 1993). To date, empirical explorations of this issue have employed variations of the *magnitude estimation* procedure from psychophysics (Stevens, 1975): Observers are presented with a stimulus event and asked to judge the perceived relationship (i.e., the perceived relative mass) via some sort of quantitative report. In the present work, we decided to take a different tack: We used the *magnitude production* procedure (Stevens, 1975). Magnitude production is the converse of magnitude estimation: Observers are given quantitative values and asked to produce them by modifying some aspect of a stimulus event (Stevens, 1975).

Method

Observers. Two observers were employed: One of the authors (SF) and a graduate student (MY) who was naive to the issues surrounding relative-mass perception. Both were volunteers.

Collision objects. Two plastic bowls, identical in manufacture and appearance, served as collision objects. They were white, with a diameter of 20.3 cm and a depth of 8.6 cm. Each was center-fit with a long bolt extending into its cavity. The bolts allowed metal plates (i.e., washers, pipe fittings and barbell accessories) ranging in weight from 5 to 2349 g to be secured to the bowls.

Collisions. Collisions were staged on a fleck-patterned linoleum floor. One bowl (the *target bowl*) was placed at rest on the floor. A second bowl (the *incoming bowl*) was launched (pushed) by an assistant so that it would strike the target bowl approximately head-on and at a medium speed (or as indicated by the observer; see below). Collisions were video-relayed from directly overhead with a Canon ES80 8-mm Camcorder suspended from the ceiling superstructure to a 20 in. (50.8 cm) Panasonic CT-2081y color video monitor in an adjacent room. Bowl diameter was about 5.72 cm on this monitor. The camera was positioned to produce a "bird's eye" view of the collisions. The target-bowl image was centered on screen (or as directed by the observer; below) and the incoming-bowl image entered stage left, traveling horizontally across the screen. Neither the launcher nor the launch event was visible on-screen.

Procedure. Observers were tested singly. The observer would be seated in front of the video monitor and presented with masking noise (via headphones) to muffle collision sounds. The observer communicated with the launcher in the collision room via a one-way electronic communication system.

For each trial, the observer was given a mass ratio (the *Goal Ratio*) from the set 1:4, 1:3, 1:2, 1:1, 2:1, 3:1, 4:1. The observer watched collisions on the monitor and dictated how the weight of the incoming bowl should be modified (e.g., 'a little heavier'; 'a lot lighter') to produce the Goal Ratio. This view→adjust→view process continued until the observer was satisfied that the actual ratio of the bowls' weights (the *Selected Ratio*) was identical to the Goal Ratio. Observers produced one Selected Ratio per Goal Ratio. The launcher was blind to Goal Ratio throughout the experiment.

Observers were encouraged to explore collision parameters--incoming bowl weight and speed, target bowl placement, collision incidence angle--to see how such changes affected apparent mass ratio. Observers were encouraged also to explore the parameters of the viewing event, that is, to try various viewing distances, lighting arrangements and postures to the same effect. It was emphasized that observers should be assertive in searching for event and viewing parameter settings that maximized their ability to complete the task (Flach, 1990).

Results and Discussion

Figure 1 plots log Selected Ratio against log Goal Ratio for each observer individually and pooled. The regression function is for the pooled data.

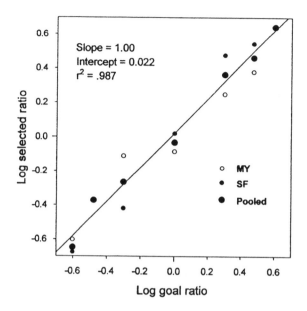

Figure 1. Selected mass ratio as a function of goal mass ratio for observers MY, SF, and their data pooled. Regression line and parameters are for the pooled data.

Because the graph is a straight-line function in log-log units, the results are interpretable with respect to Stevens' Power Law (Stevens, 1975), which is of the form:

$$y = kf^a \tag{1}$$

The regression slope is the exponent of the power function, and the antilog of the intercept is the constant k; thus, the present data yield the following relationship between physical and perceived mass ratio:

$$\text{judged ratio} = 1.05 * (\text{actual ratio})^{1.00} \tag{2}$$

The interpretation of this is straightforward. The fact that the exponent and the constant k are both unity indicates that impressions of mass ratio are a linear function of actual mass ratio. These results indicate that an accounting of the pooled relative-mass impressions need extend no further than the distal mass ratio of the colliding objects; once mass ratio is accounted for, there is nothing left to explain.

Acknowledgments. This research was supported by a grant from the Northeast Louisiana University Research Council. The second and third authors contributed equally to this project; order was determined by a coin flip. Heartfelt thanks are due Mark Yates for his participation.

References

Flach, J. M. (1990). Control with an eye for perception: Precursors to an active psychophysics. *Ecological Psychology, 2(2)*, 83-112.

Flynn, S. B. (1994). The perception of relative mass in physical collisions. *Ecological Psychology, 6(3)*, 185-204.

Flynn, S. B. (1995). Effect of velocity on judgments of relative mass. *Perceptual and Motor Skills, 81*, 979-987.

Gilden, D. L. (1991). On the origins of dynamical awareness. *Psychological Review, 98*, 554-568.

Gilden, D. L., & Proffitt, D. R. (1989). Understanding collision dynamics. *Journal of Experimental Psychology: Human Perception and Performance, 15*, 372-383.

Runeson, S., & Vedeler, D. (1993). The indispensability of precollision kinematics in the visual perception of relative mass. *Perception & Psychophysics, 53*, 617-632.

Stevens, S. S. (1975). *Psychophysics: Introduction to its perceptual, neural, and social prospects.* New York: Wiley.

Studies in Perception and Action IV
M. A. Schmuckler & J. M. Kennedy (Eds.)
© *1997 Lawrence Erlbaum Associates, Inc.*

Measuring Visible Information In Mediated Environments

Catherine M. Burns

Cognitive Engineering Laboratory, Department of Mechanical and Industrial Engineering, University of Toronto, Toronto, ON, Canada

The increased use of computer display technology has created the situation where people must work almost exclusively within a mediated environment. Their ability to complete their tasks safely and effectively becomes highly dependent on how well designed that environment is. The field of computer interface design is clearly a situation of mediated perception (Gibson, 1979; Vicente & Rasmussen, 1990). Much of the effectiveness of the interface is dependent on the skills of the mediator, the interface designer.

One of the great advantages of computers is that they can manage vast quantities of information within the confines of a relatively small box. For this reason, computerized displays are becoming popular for monitoring and controlling large scale industrial systems. The controls and displays that once required a room-sized control board can now be presented on one or two CRTs. This gain however, comes with its commensurate costs. Only small quantities of this information can be displayed at a single time while the bulk of the information remains effectively obscured. This phenomenon, depicted in Figure 1, has been likened to looking through a keyhole (Woods et al., 1990). In using these systems, people are prone to getting lost and losing the sense of what is happening in the system as a whole (Elm & Woods, 1985; Woods et al., 1990; Roth et al., 1993).

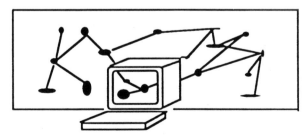

Figure 1. The keyhole view through a computer CRT.

As part of a study on improving navigation within computer displays for these large scale systems, we began by looking at literature on navigation in natural environments.   Benedikt's (1979) discussion of navigation in architectural spaces provided a close analogue to the keyhole situation described by Woods (1990).   In navigating through rooms in buildings, the environment is only partially visible with much of the environment occluded behind walls and objects. Benedikt drew from Gibson's information array the concept of an *isovist* which he defined as "a location-specific pattern of visibility" (p. 48).   Figure 2 shows an isovist in a cluttered environment. Furthermore, at each vantage point in space an isovist can be defined, creating an isovist field. Benedikt argued that these isovists, or characteristics of these isovists could act as informers to navigation.

Why consider isovists in computer displays?

In studying interface design for computer displays for large scale systems we need to understand what characteristics of the mediated environment might be affecting the performance of the display users. This calls for some relevant way of measuring the mediated environment. In particular, our recent work is directed at understanding factors that affect navigation behavior in computer displays of large scale systems which are prone to keyholing and disorientation (Elm & Woods, 1985; Woods et al., 1990; Roth et al., 1993).   Benedikt's architectural spaces parallel the keyhole discussed by Woods in that both environments are subject to areas of visibility, areas of occludedness, and movement of an observer through the environment that changes the visible information.   In both cases the patterns of visibility and occludedness are specific to the observer's position in the environment. If isovist patterns and isovist fields could act as informers to navigation as Benedikt suggested, something similar could act as an informer to navigation in mediated environments. The isovist is also quantitative and Benedikt proposed several further measures based on the original isovist measures.

What might be the "isovist" in a computer display?

By working in architectural space, Benedikt was able to simplify his discussion to two-dimensional isovists, such as what might be worked out from a floor plan or blueprint. Benedikt was also able to take advantage of the fact that light travels in straight lines to describe isovists analytically and to develop

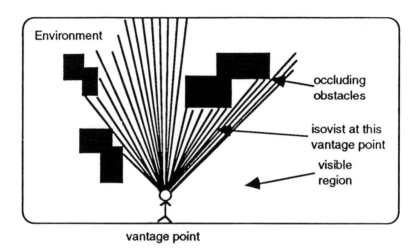

Figure 2. Benedikt's (1979) definition of isovist.

environment measures based on isovists. The mediated environment of computer displays is not as straightforward. Plain display space is not necessarily correlated with what is meaningful and informative about the environment. What is meaningful, however, are the elements of information which are displayed. In an industrial system, this corresponds to the plant variables that are displayed. Depending on the location of the user of the system, certain variables will be visible and other variables will be occluded, thereby creating a "location-specific pattern of visibility". It is possible to develop some measures such as:

Keyhole Size: the number of visible displayed variables
Size of Occluded Area: the total number of variables - keyhole size
Relative Keyhole Size: the percentage of possible variables that have been displayed
Relative Occludedness: 1 - the relative keyhole size.

Plans and Challenges

Our research intends to incorporate these measures developed from Benedikt's isovist concept as part of a larger study of navigation within computer displays. These measures, however, are admittedly naive. The meaning of the variables with respect to the behavior of the plant and the form of the display of those variables in terms of making that behavior visible are undoubtedly very important factors affecting user behavior. However, these variables, based on Benedikt's idea of isovists, offer promise for measuring aspects of the computer environment which may be affecting navigation behavior.

Acknowledgments. This work was funded through a grant from ABB Corporate Research, Heidelberg, Germany.

References

Benedikt, M. L. (1979). To take hold of space: Isovists and isovist fields. *Environment and Planning B, 6,* 47-65.

Elm, W. C., & Woods, D. D. (1985). Getting lost: A case study in interface design. *Proceedings of the Human Factors Society Annual Meeting,* 927-931. Santa Monica, CA: HFS.

Gibson, J. J. (1979/1986). *The ecological approach to visual perception.* Hillsdale, NJ: Lawrence Erlbaum Associates, Inc.

Roth, E. M., Mumaw, R. J., & Stubler, W. F. (1993). Human factors evaluation issues for advanced control rooms: A research agenda. *Proceedings of the IEEE Conference on Systems, Man, and Cybernetics* (pp. 254-259). New York, NY: IEEE.

Vicente, K. J., & Rasmussen, J. (1990). The ecology of human-machine systems II: Mediating "direct perception" in complex work domains. *Ecological Psychology, 2,* 207-249.

Woods, D. D., Roth, E. M., Stubler, W. F., & Mumaw, R. J. (1990). Navigating through large display networks in dynamic control applications. *Proceedings of the Human Factors Society Annual Meeting* (pp. 396-399). Santa Monica, CA: HFS.

Studies in Perception and Action IV
M. A. Schmuckler & J. M. Kennedy (Eds.)
© 1997 Lawrence Erlbaum Associates, Inc.

Visual Perception Of Relative Phase
And Phase Variability

Frank T. J. M. Zaal[1] & Richard C. Schmidt[2]

[1] Perception Action Laboratory, Indiana University, Bloomington, IN, U.S.A.
[2] Department of Psychology, Holy Cross College, Worcester, MA, U.S.A.

Coordinated rhythmical movement has been the cornerstone of the application of dynamical systems theory to our understanding of human movement (e.g., Kelso, 1995). It has been demonstrated that the phase relation between two oscillating limbs exhibits two naturally stable modes: an in-phase mode (0 degrees) and an anti-phase mode (180 degrees). Schmidt, Carello, & Turvey (1990) showed that these characteristics are also present when two persons coordinate their limbs with each other, suggesting that the informational coupling between the two oscillators can be of a visual nature.

Bingham, Schmidt, & Zaal (1996) performed a number of experiments in which the coordination of two oscillating balls on a computer screen was judged. The kinematics used in the displays were obtained from the actual bimanual pendulum movements. Relative phase was manipulated through the pendulums' inertial properties. Instructions defined coordination in terms of the amount of phase variability. The results indicated, however, that judgments were related to mean relative phase rather than to phase variability. Moreover, the 0 and 180 degrees conditions represented the most stable performance. Since in the displays mean relative phase and phase variability were confounded, we performed a similar study in which these two variables were manipulated separately by using numerical simulations.

Method

Twenty participants were shown two rhythmically moving balls on a computer screen (8 cycles, each lasting 1 s.). Balls could move with a mean relative phase (RP) of 0, 30, 60, 90, 120, 150, or 180 degrees. Phase variability (PV) was introduced by adding high frequency oscillation (3 Hz) at four levels (SDs: 0, 5, 10, and 15 degrees). Each combination of RP and PV was presented three times. Participants were divided in two groups: (i) judging RP, or (ii) judging PV on a scale from 0 to 10. Both groups first received instructions and demonstrations, in which examples were given of both manipulations. The subsequent "blocked" sessions of the two groups differed. For the group judging RP the trials were presented in four blocks of the same PV, with RP randomized within a block. The level of PV increased over the session. In contrast, the group judging PV were shown seven blocks of increasing RP, with PV randomized within a block. For both groups, the "blocked" session was followed by a "random" session, in which both RP and PV were randomized. Here we present data from these "random" sessions. Within-cell means and SDs were computed for each participant. The analyses involve the inter-participant means of these measures.

Judging mean relative phase

Participants were well able to perceive the differences in RP (Figure 1). A repeated measures ANOVA with factors Phase (7 levels) and Variability (4 levels) showed a significant Phase effect. Linear regressions on the individual participant's data yielded R^2 values from .62 to .95. The interaction was also significant ($F(18,162) = 2.56$; $p < .001$). Simple effects analyses indicated that added PV increased the RP judgments in the 0-degree (in-phase) condition significantly ($p < .001$) and slightly affected the judgments in the 180-degree (anti-phase) condition ($p < .05$).

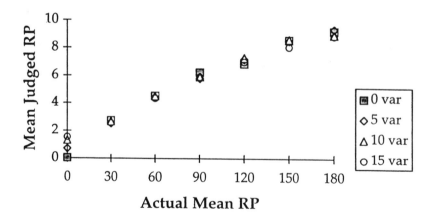

Figure 1. Mean relative phase judgments in group RP's "random" session.

Standard deviations of judgments were affected by the actual RP in the displayed movement. An ANOVA showed a significant Phase effect ($F(6,54)$ = 8.37; $p < .001$). The judgments in the 0-degree conditions were most stable (i.e., SD was smallest). The relation between the stability of the judgments and RP proved to be an inverted U-shape, with the 180-degrees conditions being less stable than the 0-degree conditions.

Judging phase variability

Except for the conditions in which RP was 0 degrees, participants were not very well able to judge the added PV. In these conditions, stability of judgments decreased (SDs increased) with increasing PV. Figure 2 shows the PV judgments as a function of the RP in the displays. An ANOVA on the mean judgments resulted in a significant Phase effect ($F(6,54)$ = 8.35; $p < .001$), a significant Variability effect ($F(3,27)$ = 21.71; $p < .001$), and a significant interaction ($F(18,162)$ = 2.97; $p < .001$). Simple effects analyses showed that the significant Variability effect was mainly caused by the differences in the 0-degree conditions ($p < .001$). The simple effects for Phase were significant at all levels of Variability ($p < .001$ for the three lower levels of variability; $p < .05$ for the highest level).

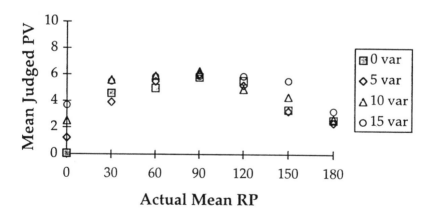

Figure 2. Phase variability judgments in group PV's "random" session.

Conclusion

Judgment of variability seems to be overpowered by mean relative phase effects. Movement away from the two stable 0- and 180-degree relative phases is perceived as more variable, implying that in natural movement only these stable states can be under perceptual control.

Acknowledgments. We would like to thank Geoffrey Bingham for the opportunity to perform this study in the Perception-Action Laboratory.

References

Bingham, G. P., Schmidt, R. G., & Zaal, F. T. J. M. (1996). *Visual perception of relative phase*. Paper presented at the 37th Meetings of the Psychonomic Society. Chicago, IL, November 2, 1996.

Kelso, J. A. S. (1995). *Dynamic patterns: The self-organization of brain and behavior*. Cambridge, MA: MIT Press.

Schmidt, R. G., Carello, C., & Turvey, M. T. (1990). Phase transitions and critical fluctuations in the visual coordination of rhythmic movements between people. *Journal of Experimental Psychology: Human Perception and Performance, 16*, 227-247.

Studies in Perception and Action IV
M. A. Schmuckler & J. M. Kennedy (Eds.)
© 1997 Lawrence Erlbaum Associates, Inc.

Judging Coordinatedness Of Stimuli

Gil Hupert-Graff[1] & Joachim Meyer[1,2]

[1] Research Center for Work Safety and Human Engineering Technion,
Haifa, Israel
[2] Dept. of Industrial Engineering, Ben Gurion University of the Negev,
Beer Sheva, Israel

Research on people's ability to produce coordinated movements has shown that the relative difficulty of maintaining coordination is related to the position of the ratio of frequencies in the Farey tree structure (e.g., Peper, Beek, & van Wieringen, 1995; Treffner & Turvey, 1993). The Farey tree is a number theoretical construction in which consecutive levels are devised by taking "parent" ratios p/q and p'/q' and computing the Farey mediant between them, which is $(p+p')/(q+q')$. Parent levels are more stable frequency ratios, and unstable performance of lower levels tends to converge to them.

The goal of the experiment reported here is to test the hypothesis that the evaluation of coordinatedness of events also obeys the hierarchy of the Farey tree. This may serve as evidence for the use of equivalent information for the control of movements and for the forming of intuitive judgments.

Method

Participants. Eight volunteers (2 men and 6 woman) without specific musical training or knowledge participated in the experiment.

Instruments and Procedure. The experiment was conducted on 486 DX2 (66 MHz) PCs. The program showed two red circles (each with 20 pixels diameter), placed on a white background on both sides of the center of the screen. Each circle pulsated at a different frequency. The duration of the on-time was always 100 msec and frequencies were changed by altering the time between pulses.

Participants were exposed to the 16 frequency ratios of the Farey tree up to level 3 in randomized order. The ratios were the parent ratio 1:1 (level -1), the ratio 1:2 (level 0), the ratios 1:3 and 2:3 (level 1), the ratios 1:4, 2:5, 3:5 and

3:4 (level 2), and the ratios 1:5, 2:7, 3:8, 3:7, 4:7, 5:8, 5:7 and 4:5 (level 3). The phase difference was always 0, and the slower frequency was always 1 Hz. The stimuli were shown for either 10 or 20 seconds, with the faster pulsating circle either at the right or at the left. After seeing the display, participants were asked to evaluate the coordinatedness of the lamps on a scale ranging between 1 (no coordination) and 100 (perfect coordination).

Participants completed a practice block with 32 trials and two experimental blocks with 64 trials each, holding all possible combinations of the values of the 16 frequency ratios, the two trial durations and the two positions of the rapid lamp.

Results and Discussion

In all following analyses, data collected during the practice block were excluded. Participants were instructed to consider the ratio 1:1 as 100. In order to prevent this instruction from biasing the statistical results, evaluations of the ratio 1:1 were excluded from the statistical tests.

The main purpose of the experiment was to test the question whether the assessed coordinatedness of frequencies ratios also declines with Farey levels. A two-way ANOVA was conducted with the evaluation as the dependent variable and the Farey level and subject (the last one entered as a random variable) as independent variables. Both main effects and the two-way interaction were significant with $p < .005$. Figure 1 presents the participants' mean evaluations of coordination as a function of the Farey level (with points representing the mean of all evaluations of stimuli for a given level). It is clear that all participants' evaluations decline as a function of Farey level. Also, participants adopted scales that differ significantly from each other.

A more detailed analysis of the responses to the different frequency ratios is warranted, since not only the Farey level, but also other factors may affect estimated coordinatedness. This receives support from Treffner & Turvey's (1993) finding that the difficulty of maintaining coordination movements for different ratios within a Farey level may not be the same. Figure 2 shows the mean judgments of coordinatedness for the 16 frequency ratios. Frequencies are ordered primarily by Farey level, secondarily by the stability of the nearest parent (the parent from the above Farey level) and thirdly by the stability of the other parent. This way of ordering reflects an intuitive assumption: ratios inherit their stability from their parents, while the nearer parent has more

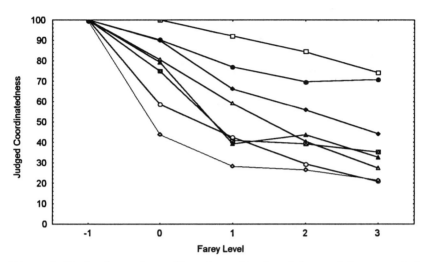

Figure 1. Evaluations of coordinatedness for the eight participants and the Farey levels.

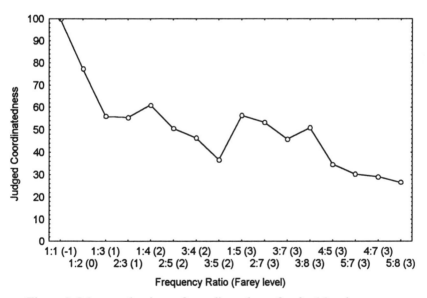

Figure 2: Mean evaluations of coordinatedness for the 16 ratios.

impact. The two way ANOVA with the ratio and the subject as independent variables again revealed significant main-effects and a significant interaction.

Figure 2 shows that evaluations of ratios in the same Farey level indeed differ. In line with Treffner and Turvey's (1993; Exp. 3) results the harmonic ratio (1:x) received the highest evaluation, and the Fibonacci ratio received the lowest evaluation. Our results reveal additional differences between other ratios in the same Farey level.

Summary

Judgments of coordinatedness and the actual performance of coordinated movements show the same regularities. This lends some support to the claim that intuitive judgments rely on the same or similar mechanisms that are used for action.

The perceptual judgment of relatedness may provide us with information about the mechanisms by which coordination is achieved that may be difficult to obtain through actual action, due to the physical constraints that apply to movement that limit the accuracy of motions. The Farey tree alone cannot account for the differences between frequency ratios.

References

Peper, C. E., Beek, P. J., & van Wieringen, P. C. W. (1995). Multifrequency coordination in bimanual tapping: Asymmetrical coupling and signs of supercriticality. *Journal of Experimental Psychology: Human Perception and Performance*, 21, 1117-1138.

Treffner, P. J., & Turvey, M. T. (1993). Resonance constraints on rhythmic movements. *Journal of Experimental Psychology: Human Perception and Performance*, 19, 1221-1237.

Studies in Perception and Action IV
M. A. Schmuckler & J. M. Kennedy (Eds.)
© *1997 Lawrence Erlbaum Associates, Inc.*

Heading Perception During Combined Observer Translation And Rotation

Li Li & William H. Warren

Department of Cognitive & Linguistic Sciences, Brown University,
Providence, RI, U.S.A.

How do human observers recover direction of heading during translation and rotation? This has been an intriguing problem in the field of perception of self-motion. Initial research by Warren & Hannon (1990) demonstrated that retinal flow contained sufficient information to decompose rotation and translation, but subsequent work by Royden, Crowell, & Banks (1994) found that extra-retinal information was necessary to determine eye rotation at rotation rates higher than 1 deg/sec. However, both studies used minimal random-dot displays of single planes or clouds. Warren et al. (1996) compared random-dot and texture-mapped displays that added complex 3D structure, dynamic occlusion, and reference objects, and showed that during simulated translation and rotation of the observer, random-dot displays yielded large heading errors as rotation rate increased (15 deg at 7 deg/s), but texture-mapped displays yielded much smaller mean errors (4 deg at 7 deg/s). This indicates that as the display is enriched, the visual system can determine direction of heading solely from the retinal flow. What are the sufficient sources of information in the complex texture-mapped scene that contribute to successful decomposition of translation and rotation? In the present studies, we try to answer this question by manipulating edge parallax, global parallax, radial foreground flow, and the presence of reference objects.

Method

Displays. Displays simulated observer translation over a ground plane at 2 m/s with a fixation point off to one side. There were 5 display types: (1) Occluding tombstones on a textured ground plane provided optical information from edge parallax, dense global parallax, radial foreground flow, and reference objects (Figure 1a); (2) Non-occluding posts on a textured ground plane provided dense global parallax, radial foreground flow, and reference objects (Figure 1b); (3) Textured ground plane alone provided dense global parallax and radial foreground flow (Figure 1c); (4) Occluding tombstones alone provided edge and global parallax and reference objects (Figure 1d); and (5) Non-occluding posts alone provided global parallax and reference objects (Figure 1e). All the displays were generated on a Silicon Graphics Crimson Reality workstation at 30 frames per second, and were projected on a large screen (112° H x 95° V). All subjects viewed the displays binocularly.

Viewing Conditions. There were two viewing conditions. In the *Simulated Rotation* condition, the fixation point was attached to a tombstone/post at eye level and remained stationary on the screen. The displays simulated optic flow at rotation rates of 0, ±1, ±3, ±5, and ±7 deg/s respectively. This placed optical and extra-retinal information about eye rotation in conflict. In the *Actual Rotation* condition, subjects tracked a moving fixation point at rotation rates of ±1 and ±5 deg/s respectively. In both conditions, the rotation was about the vertical axis.

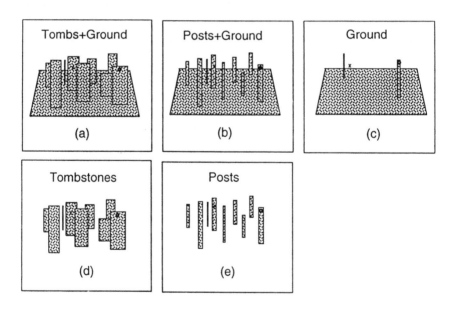

Figure 1. Five types of displays used in the experiments. (a) Occluding tombstones on a textured ground plane; (b) Non-occluding posts on a textured ground plane; (c) Textured ground plane alone; (d) Occluding tombstones alone; (e) Non-occluding posts alone.

Design and Procedure. Four experienced observers viewed all five display types. In addition, nine new naive observers viewed each one. For each eye rotation rate tested, there were 30 trials, 1.5 sec in duration. Observers were asked to track the fixation point during the course of the trial and adjust a probe at 10 m to indicate perceived heading at the end. Fifty-four practice trials for the Simulated condition were run without feedback before the experiments commenced. The dependent measure (heading error) was the angle between the correct heading and the judged heading.

Results

1. In the Simulated Rotation condition, mean heading error was small at all rotation rates as long as the textured ground plane was present, with or without added tombstones or posts. However, with tombstones alone or posts alone, error increased substantially with rotation rate (Figure 2a). This pattern of results was reproduced in simulations of a heading model based on differential motion (Rieger & Lawton, 1985; see Figure 2b).

2. In the Actual Rotation condition, mean heading error was small at all rotation rates for all five display types. The absence of a densely textured ground plane did not affect observers' heading judgments.

Conclusions

1. Dense global parallax and radial foreground flow provide sufficient information   to perceive heading during simulated eye rotation. We are currently testing whether global parallax or foreground flow alone is sufficient for accurate performance.

2. With active eye movements, observers can also use extra-retinal information to determine direction of heading during translation and rotation. Thus, perception of heading during eye movements uses both optical flow and eye position information.

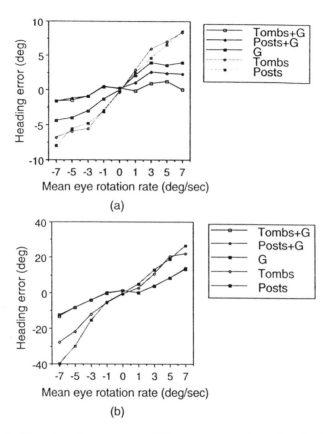

Figure 2. Mean heading errors at different eye rotations for the five types of displays (a) in the simulated condition, and (b) generated by the heading model with differential motion.

References

Rieger, J. H., & Lawton, D. T. (1985). Processing differential image motion. *Journal of the Optical Society of America, A, 2*, 354-360.

Royden, C. S., Crowell, J. A., & Banks, M. S. (1994). Estimating heading during eye movements. *Vision Research, 34*, 3197-3214.

Warren, W. H., & Hannon, D. J. (1990). Eye movements and optical flow. *Journal of the Optical Society of America, A, 7*, 160-169.

Warren, W. H., Li, L., Ehrlich, S. M., Crowell, J. A., & Banks, M. S. (1996). *Perception of heading during eye movements used both optic flow and eye position information.* Presented at ARVO.

Studies in Perception and Action IV
M. A. Schmuckler & J. M. Kennedy (Eds.)
© 1997 Lawrence Erlbaum Associates, Inc.

Robustness Of Heading Perception Along Circular Paths

Brett R. Fajen & Nam-Gyoon Kim

CESPA, University of Connecticut, Storrs, CT, U.S.A.

Human observers are quite accurate in perception even under severely impoverished conditions. For example, when driving in rain, accurate heading perception is still possible despite the presence of raindrops on the windshield. Indeed, Warren, Blackwell, Kurtz, Hatsopoulos, & Kalish (1991) demonstrated the robustness of heading perception in their study. Specifically, they constructed displays depicting linear and circular translation parallel to a ground plane made of random dots whose directions and magnitudes were manipulated. In "velocity field" displays, both vector directions and magnitudes were preserved. In "direction field" displays, vector directions were preserved but magnitudes were randomized. In "speed field" displays, vector magnitudes were preserved but directions were randomized. Performance was reliable with "velocity field" and "direction field" displays, but only at chance with "speed field" displays. These researchers contended that the information for heading perception is the instantaneous pattern of vector directions. Furthermore, the reliable performance with "direction field" displays was interpreted as evidence for the robustness of the visual system, the ability to tolerate large amounts of "directional noise."

The present study extended Warren et al.'s study in the following ways. First, they examined "speed field" displays only with respect to linear translation, whereas we extended it to circular translation. Second, they manipulated directional noise by varying direction, whereas we manipulated the signal-noise-ratio. Third, we contrasted "speed field" displays to a flow field containing snowy-type noise, a condition comparable to driving in snow. Lastly, Warren et al. evaluated heading accuracy indirectly by fitting each subject's data (percent correct) with an ogive and then regressing against heading angle to produce a heading threshold. We determined heading threshold directly by having participants indicate the exact location of the path and recording the difference between actual heading and perceived heading.

Method

Displays were generated on a Silicon Graphics Indigo^2™ and presented on a window of 1280 x 1080 pixels drawn at the rate of 60 frames/s. Displays simulated observer movement parallel to the ground plane along a circular path at a tangential speed of 13.2 m/s (or 30 mph). Each display lasted about 2 s (120 frames). A ground plane was made of 40 white pixels displayed on a black background. The trajectory of each dot constituting "signal" traced a circular path whose center of rotation shared that of the observer's path.

Both types of noise dots followed circular trajectories with randomized radii and centers of rotation. In the "ground noise" condition (equivalent to the "speed field" displays of Warren et al., 1991), noise dots were confined to the ground plane at one eyeheight below the point of observation. In the "snow noise" condition, the vertical component was varied such that noise dots started at a random height less than 30 m and decreased by 0.1 m/frame. Noise dots interacted with signal dots such that the hypothesized information for heading (i.e., the instantaneous pattern of vector directions) was preserved in the latter, but not the former.

A blue horizontal bar was placed at a simulated distance of 20 m from the observer and present throughout each trial. At the end of each trial, participants selected the point on the horizontal line, using the computer mouse, at which they thought they would cross if they were to continue on their current path. The difference in degrees between the point selected and actual heading was used to determine heading accuracy.

Three variables were controlled: radius of the observer's path (R), noise type, and SNR. R varied among ±60, 80, 120 or 240 m (plus for a right-hand turn and minus for a left-hand turn). SNR varied among 1, 0.5, 0.33, 0.25 and 0.17 (40, 80, 120, 160 or 240 noise dots, respectively). This yielded a 2 (noise type) x 8 (R) x 5 (SNR) design with a repetition for 160 trials. All variables were within-subject variables.

Ten undergraduate students at the University of Connecticut participated in the experiment.

Results and Discussion

Results were collapsed over the sign of R and entered into an ANOVA. Noise type, $F(1,9) = 118.86$, $p < .0001$, SNR, $F(4,36) = 5.18$, $p < .01$, and R, $F(3,27) = 22.15$, $p < .0001$, were reliable, as were noise type x SNR, $F(4,36) = 6.75$, $p < .001$ (Figure 1a), and noise type x R, $F(3,27) = 10.78$, $p < .0001$ (Figure 1b).

Performance was extremely poor in the ground noise condition (M = 5.1°), whereas performance in the snow noise condition (M = 2.7°) was well within the acceptable range of 2°-4° necessary for a proper braking at the simulated speed (Kim & Turvey, 1997). The effect of R was also consistent with prior findings (Kim & Turvey, 1997; Warren et al., 1991). Increased noise density had a detrimental effect in the ground noise condition, but was negligible in the snow noise condition.

Separate ANOVA's were conducted for both types of noise. In the snow noise condition, R, $F(3,27)$ = 5.02, p < .01, was significant, but SNR, F < 1, and SNR x R, F < 1, were not. In the ground noise condition, SNR, $F(4,36)$ = 7.76, p < .0001, and R, $F(3,27)$ = 25.18, p < .0001, were significant, but SNR x R, F < 1, was not. In the former, performance did reach an acceptable level of 3.8° with SNR = 1. With a standard error of 0.4°, however, its upper boundary of 4.2° failed to reach the acceptable level.

Taken together, results corroborate the previous findings that perceptual systems are robust against substantial amounts of noise. However, the robustness is only to the extent that information such as the instantaneous pattern of vector directions is available in the flow field (e.g., the snow noise condition). When it is absent (e.g., the ground noise condition), perception fails.

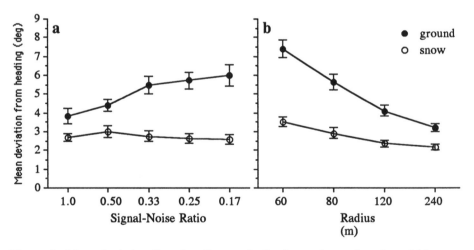

Figure 1. Mean deviation from heading angle (in degrees) as a function of (a) NR, and (b) radius (m), for both types of noise. Vertical bars indicate standard errors.

References

Kim, N.-G., & Turvey, M. T. (1997). *Curvilinear heading and global optical flow.* Manuscript submitted for publication.

Warren, W. H., Blackwell, A. W., Kurtz, K. J., Hatsopoulos, N. G., & Kalish, M. L. (1991). On the sufficiency of the velocity field for perception of heading. *Biological Cybernetics, 65,* 311-320.

Section I: *Perception*

I.B: *Audition*

Studies in Perception and Action IV
M. A. Schmuckler & J. M. Kennedy (Eds.)
© *1997 Lawrence Erlbaum Associates, Inc.*

Rotational Inertia Constrains Perception
Of Object Length By Sound

Krista L. Anderson, Andrew J. Peck, & Claudia Carello

CESPA, University of Connecticut, Storrs, CT, U.S.A.

The identification of sound source events such as rustling leaves or leaf blowers is reasonably commonplace. Despite the propensity of listeners to provide source identifications, psychoacoustic research has been concerned with the perception of properties of the sound (e.g., pitch, loudness) rather than perception of properties of the sound-source (e.g., size, shape, material). Nonetheless, it is sources that animals and humans perceive and source properties that have consequences for behavior (Gaver, 1993). Our research concerns accuracy in the perception of a sound source, not in terms of identifying the event—a wooden dowel dropping onto a hard surface—but assessing a metrical property of the object itself—its size. The goal of the present research is twofold: (1) providing an empirical evaluation of the basic capability of size perception by sound (in particular, the lengths of dropped wooden dowels), and (2) identifying the physical properties of the objects that constrain that perception.

The first goal is satisfied by the simple experiments described in Figure 1. Two groups of naive listeners were presented either with relatively large rods or relatively small rods. Both groups rank-ordered rod lengths appropriately within each radius set. Those who heard the larger rods also provided reasonably accurate length estimates (averaging from 24 to 95 cm). But the length discrimination for the small rods seems to be little better than half that of the larger rods. Far from indicating shortcomings of human listeners, however, this difference points to how we will satisfy our second goal, identifying the relevant physical properties of the rods.

We must seek a physical property that will both distinguish the rods from one another and anchor their perceived length in the appropriate metrical range. Stiffness, elasticity, and density seem inadequate to fulfill either function; they can be assumed to be the same across the objects in our experiments, given that the rods were all the same material. Rotational inertia, in contrast, varies with the length, radius, and mass of the rods. The contribution of rotational inertia to dynamic touch is already well known (Turvey, 1996). The major constraint on perceived length by wielding is rotational inertia, in particular, its quantification in the inertia tensor. It is affected by how length and radius distribute the mass relative to the rotation point. In dynamic touch, perceived length scales as the 1/3 power of the largest principal moment of inertia, I_1. While this has the consequence of pushing perceived lengths away from actual lengths, it is rooted in the dimensional relationship of actual length to the tensor. I_1 is proportional to the product of mass and the squared length. Mass, in turn, is proportional to volume, which is proportional to the product of length and diameter squared (for objects of cylindrical symmetry). For rods of constant diameter, mass is simply proportional to length. This means that I_1 is proportional to length cubed or, alternatively, length is proportional to the cube root of I_1. Since actual length is, therefore, tightly coupled to the inertia tensor, perceived lengths constrained by that tensor will be tightly coupled to actual length.

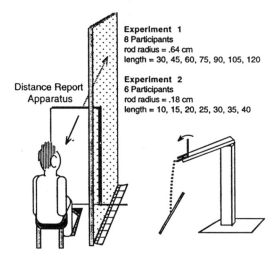

Figure 1. An adjustable vertical surface could be positioned from 0 to 200 cm by a listener. Each rod dropped from a fixed height. On a given trial, a rod was dropped 5 times. Participants were instructed to listen to the rods and move the adjustable surface out from the front edge of the desk to a position that could just be reached with the rod. The seven rod lengths in each experiment were presented three times in random order.

For nonconstant radii, as in the present experiments, the 1/3 scaling alone would lead to perceived lengths overly influenced by mass increases due to radius. Again, the relationship of actual length to the tensor shows how this scaling is modulated. When radius varies, actual length is related not only to I_1 but also to the smallest principal moment of inertia, I_3. In particular, for rods of varying lengths and radii, actual length scales positively to I_1 and negatively to I_3. This scaling has been found to characterize perceived length by wielding (Fitzpatrick, Carello, & Turvey, 1994). Because the rods of the present experiments differed in radius, the full tensor is relevant: A positive scaling of acoustically perceived length to I_1 and a negative scaling to I_3 was obtained. The combined data of the two experiments show that perceived length is a function of the power equation obtained from a multiple regression of log perceived length onto log I_1 and log I_3 ($r^2 = .97$). The exponent on I_1 showed the positive 1/3 scaling that is commonly found in experiments on dynamic touch. The negative exponent on I_3 was characteristic of dynamic touch experiments in which the radius of wielded rods varies. In particular, this relationship indicates that acoustically perceived lengths of small radius rods are compressed, not because they are less discriminable or pushing the limits of resolving power but because of their magnitudes with respect to a major physical variable constraining a rod's reactions on striking and, therefore, the sounds it produces.

The foregoing arguments and analyses indicate that, for the objects examined, the same physical quantity constrains perception of length by ear and by hand and it does so in the same way. This is more than coincidence; it reflects the variables that can influence their respective media. It is not yet clear whether this commonality will persist over other object variations. In any event, these lines of research support a characterization of the nervous system in terms of extracting physical invariants from its interactions with the physical world (Fitzpatrick et al., 1994).

Acknowledgments. The research reported here was supported by Grant SBR 93-09371 from the National Science Foundation. The authors thank M. T. Turvey for suggesting that the inertia tensor might influence hearing length as it influences perceiving length by dynamic touch.

References

Fitzpatrick, P., Carello, C., & Turvey, M. T. (1994). Eigenvalues of the inertia tensor and exteroception by the "muscular sense," *Neuroscience, 60*, 551-568.

Gaver, W. W. (1993). What in the world do we hear? An ecological approach to auditory event perception. *Ecological Psychology, 5*, 1-29.

Turvey, M. T. (1996). Dynamic touch. *American Psychologist, 51*, 1134-1152.

Studies in Perception and Action IV
M. A. Schmuckler & J. M. Kennedy (Eds.)
© *1997 Lawrence Erlbaum Associates, Inc.*

Auditory Interceptive Timing And Familiarity With Acoustic Environment

Kiyohide Ito

Institute of Special Education, University of Tsukuba, Tsukuba, Ibaraki, Japan

People intercept moving objects by picking up some information in the acoustic array as well as the optic array. Rosenblum et al. (1987) explained about the acoustic variables related to the accuracy in estimating the time of arrival (Ta time to arrival)(1987) and indicated that feedback increased the accuracy of Ta judgment (1993). Schiff & Oldak (1990) reported that blind people had the similar level of accuracy in the acoustic Ta judgment to the sighted person's optic Ta judgment. This suggests the blind people are equally capable of judging Ta using only acoustic information.

The blind person, in their real life, is often required to couple perception and action more than judging Ta. The blind baseball player judges the timing of swinging the bat by the sound of the approaching ball on the ground. In this case, it is considered to be difficult for the blind people to perform tasks without judging Ta accurately and coordinating the two conducts, namely interceptive action of hitting a ball and acoustical perception of detecting the moving ball.

This study aims to find the difference in the accuracy between simple Ta judgement and interceptive actions by blind people and to observe how interceptive timing errors are changing by repeating the task with no perceptual feedback assuming that the errors would decrease when familiarized with the circumstances (Coleman, 1962).

Experiment 1

Method

Ten blind people, nine males and one female with the age range of 16 to 31, participated and were asked to perform an interceptive Pendulum-hitting task and a judging Ta task in an echoic room using the apparatus shown in

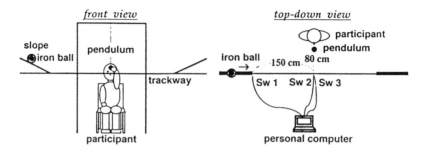

Figure 1. Timing switches (Sw) 1 & 2 are automatic and Sw 3 is manually operated.

Figure 1. In the first task, each participant was instructed to intercept the approaching iron ball (38 mm dia.) with a constant velocity on the U-shaped iron trackway (18 x 2700 mm) by swinging a pendulum and, in the second task, to press the switch (Sw3) when s/he thought it was passing in front of her/him. Interceptive timing errors and judgment errors were measured by the difference between actual time (Sw1 to Sw2) and perceived time (Sw1 to Sw3). Participants performed 20 trials in each task under two different conditions: S (ball velocity 1.0 m/s, actual Ta 1.5 s) and L (ball velocity 0.5 m/s, actual Ta 3.00 s) without getting any feedback or comments on each result of their task. They were told to keep looking forward without moving their head, not to use any means of judging time like number-counting and only to concentrate on the approaching sound of the iron ball.

Results and Discussion

Timing error and judging error were measured by the percentage difference of perceived time from actual time. Table 1 indicates that significant differences were recognized between the two tasks. Timing error in Pendulum-hitting was about twice as large as that of Ta-judging. This is because participants could not obtain any perceptual information about the pendulum which produces no sound except the acoustic information for localizing the moving sound made by the iron ball.

Table 1
Timing Error in Each Task Under the Two Conditions (n = 10)

		S Condition		L Condition	
		CE	VE	CE	VE
Ta	Mean	12.26	6.81	11.61	6.00
	Standard Deviation	4.08	1.66	3.65	2.23
IT	Mean	20.04	11.49	18.47	12.09
	Standard Deviation	6.43	4.22	9.27	5.66

Note. CE refers to constant timing error, VE to variable timing error (Tresilian, 1994). Ta refers to the judging time-to-arrival task to press the switch and IT to the interceptive timing task to hit the ball by the pendulum.

Experiment 2

Method

Four blind people, two males and females, were asked to perform 100 trials of only the Pendulum-hitting task with the ball velocity of 1.0 m/s and the actual Ta of 1.5 s without any feedback as in Experiment I.

Result and Discussion

All trials were divided into 10 divisions (Div. 1 to 10) with 10 trials each. Mean timing error for each participant ranged between 27.738 and 5.370 in Div. 1 and 7.460 and 1.940 in Div. 10. Standard Deviation error ranged between 8.666 and 5.249 in Div. 1 and 4.985 and 3.280 in Div. 10. All participants except #2, whose task seemed to have a ceiling effect and did not improve, showed a significant difference between Div. 1 and 10. Why the accuracy of interceptive timing increased is considered to have two reasons: 1) The participants have, by some means, obtained the perceptual feedback associated with the timing error, and 2) That they were familiarized with the acoustic environment where the task was performed. They were quite unfamiliar with the moving sound of iron balls and the echoic room for the experiment. Therefore, it is considered that the participants learned to coordinate the action of swinging the pendulum and acoustical perception of detecting the sound produced by the moving object while being perceptually

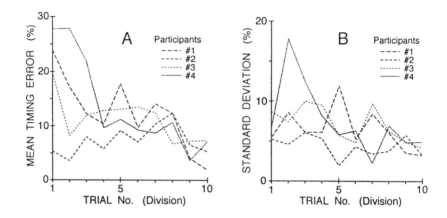

Figure 2. Profiles of A) mean and B) standard deviation of the timing error of the Pendulum-hitting task.

familiarized with the sound intensity, the interaural intensity difference, the interaural time difference and the ratio of direct and reverberant sound.

Conclusion

When elapsed time for interceptive tasks cannot be estimated perceptually, its timing error is larger than that of judging time-to-arrival. However, after repeating the trials, the accuracy in timing increased. Coupling of auditory perception and action was needed for listeners to succeed in the task and learning by trial and error brought higher achievement. Therefore, familiarity with acoustic environment is considered to play some kind of role in this coupling. The current study, however, has a fairly small number of participants and unsolved questions still remain. Hence, further study is being continued.

Acknowledgments. I am very grateful to Masato Sasaki for helpful comments, Kazuhiko Mamada and Tomohiro Haraikawa for technical assistance, Emi Miyamoto and Tanahashi for experimental assistance, and Junko & Johsei Nagakawa for editorial assistance.

References

Coleman, P. D. (1962). An analysis of cues to auditory depth perception in free space. *Psychological Bulletin, 60*, 302-315.

Rosenblum, L.D., Carello, C., & Pastore, E. (1987). Relative effectiveness of three stimulus variables for locating a moving sound source. *Perception, 16*, 175-186.

Rosenblum, L. D., Wuestefeld, A. P., & Saldaña, H. M. (1993). Auditory looming perception: Influences on anticipatory judgments. *Perception, 22*, 1467-1482.

Schiff, W., & Oldak, R. (1990). Accuracy of judging time to arrival: Effects of modality, trajectory, and gender. *Journal of Experimental Psychology: Human Perception and Performance, 16*, 303-316.

Tresilian, J. R. (1994). Approximate information sources and perceptual variables in interceptive timing. *Journal of Experimental Psychology: Human Perception and Performance, 20*, 154-173.

Studies in Perception and Action IV
M. A. Schmuckler & J. M. Kennedy (Eds.)
© *1997 Lawrence Erlbaum Associates, Inc.*

Acoustic Perception Of Aperture Passability

Michael K. Russell

CESPA, University of Connecticut, Storrs, CT, U.S.A.

Traditionally, investigations into acoustic perception have focused almost exclusively on either the perception of distance or sound location/localization. More recently, investigations into audition have begun to take a more ecological approach with an increased focus on "everyday listening" than on "musical listening" (Gaver, 1993). That is, studies into audition are focusing more on the environment in which perception occurs, the types of sounds which occur in the organism's natural environment, as well as the types of task associated with acoustic perception.

A recent recurring finding is that the same perceptual task can be accomplished visually and acoustically and in a comparable manner. The ability of organisms, human and nonhuman, to use the change in spatial layout as information about time-to-contact is possible acoustically and visually. The ability of human observers to perceive the reachability of an object can also be performed visually or acoustically. Nevertheless, similarities between vision and audition have only been briefly addressed from a theoretical perspective (e.g., Lee, 1990).

The present study further explored the relation between audition and vision by investigating the ability of observers to determine the passability of an aperture using acoustic information. Previous investigations have found aperture passability in the visual realm to be based on body-scaled information. Warren and Whang (1987) using humans, and Ingle and Cook (1977) using frogs, found that the critical boundary between passable and impassable apertures occurred with gaps 1.3 times greater than the observer's widest body part. If similarities exist between acoustic and visual perception of aperture passability, then acoustic perception should also be body-scaled.

Method

The seven participants were volunteers and students at Trinity College, Hartford, CT and all reported having normal hearing. Mean participant shoulder width was 47.2 cm.

The sound stimulus was a mallard (<u>Anas platyrhynchos</u>) hen assembly call recorded in the wild. Sounds were presented using an Apple Power Macintosh 7200, Realistic SA-150 amplifier, and a Realistic speaker (11 x 18 x 10.5 cm), at a zero degree azimuth to the observer's midline (Figure 1).

The procedure was adapted from Warren and Whang (1987). The boundaries to the aperture were established by the above mentioned speaker and a wall. Observers stood 2 m from the aperture, with eyes closed and the right side of their body aligned with the wall. The 3.0 sec assembly call could be replayed by the observer, although the large majority of trials involved a single call broadcast. Aperture size, the distance between speaker and wall, ranged from 35 to 90 cm, in 5 cm increments. For each aperture, they were asked to verbally state whether or not they could pass through the aperture. The 12 apertures sizes were presented four times each in random order for a total of 48 trials.

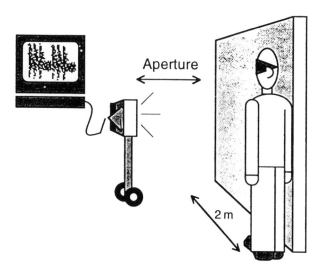

Figure 1. Schematic drawing of the testing arrangement.

Results

An ANOVA on the mean participant data yielded a significant effect of aperture size (F (11,72) = 7.54, p < 0.001). As can be seen in Figure 2, with an increase in actual aperture size, the percentage of "no" responses decreased.

In order to determine if perception of aperture passability is body scaled, the ratio of aperture size to mean shoulder width, A/S, was calculated. As can be seen in Figure 2, observers were more likely to report being able to pass through the aperture when the aperture to shoulder width was greater than 1.0.

Discussion

As stated previously, visual perception of aperture passability was indexed by A/S 1.3 for active humans and non-humans. In addition, Warren and Whang (1987) calculated the critical aperture to shoulder width for static observers to be 1.16. The results of the present study suggest not only that acoustic perception of aperture passability is possible, but also that it is remarkably similar to aperture passability based on visual information. Similar to what was documented by Warren and Whang, the present study determined static observers being more likely to report an aperture as passable when the ratio of aperture width to shoulder width was greater than 1.0. Since the present study and previously published findings have documented similarities between visually and acoustically based perception, future studies may wish to investigate the factor(s) affecting the acoustic basis of perception, as well as the possibility of identifying a single unifying informational basis to perception that is amodal.

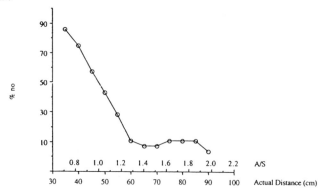

Figure 2. Mean percentage of "impassable" judgments as a function of aperture width and aperture width normalized for shoulder width (A/S).

References

Gaver, W. W. (1993). What in the world do we hear?: An ecological approach to auditory event perception. *Ecological Psychology, 5*, 1-29.

Ingle, D., & Cook, J. (1977). The effect of viewing distance upon size preference of frogs for prey. *Vision Research, 17*, 1009-1019.

Lee, D. (1990). Getting around with light or sound. In R. Warren & A. H. Wertheim (Eds.), *Perception and control of self-motion* (pp. 487-505). L. Erlbaum Associates: Hillsdale, N.J.

Warren, W. H., Jr., & Whang, S. (1987). Visual guidance of walking through apertures: Body-scaled information for affordances. *Journal of Experimental Psychology: Human Perception and Performance, 13*, 371-383.

Studies in Perception and Action IV
M. A. Schmuckler & J. M. Kennedy (Eds.)
© 1997 Lawrence Erlbaum Associates, Inc.

Acoustic Perception Of Sound Source Occlusion

Michael K. Russell

CESPA, University of Connecticut, Storrs, CT, U.S.A.

As noted by Gibson (1979), "the earth is generally cluttered" and "surfaces are generally opaque" (p. 78). Occlusion and disocclusion arise, with important consequences for perceiving and acting. Replacing "opaque" with "solid" highlights the possibility of acoustic occlusion.

Little attention has been given to the acoustic aspect of occlusion and disocclusion. To the contrary, most investigations of the acoustic perception of distance or location/localization have been conducted in uncluttered environments. Although the characterization of clutter for acoustics is usually in terms of reflecting surfaces rather than occluding surfaces, casual observation suggests that both biological and nonbiological sounds are detected, located, and tracked going behind and emerging from clutter. Thus, the possibility exists that the acoustic perceptual system is capable of detecting occlusion. The present experiments assessed this capability. In particular, can listeners detect the presence of an occluding object?

The Experiments

In addition to the absence of clutter in typical experimental designs (sometimes exacerbated by the use of anechoic chambers), the use of pure tones or broadband noise also contrasts with the natural environment whose sounds have both linear and nonlinear components. Duck calls are instances of such natural sounds and were used here. Experiment 1 used a call recorded in the wild; Experiment 2 used a call recorded in the laboratory (for clarity).

Method

Students at Trinity College, Hartford, CT, volunteered to participate; four in Experiment 1 and five in Experiment 2. All reported having normal hearing.

The sound stimulus for Experiment 1 was a mallard (Anas platyrhynchos) hen assembly call recorded in the wild. The sound stimulus for Experiment 2 was a laboratory-recorded mallard duckling contentment call. Sounds were presented using an Apple Power Macintosh 7200, Realistic SA-150 amplifier, and a Realistic speaker (11 x 18 x 10.5 cm), at a zero degree azimuth to the observer's midline.

The speaker was wholly or partially occluded (see below) by a wooden plank (13.5 x 43 x 2 cm) placed 2 cm in front of it.

Participants, seated 2.4 m from the speaker with eyes closed, were asked to state "yes" or "no" as to the presence of an occluding surface. The 3.0 sec assembly call and the 1.2 sec contentment call could be replayed by the observer, although the large majority of trials involved a single call broadcast. Neither feedback nor practice were given.

Complete occlusion and no occlusion were examined along with partial occlusion (25 and 50% of the speaker hidden by the plank). Since an ear bias has been documented (e.g., Mandal, Pandey, Singh, and Asthana, 1992), partial occlusion was assessed independently for the right and left sides of the speaker. Thus, participants were exposed to six occlusion arrangements (0, right 25, left 25, right 50, left 50, and 100%), four times each, yielding a total of 24 trials.

Results

For Experiment 1, the effect of occlusion was not significant in a one-way ANOVA on the mean participant data ($p > 0.35$; Figure 1). A post-hoc Tukey test revealed all occlusion arrangements were perceptually comparable ($ps > .05$).

For Experiment 2, the ANOVA on the mean participant data yielded a significant effect of occlusion [$F(5,24) = 3.44$, $p < 0.05$; Figure 2]. A post-hoc Tukey ($p < 0.05$) test revealed significant differences between 0 and 100%, and between right 25 and 100%, occlusion.

Discussion

The present study demonstrated that listeners can detect occlusion acoustically; the more occluded the sound source, the more likely were observers to report the presence of an occluding surface. Nevertheless, the ability to detect occlusion was dependent on the sound stimulus and the side of

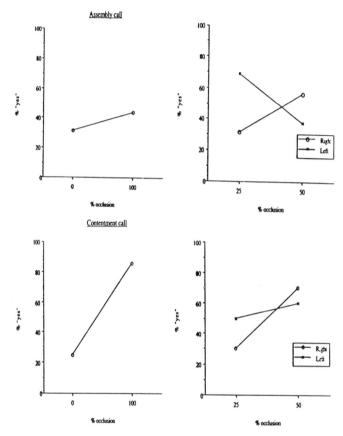

Figure 1. Mean percentage of "yes" responses as a function of percent sound source occlusion.

occlusion. The critical difference between such stimuli remains to be seen. Nevertheless, the point should be underscored that the acoustic perception of occlusion is possible. Future studies will investigate the factor(s) affecting the perception of occlusion.

References

Gibson, J. J. (1979). *The ecological approach to visual perception*. Boston, MA: Houghton-Mifflin.

Mandal, M. K., Pandey, G., Singh, S. K., & Asthana, H. S. (1992). Degree of asymmetry in lateral preferences: Eye, foot, ear. *Journal of Psychology, 126*, 155-162.

Studies in Perception and Action IV
M. A. Schmuckler & J. M. Kennedy (Eds.)
© *1997 Lawrence Erlbaum Associates, Inc.*

Constraints On A Nonspeech McGurk Effect

Lawrence Brancazio[1], Cathi T. Best[2], & Carol A. Fowler[1]

[1] University of Connecticut and Haskins Laboratories, Storrs, CT, U.S.A.
[2] Wesleyan University and Haskins Laboratories, U.S.A.

An auditorily-presented speech syllable (for example, the syllable /ba/), dubbed on the visual image of a different speech syllable (e.g., /da/), is heard as the visually-presented syllable or some combination of the two (the "McGurk effect"). Saldaña & Rosenblum (1993) tested a nonspeech analogue of the McGurk effect by pairing audio signals of violin plucks with video presentations of bows, and vice versa. They found a smaller effect of visual mismatch for plucks and bows than for consonants.

We tested for a McGurk effect with stimuli that are kinematically and acoustically similar to speech: clicks used in African languages, which are perceived as nonspeech mouth sounds by native English speakers (Best, McRoberts, & Sithole, 1988). We used bilabial, dental, and lateral clicks, both coarticulated with a following vowel and in isolation. For comparison, we used the English syllables /pa/, /ta/, and /ka/, and their excised release bursts. We tested whether a strong McGurk effect can be found for nonspeech stimuli that share kinematic properties with speech; and whether dynamic acoustic information (found in formant transitions between a consonant release and a vowel), paired with dynamic visual information (as the vocal-tract articulators move from a consonant closure to a vowel configuration), is necessary for the effect to occur.

Method

An AXB paradigm was used. The test (X) token was presented auditorily, and the comparison (A and B) tokens were presented audio-visually. The audio presentation of one comparison token was from the same category as the test token, and the other was different. In the Match condition, both comparison audio tokens were matched with congruent visual stimuli (audio /pa/ matched with video /pa/). In Mismatch, the visual stimuli were switched between the A and B tokens. In the English stop consonant conditions, /pa/-/ta/ and /pa-ka/ comparisons were used; in the click conditions, bilabial - dental and bilabial - lateral comparisons were used. In a third trial-type, Different-Audio, the A and B tokens were acoustically identical, and from a different category than the X token. A or B had a video token that matched its audio token, and the other had a video token that matched the X audio token.

Two test sequences were shown to each group, English syllables, English excised bursts, click syllables, and uncoarticulated clicks (n = 24): an Audio-alone test of discriminability, and an Audio-visual test (including randomized Match, Mismatch, and Different-Audio trials). Participants decided which comparison token *sounded* more like the test token. The effect of visual presentation upon judgments was determined by subtracting the percentage of correct audio-match judgments in the Mismatch condition from the percentage of correct judgments in the Match condition, and by the percentage of trials above 50% in Different-Audio where the comparison token with the video matching the test token was heard as more similar to the test token.

Results

a. *English stop consonants.* In the Audio-alone condition, discrimination was higher for full syllables than for excised bursts, and among excised bursts, /ka/ had the most errors. In the Audio-visual condition, the Match-Mismatch effect was significantly greater in the full-syllable condition than in the excised-burst condition [$F(1,45) = 15.32$, $p < .001$]. Results by condition (with significant effects marked) are shown in Figure 1. In Different-Audio, the audio token with the video matching the test token was selected significantly more often than chance in all four full-syllable conditions. The video effect was greatest for the full-syllable audio /pa/ paired with video /ta/, which was judged as similar to audio /ta/. There were no significant video effects in any of the excised-burst conditions.

b. *Clicks.* In the Audio-alone condition, discrimination was higher for full syllables than for isolated clicks, and among isolated clicks, the bilabial was often confused with the dental. In the Audio-visual condition, the Match-Mismatch video effect was significant for the bilabial-dental contrast, but not for the bilabial-lateral [$F(1,45) = 31.75$, $p < .0001$]. In the full-syllable condition, the bilabial-dental effect was significant for either test token, but it was significant only for bilabial in the isolated-click condition (see Figure 1). In Different-Audio, in the full-syllable condition, there were significant

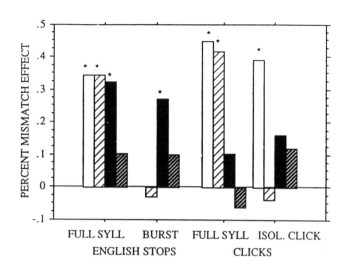

Figure 1. Difference in percent audio match selection between match and mismatch trials. White bars are /pa/-/ta/ and bil.-dent. contrasts; shaded bars are /pa/-/ka/ and bil.-lat. Solid bars are for the first of the pair as test token, striped bars are for the second of the pair. * indicates significant effects (*p* < .01).

video effects for audio bilabial paired with video dental (A.bil-V.dent), for A.dent-V.bil, and for A.lat-V.bil. In the isolated click condition, the only significant video effect was for A.dent-V.bil.

Summary. The mismatch effect (both in the Mismatch and Different-Audio trials) was weak when only the initial portion of the acoustic signal was presented. The mismatch effect was as great for clicks as it was for English consonants. With excised bursts and isolated clicks, the effect occurred only when acoustic discriminability was relatively poor: the bilabials were mistaken as dental in the audio-alone condition, and the corresponding mismatch effects were significant. In contrast, bilabials and laterals were highly distinguishable, as were /pa/ and /ta/ bursts, and there were no mismatch effects for these comparisons.

Discussion

Overall, the results suggest that a robust McGurk effect may require a dynamic acoustic signal (the transitions), as well as a dynamic visual signal (Rosenblum & Saldaña, 1996). When only an initial acoustic release burst is present, the effect is weaker; it occurs only when the acoustic signal is confusable with the acoustic signal normally produced by the visual event. Possibly the time-scale of the acoustics must be commensurate with the time-scale of the dynamic visual information for a strong McGurk effect. Given an appropriate acoustic signal, however, the McGurk effect may be as strong for nonspeech events as for speech.

Acknowledgments. This research was supported by NICHD Grant HD-01994 to Haskins Laboratories.

References

Best, C. T., McRoberts, G. W., & Sithole, N. M. (1988). Examination of perceptual reorganization for nonnative speech contrasts: Zulu click discrimination by English-speaking adults and infants. *Journal of Experimental Psychology: Human Perception and Performance, 14,* 345-360.

Rosenblum, L. D., & Saldaña, H. M. (1996). An audiovisual test of kinematic primitives for visual speech perception. *Journal of Experimental Psychology: Human Perception and Performance, 22,* 318-331.

Saldaña, H. M., & Rosenblum, L. D. (1993). Visual influences on auditory pluck and bow judgments. *Perception & Psychophysics, 54,* 406-416.

Studies in Perception and Action IV
M. A. Schmuckler & J. M. Kennedy (Eds.)
© *1997 Lawrence Erlbaum Associates, Inc.*

Metaphor In The Surround: Adult Metaphoric Utterances And The Emergence Of Metaphor

Cathy Dent-Read

Center for the Study of Women, University of California,
Los Angeles, CA, U.S.A.

Metaphor, although usually considered a verbal phenomenon, can also be expressed pictorially and in action (Kennedy, 1982; Dent & Rosenberg, 1990). We argue that metaphoric resemblance is perceptible and that "seeing-as" is the process of detecting the qualities of one kind of object or event in another (Dent, 1984; Dent & Rosenberg, 1990; Dent-Read & Szokolszky, 1993; Dent-Read, 1997). Further, metaphor is an expression of "seeing-as" that guides the listener. I have documented the development of metaphor in my daughter from her first words through 15 months (Dent-Read, 1997). Here, I document the metaphors, expressed in action and/or language that she experienced in this period to ascertain the forms the metaphors took and the frequency of metaphors experienced in relation to those expressed.

Method

The data consist of short narrative entries in a diary of the child's language use. Recording began with her first word (age 10 months) and continued to five years. In addition, entries on metaphors addressed to her or used in her hearing were made. Narratives described the verbal and action contexts and components for the metaphors.

The metaphors used by adults were grouped into categories similar to those previously analyzed (Dent-Read, 1997) -- type, form, and content. Type is either action, verbal or both; form is either metaphor or simile ("like" is used); and content is either object or event. Adult metaphors were scored as addressed to the child or not. Only data from the first 15 months are examined; detailed methods are published elsewhere (Dent-Read, 1997).

Results

Adult metaphors were not recorded until 9 months after the child's first word. Metaphors were likely used prior to her use of language, but before the start of the study. Adult metaphors began when hers did -- 1 year 7 months of age. The overall frequency of metaphors used by adults and the child is presented in Figure 1. At the age when the child first started using metaphor, the first adult metaphors were recorded. Adult metaphors are more frequent than the child's, then decrease, then increase again. Only 3 of the adults' metaphors were not directed to the child. The child's reactions to the metaphors varied. Most often she said nothing, sometimes she repeated the vehicle term, sometimes she denied the assertion.

The metaphors divided into object and event are given in Figure 2. Adults more often used event metaphors in the ratio of 28:16. This pattern fits with previous experimental data, but not with this child's use of metaphor, where event metaphors did not predominate either in timing or in frequency over object metaphors.

Adult verbal metaphors were in the form of metaphors rather than similes in the ratio 31:10. The child's metaphors in this period were mostly single word utterances, i.e., use of vehicle only. She began to use the word "like" for comparison, but did not use it in metaphors during the study.

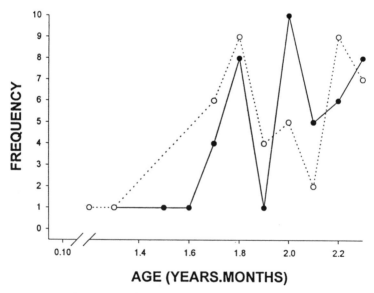

Figure 1. Total frequency of child and adult metaphor.

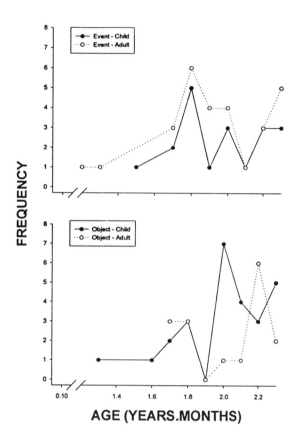

Figure 2. Frequency of child and adult metaphors based on event or object resemblance.

Finally, only three of the adult metaphors were action metaphors. Experience with pictorial metaphor was not recorded as it was too frequent; children's picture books contain many visual metaphors. The child used action metaphors more often than her parents, but these did not predominate either in timing or in frequency over verbal metaphors.

Discussion

These data form the first characterization of metaphors in the ambient social surround of a young child learning language. A record of every metaphor she heard is nonexistent because she was cared for outside her home 12-15 hours per week and metaphors in books were not recorded. The metaphors recorded, which contain the predominance of metaphors addressed to her, or overheard, show no consistent relation over time in frequency of adult and child metaphors.

The pattern of results for object vs. event metaphors in child and adult metaphors is intriguing. For event metaphors, frequency patterns between adult and child metaphors show a strikingly similar pattern over time, with adults generally slightly higher in frequency. Neither adult recalls being aware of the frequency of the child's metaphors during the study -- frequencies were not tabulated contemporaneously. Object metaphors show no such pattern. Adults may more easily notice resemblance between events, and see qualities of one in another as in previous experimental studies, which may account for their more frequent use of event metaphors. If child and adult form a mutual reciprocal system, then adults may influence the child to use event type metaphors, but she does not influence them to use object metaphors.

References

Dent, C. (1984). The developmental importance of motion information in perceiving and describing metaphoric similarity. *Child Development, 55,* 1607-1613.

Dent, C., & Rosenberg, L. (1990). Visual and verbal metaphor: Developmental interactions. *Child Development, 61*, 983-994.

Dent-Read, C. (1997). A naturalistic study of the development of metaphor: Seeing and seeing-as. In C. Dent-Read & P. Zukow-Goldring (Eds.), *Evolving explanations of development: Ecological approaches to organism-environment systems.* Washington, DC: American Psychological Association.

Dent-Read, C., & Szokolszky, A. (1993). Where do metaphors come from? *Metaphor and Symbolic Activity, 8*, 227-242.

Kennedy, J. (1982). Metaphor in pictures. *Perception, 11*, 589-605.

Studies in Perception and Action IV
M. A. Schmuckler & J. M. Kennedy (Eds.)
© *1997 Lawrence Erlbaum Associates, Inc.*

Auditory And Haptic Information Support Perception Of Size

John Pittenger, Jason Jordan, Angela Belden, Piper Goodspeed & Frank Brown

Department of Psychology, University of Arkansas at Little Rock, Little Rock, AR, U.S.A.

This study follows-up on work presented at ICPA-8. Pittenger, Guski, & Heine (1995) showed that both acoustic and haptic information made available by shaking cylinders containing ball bearings supported perception of the number of balls in those containers. Guth, Rieser, & Yen (1995) presented a demonstration, but not data from parametric studies, showing that people who stirred dishes of beads could discriminate among the sizes of the beads.

In the present study, size discrimination was assessed using both the stirring and shaking techniques for producing haptic and auditory information. Subjects were tested in the information conditions; Haptic (in which the subject stirred or shook containers of balls while listening to a masking noise), Auditory (in which the experimenter stirred or shook the containers while the subject listened) and Full (in which the subject shook or stirred the containers in the absence of masking noise).

Method

Eight sizes of steel shot (which provided fine gradations of size from .14 to .21 inch diameter) and seven sizes of plastic beads (which provided a wide range of sizes, 2.4 to 10 mm diameter) were employed. For the shaking method, 3/4 inch of shot or beads were placed in opaque plastic cylinders (different sizes in different cylinders). Subjects lifted and shook the cylinders. For the stirring method, glass bowls were filled with 1 inch of balls and were stirred with a stick inserted though the top of the opaque cloth cone that covered each bowl.

Each subject was tested under all three information conditions. Method (stir vs shake) and Material (shot vs. beads) were between-subjects factors.

Subjects were instructed to place the containers in a line in order of the size of the balls they contained. Accuracy was stressed and subjects were encouraged to check and revise their orderings. No feedback was provided to subjects until after testing was completed.

Ninety-six college students participated, 24 in each of the 4 combinations of method and material.

Results and Discussion

For each trial, the Spearman rank-order correlation coefficient between the observed and the correct size order was computed. A MANOVA which treated the coefficients for the three information conditions as dependent measures was conducted. Significant effects of Material (shot vs. beads), Method (shake vs. stir), Information, Material*Method, and Material*Information were found. The relevant means are presented in Table 1.

The most striking finding is the high accuracy with which the subjects were able to perceive the relative sizes of the balls on the basis of the vibrations heard and/or felt as the containers were shaken or stirred. This is demonstrated by the high positive values of the correlations and by counts of the number of inversions needed to correct the observed orders. These counts were made as follows; If the correct order was 1 2 3 4 5 6 7 and the subject placed them in 2 1 3 4 5 6 7, then one inversion was needed. Two inversions would be needed for 2 1 4 3 5 6 7 and for 3 1 2 4 5 6 7. Mean Spearmans of .97 and up correspond to means of fewer than 1.0 inversions, while mean Spearmans between .92 and .95 correspond to mean inversions below 2.0. For sets of 7 and 8 containers, these small numbers of inversions reflect nearly perfect performance.

Looking at the effects of material and method, note that shot (for which diameters of successive sizes differed by .01 or .02 inches) were more difficult to order than beads (which differed by steps of 0.6 to 2.0 mm). Also, stirring produced generally less accurate orders than did shaking. We suspect this is due to the greater range of patterns, amplitudes, and frequencies of motion possible with shaking. The interaction of material and method can be understood by noting that stirring leads to reduced accuracy only for shot, i.e., for the more difficult-to-order sets of stimuli.

The main effect of Information is interesting. Ordering based on sound information alone is just as accurate as ordering based on both sound and haptic information (i.e., in the full information condition). That is, access to haptic information in addition to sound information does not improve performance. However, haptic information alone does lead to performance at a

Table 1

Mean Spearman Correlation Coefficients Between Observed and Correct Size Orders

Information Condition	Shaking		Stirring	
	Shot	Beads	Shot	Beads
Full	.94	.97	.80	.99
Sound	.95	.97	.82	.99
Haptic	.60	.94	.57	.97

level better than chance. Information and material interacted, in that performance in haptic trials was especially poor for shot. For beads, haptic trials were only slightly less accurate than the full and sound trials.

While performance with shot in haptic trials was the weakest found in this study, many subjects were still at better-than-chance levels. Of the 48 subjects tested with shot in the haptic condition, 22 had Spearman coefficients significant at the .05 level and 34 had coefficients significant at the .20 level. These frequencies are far above those expected if all subjects were ordering the containers at random.

References

Guth, D., Rieser, J., & Yen, L. (1995, July). *Toward understanding long canes as perceptual tools: Tapping, scraping, and stirring to identify stuff by sound and touch.* Presented at the 8th International Conference on Perception and Action, Marseille.

Pittenger, J., Guski, R., & Heine, W.-D. (1995, July). *Shake, rattle and roll: Non-visual information supports perception of number.* Presented at the 8th International Conference on Perception and Action, Marseille.

Section I: *Perception*

I.C: *Haptics and Touch*

Studies in Perception and Action IV
M. A. Schmuckler & J. M. Kennedy (Eds.)
© *Lawrence Erlbaum Associates, Inc.*

Local Attitudes Are The Effective Stimuli For Haptic Curvature Discrimination

Sylvia C. Pont, Astrid M. L. Kappers, & Jan J. Koenderink

Helmholtz Instituut, Universiteit Utrecht, The Netherlands

The thresholds for static haptic curvature discrimination at different locations on the hand and for stimuli varying in length up to 20 cm reveal a single trend. This trend suggests that the effective stimulus for the discrimination of curvature in the range -4/m to +4/m is the total difference of local surface attitude (the slope difference) between the outermost contact positions on the stimulus (Pont, Kappers, & Koenderink, in press).

We want to test whether curvature discrimination is indeed based on local surface attitude differences, or whether local curvature or height differences also play a role in this process.

Method

Three naive, paid subjects participated in the experiments.

The stimuli were three geometrically different series of strips with a length of 20 cm, a width of 2 cm, and a peak or trough height of 5 cm. The "zeroth-order stimuli" (Figure 1, left) had a 2.5 cm wide raised or sunken part in the middle (range -10mm to +10mm). These strips are described by the zeroth-order geometrical structure, namely height difference. The "first-order stimuli" had an attitude ranging from -3.4° to +3.4° relative to the horizontal, on both sides, and a 2.5 cm wide horizontal platform in the middle. These strips (Figure 1, middle) have geometrical properties up to the first-order (local attitude difference). The third set consisted of circularly curved strips. These "second-order stimuli" (Figure 1, right) contain components up to the second-order, namely curvature (range -4/m to +4/m). Figure 1 B shows the three stimuli ranges, from the most "concave" versions (at the rear) to the most "convex" ones (at the front).

Figure 1. The three sets of stimuli.

The (unseen) strips were touched statically and always in the same place: perpendicular to the subject's fingers, under the distal joints of the index, middle and ring fingers, with the middle finger at the middle of the strips. The subjects had to indicate which of two successively presented strips was more "convex".

We tested the following combinations of the index ("I"), middle ("m"), and ring ("r") finger: "imr", "ir", "im", "mr", "i" and "r". The conditions "ir", "i" and "r" were not tested for the zeroth-order stimuli, because under these conditions the only remaining cue would be the height difference between successively presented strips. A control condition "m" was tested with the second-order stimuli to find out whether the subjects could discriminate curvature locally in the range -4/m to +4/m.

A flat reference strip was combined with seven "convex" and seven "concave" test strips. All combinations were presented eight times in a random sequence. Each experimental condition (112 trials) was tested three times on different days.

Psychometric curves were determined for the percentages of judgments in which the test strips were judged to be more convex than the reference strip as a function of the curvature (or attitude or height difference) of the test strips. The basic dependent variable is the discrimination threshold at 84% correct.

The discrimination thresholds for the second-order stimuli in terms of curvature were transformed into values in terms of the first- and zeroth-order (height difference and local attitude), using the contact lengths of the fingers on the strips.

Results and Discussion

The discrimination thresholds with standard errors for subject HB are represented in Figure 2. The results for the other two subjects are similar. The results for the zeroth- and the second-order stimuli in terms of height difference are depicted in the right panel. The thresholds for the zeroth-order stimuli are clearly much higher than those for the second-order stimuli in units of height differences. Thus, the height difference cannot be a cue for curvature discrimination.

The left panel shows the values for the first- and the second-order stimuli in terms of local attitude. The discrimination thresholds for the curved strips are similar to those for the first-order strips. This means that the second-order geometrical structure, namely the local curvature, does not contribute markedly to discrimination of curvature. This was confirmed by the control experiment in which condition "m" was tested for the second-order stimuli: the thresholds exceeded the measuring range, from which it is clear that in our measuring range the subjects cannot determine curvature locally.

We conclude that the effective stimuli for the discrimination of curvature in the range -4/m to +4/m are local attitudes. Height differences and local curvature do not play a role in this process.

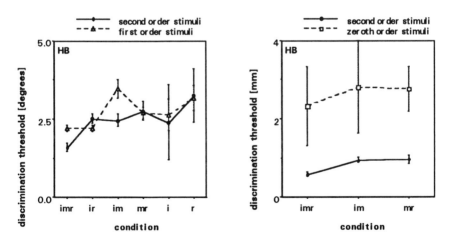

Figure 2. Discrimination thresholds for subject HB. The connections between the thresholds for the different conditions are added simply for visualization.

The thresholds for the conditions "imr" and "ir" are, overall, lower than the rest. The performance thus improves if the stimulation consists of two non-horizontal attitudes instead of one. The thresholds for the conditions "i" and "r" are in the order of 2 to 4 degrees. Thus, a local attitude difference between successively presented strips of only 2 to 4 degrees can be discriminated by means of static touch with one finger. This discriminatory power provides the basis for curvature discrimination in our measuring range.

Acknowledgments.   We are grateful to the Netherlands Organization for Scientific Research (NWO).

References

Pont, S. C., Kappers, A. M. L., Koenderink, J. J. (in press). Haptic curvature discrimination at several regions of the hand. *Perception & Psychophysics.*

Studies in Perception and Action IV
M. A. Schmuckler & J. M. Kennedy (Eds.)
© *Lawrence Erlbaum Associates, Inc.*

Influence Of Orientation On The Haptic After-Effect Of Cylindrical Surfaces

**Ingrid M. L. C. Vogels, Astrid M. L. Kappers,
& Jan J. Koenderink**

Helmholtz Instituut, Universiteit Utrecht, The Netherlands

The perceived curvature of a surface is strongly influenced by a previously touched surface (Vogels et al., 1996). The judged sign of the curvature (convex/concave) is biased in the direction opposite to that of the preceding curvature. The magnitude of this haptic after-effect of curved surfaces increases with curvature: after a spherical surface has been touched for 5 s the after-effect on a subsequently touched surface is about 20% of the curvature of the first surface. The strength of the after-effect is also enhanced by the duration of contact with the first surface: the time constant of buildup is about 2 s. The after-effect decreases with increasing time-lapse between the touching of the two surfaces: the time constant of decay is about 40 s.

So far, only the after-effect of spherical surfaces has been investigated. In the experiments reported here we study the after-effect of cylindrical surfaces. These surfaces can be described as:

$$z(x,y) = -1/2 \ k \ x^2 \qquad (1)$$

where k is the principal (extreme) curvature of the surface which has the largest absolute value. The curvature along the y-axis is $0/m$[1], i.e., flat. Since cylindrical surfaces are not rotation invariant about the surface normal, the curvature distribution, and therefore the posture of the hand, depend on the orientation of the surface. We investigated whether the after-effect of a cylindrical surface depends on its orientation relative to the hand .

---

[1] Curvature is defined as reciprocal radius.

Method

Three naïve paid subjects participated (WR, RR and WH). The stimuli had a cylindrical upper surface, according to equation 1. The size of the stimuli was such that the edges of the surfaces could not be felt. Stimulus curvature ranged from -4/m (concave) to 4/m (convex).

In each trial subjects had to touch two surfaces presented successively: a conditioning surface (for 10 s) and a test surface. The orientation of the two surfaces was the same within one trial but was varied between trials. Blindfolded subjects were asked to judge the curvature of the test surface along the axis of the principal curvature with the largest absolute value. Their judgments were restricted to "convex" or "concave". The axis could be oriented either along the middle finger (0 deg) or across the middle finger (90 deg). Subjects were not allowed to move their hand over the surfaces.

The conditioning curvature could be: -4, -2, -1, 0, 1, 2, or 4/m. Each conditioning surface was combined with seven differently curved test surfaces and each combination was presented 10 times. A psychometric function was fitted to the percentage of convex judgments for each conditioning surface. We refer to the 50% point of the psychometric curve as the "phenomenal flatness", since we assume that the surface which is judged to be convex in 50% of the cases is perceived as flat. The difference between the 50% and 85% points is called the threshold.

Results

In Figure 1 the phenomenal flatness is given as a function of the conditioning curvature for the two orientations and for all subjects. We fitted linear functions to the data points, which yielded correlation coefficients of about 0.9 (see Table 1). The offset corresponds to the phenomenal flatness after the touching of a flat surface and is subject-dependent. For subject RR the offset depends on the orientation of the test surface. The slope represents the magnitude of the after-effect and is on average 0.18. Although the slope is always larger in the case of an orientation of 90 deg, this is only significant for one subject (RR). When we plot the phenomenal flatness for 0 deg against the phenomenal flatness for 90 deg and fit a linear function we find that the ratio of the after-effects for the two orientations are 1.20 (WR), 1.39 (RR) and 1.26 (WH).

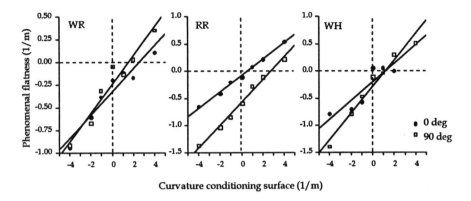

Curvature conditioning surface (1/m)

Figure 1. Phenomenal flatness as a function of the conditioning curvature for a surface orientation of 0 deg (filled circles) and 90 deg (open squares).

The thresholds of the psychometric curves did not vary systematically with the conditioning curvature. For subject RR the threshold was significantly larger when the curvature to be judged was oriented along the middle finger (90 deg).

Discussion

Our experiment shows that the perception of curvature along the axis of the largest absolute curvature of a cylindrical surface is influenced by the conditioning curvature of a previously touched surface. The influence tends to be slightly larger when the curvature is presented across the middle finger than when it is presented along the middle finger. However, this anisotropy is rather weak and not always significant. Therefore, this experiment demonstrates that orientation does not have a strong influence on the haptic after-effect of curved surfaces. Since the posture of the hand and the pressure on the skin depend on the orientation of a surface, we conclude that these stimulations are only of minor importance for the after-effect.

Vogels, Kappers, & Koenderink

Table 1

Offsets (1/m), Slopes and R^2-values of the Linear Functions Fitted to the Data Points of Figure 1.

subject	offset	0 deg slope	R^2	offset	90 deg slope	R^2
WR	-0.33	0.13	0.92	-0.24	0.16	0.94
RR	-0.08	0.15	0.99	-0.57	0.21	0.98
WH	-0.20	0.17	0.88	-0.28	0.24	0.96

Acknowledgments. This research was supported by the Netherlands Organization of Scientific Research (NWO).

References

Vogels, I. M. L. C., Kappers, A. M. L., & Koenderink, J.J. (1996). Haptic after-effect of curved surfaces. *Perception, 25,* 109-119.

Studies in Perception and Action IV
M. A. Schmuckler & J. M. Kennedy (Eds.)
© *Lawrence Erlbaum Associates, Inc.*

The Perceptual Recovery Of Texture Gradients
By Active Touch

Barry Hughes

Department of Psychology, University of Auckland, Auckland, New Zealand

Haptic texture perception is an instance of a structure-from-motion problem: perceiving a surface by touch produces a proximal event that is a function of the surface structure, the coding properties of the cutaneous receptors, and the kinematic characteristics of the actively moved area of skin. Previous research has typically involved roughness judgments using regular distributions of texture elements (see, e.g., Johnson & Hsiao, 1992; Loomis & Lederman, 1986). It is theoretically and practically useful to evaluate texture perception under other conditions (Hughes & Jansson, 1994). At issue here is whether changing the spacing of the texture elements at a rate commensurate with the inevitable changes in the velocity of the finger pad during cyclical sweeps across the surface, alters perceptual accuracy. Does, for example, a sinusoidal velocity profile over a sinusoidal spatial gradient in the opposite direction result in accurate recovery of the gradient or would the two gradients subtract to produce the perception of a nongradient? Existing models suggest not, at least for direct touch since the information sufficient for texture recovery is contained in spatial (rather than temporal) distributions (rather than averages) of cutaneous activity (especially via slowly adapting mechanoreceptors; Connor & Johnson, 1992; Hsiao et al., 1993). The perceptual importance of movements appears to reside in their generating and sustaining these cutaneous events. Vibrotactile events, by contrast, tend to activate motion-sensitive, rapidly adapting and Pacinian afferents (Gardner & Palmer, 1989); for these events, access to movement information may assist in the recovery of structure.

Method

On each trial of two experiments, participants (n = 24) were asked to discriminate one of 20 surfaces that contained bidirectional spatial gradients from nongradients of the same mean frequency (range: 0.36 - 0.52 cycles per mm) but no gradient. Direct finger pad exploration of raised elements (0.5mm high, 0.5mm wide) or Optacon exploration of flat images (0.5mm wide elements) were both used. In addition, the experiments involved variations in the type, direction, and magnitude of the gradient, and in the element structure. Examples of surfaces are shown in Figure 1. Subjects explored laterally and cyclically across the surfaces for a duration of between 5 and 7 s, following which they judged whether or not the surface contained a gradient. No constraints were placed on movement speed or force. All visual and auditory information was removed. No accuracy feedback was provided.

Results and Discussion

Figures 2 and 3 show the mean perceptual sensitivity indices for each experiment. The effects of gradient magnitude and mode were significant in all cases, including their interaction: the rate of increase in sensitivity with magnitude was 2 - 3 times greater with direct touch. This is likely due to the

Experiment 1   **Experiment 2**

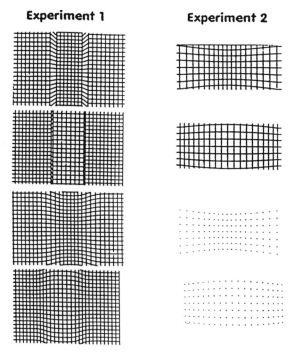

Figure 1. Depictions of the surfaces used in Experiments 1 (left panel) and 2 (right panel).

dominance of high-acuity SA afferent discharge in direct touch. Perceptual sensitivity is far lower for within-surface frequency changes than between-surface differences: uniform surfaces differing in density by 3% can be reliably discriminated (Lamb, 1983); here the gradient needed to incorporate a total change of at least 18% to be detectable. The reduced use of SA afferents

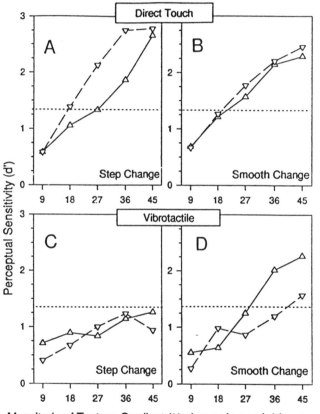

Figure 2. Mean perceptual sensitivity in Experiment 1 as a function of the exploration mode (direct touch, A and B; vibrotactile, C and D), gradient type (step-changes, A and C; smoothed step-changes, B and D), gradient magnitude and direction -- the direction of the triangle indicates whether the spatial separation of elements increased (upward) or decreased (downward) from edge to center. The dotted line corresponds to d' = 1.35, a standard benchmark of reliable sensitivity.

in the vibrotactile condition diminishes performance; even if available, movement information does not seem to be effectively used.

The effect of gradient direction was not reliable when the texture gradients were step-functions but it was highly reliable when they were sinusoidal: gradients where the spatial frequency increased from edge to center (when the finger pad is changing velocity) were easier to detect than those in the opposite direction. This was so irrespective of the mode of exploration. These effects cannot be attributed to differential response biases: despite the likelihood that

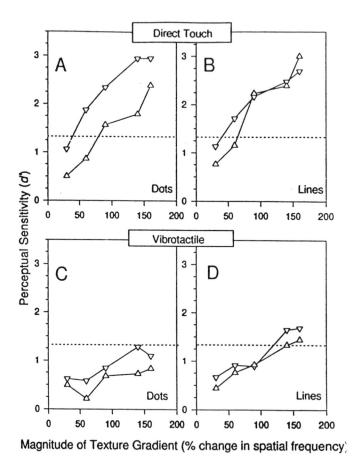

Figure 3. Mean perceptual sensitivity in Experiment 2 as a function of the exploration mode (direct touch, A and B; vibrotactile, C and D), element type (dots, A and C; gridlines, B and D), gradient magnitude and direction. Symbol and line use as in Figure 2.

all explorations generated a set of spatiotemporal proximal gradients, the participants revealed no corresponding tendency to disproportionately attribute this proximal gradient to a spatial gradient in the distal surface; indeed any bias was to report no gradient.

The corpus of research on texture by touch suggests, contrary to these data, that the magnitude but not direction of the gradient should affect detection in the direct touch condition. However, the data do not indicate that certain spatial gradients are impossible to detect if they are the reverse of the velocity profile, only that they are more difficult to recover. While this confirms previous results where active and passive touch reveal subtle but statistically reliable effects on roughness estimates, it emphasizes the ultimate necessity of considering the role of movement information (kinematic and dynamic) in modeling touch and texture interactions.

Acknowledgments. Grants from the New Zealand Lottery Science Board and the University of Auckland Research Committee supported this research. Lars Bäckström was responsible for software development; Anil Gaundar, Sau Han Wong, Christa Mair, and Matthew Millar assisted with data collection.

References

Connor, C. E., & Johnson, K. O. (1992). Neural coding of tactile texture: Comparison of spatial and temporal mechanisms for roughness perception. *Journal of Neuroscience, 12,* 3414-3426.

Gardner, E. P., & Palmer, C. I. (1989). Simulation of motion on the skin: II. Cutaneous mechanoreceptor coding of the width and texture of bar patterns displaced across the Optacon. *Journal of Neurophysiology, 62,* 1437-1460.

Hsiao, S. S., Johnson, K. O., & Twombly, I. A. (1993). Roughness coding in the somatosensory system. *Acta Psychologica, 84,* 53-67.

Hughes, B., & Jansson, G. (1994). Texture perception via active touch. *Human Movement Science, 13,* 301-333.

Johnson, K. O., & Hsiao, S. S. (1992). Neural mechanisms of tactual form and texture perception. *Annual Review of Neuroscience, 15,* 227-250.

Lamb, G. D. (1983). Tactile discrimination of textured surfaces: Psychophysical performance measurements in humans. *Journal of Physiology, 338,* 551-565.

Loomis, J. M., & Lederman, S. J. (1986). Tactual perception. In K. Boff, L. Kaufman, & J. Thomas (Eds.), *Handbook of Human Perception and Performance,* Vol. I (pp. 31.01-31.41). New York: Wiley.

Studies in Perception and Action IV
M. A. Schmuckler & J. M. Kennedy (Eds.)
© *Lawrence Erlbaum Associates, Inc.*

Effects Of Volume On Perceived Heaviness

Eric L. Amazeen

Faculty of Human Movement Sciences, Vrije Universiteit,
Amsterdam, The Netherlands

It is a well-documented fact that variations in an object's volume will produce variations in the perception of its heaviness. This effect is often identified with the size-weight illusion, a phenomenon in which, for a fixed mass, an increase in volume results in a decrease in perceived heaviness. The major class of interpretations of this illusion can be referred to as perceptual-coupling models. According to such models, it is the perception of increased volume that, through a cognitive coupling to sensed mass, produces a decrease in perceived heaviness. Therefore, a perceptual-coupling model should predict that any increase in volume that produces an increase in perceived volume will also produce a decrease in perceived heaviness.

Recent research has identified another interpretation of the size-weight illusion, namely that it follows from the dependence of weight perception on the patterns of resistance that the object presents to the rotational forces associated with lifting and holding (Amazeen & Turvey, 1996). This pattern of resistance is quantified by the inertia tensor, I_{ij}. The eigenvalues (I_1, I_2, and I_3) of I_{ij} represent the magnitudes of resistance about each of three axes that the object will present to the forces imposed by the actor-observer. The results of Amazeen and Turvey (1996) showed that perceived heaviness scaled positively to I_1 and negatively to I_3. The size-weight illusion follows from the fact that certain increases in volume produce an increase in I_3 and, therefore, a decrease in perceived heaviness.

New predictions can be made from this inertial model concerning the relation between volume and perceived heaviness. Since different types of volume manipulations will produce different variations in I_{ij}, then they should also produce different variations in perceived heaviness. For instance, increasing length results in an increase in I_1 whereas increasing width results in an increase in I_3. Thus, the inertial model would predict a decrease in perceived heaviness accompanying the increase in width (due to the negative scaling of perceived heaviness to I_3) but an increase in perceived heaviness accompanying an increase in length (due to the positive scaling to I_1). These predictions were tested in the present experiment.

Method

Fifteen participants rated the perceived heaviness for a set of 18 stimuli that varied in mass (309 g, 460 g, 660 g), volume (1520 cc, 3792 cc, 15096 cc), and in the style of volume change (varying either length or width). These objects were styrofoam cylinders with wooden handles. The cylinders were composed of 4.8 cm thick styrofoam disks that were glued together. By evenly distributing lead shot between the layers of styrofoam disks, the masses of the stimuli could be manipulated independently of the sizes. Participants held these stimuli with their right hand extended through a curtain in order to occlude their view of the stimuli during and between trials. Each trial consisted of first having the participant wield the standard, to which was assigned an arbitrary weight of 100, followed by the experimental object to which the participant assigned a value relative to the standard.

Results

Perceived heaviness increased with mass, $F(2,28) = 12.16$, $p < .0005$, but there was no main effect of volume, $F(2,28) = 2.34$, $p > .10$. A multiple regression of perceived heaviness onto mass and volume also showed a significant effect of mass, $p < .0005$, but a non-negative and non-significant coefficient on volume, $p > .50$. An increase in volume did not produce a uniform decrease in perceived heaviness. Figure 1 depicts the effects of volume on perceived heaviness, $F(2,28) = 6.87$, $p < .005$; an increase in width produced a decrease in perceived heaviness whereas an increase in length produced an increase in perceived heaviness. A simple effects analysis showed that the effects of width and length were both significant, $p < .05$. Of the 15 participants, 14 reported a decrease in heaviness as the stimuli increased in width and 12 participants reported an increase in heaviness when the increase in volume resulted from an increase in length. A multiple regression of perceived heaviness onto the inertial parameters of mass, I_1, and I_3 (all in log coordinates) accounted for almost all of the variance in mean judgments of

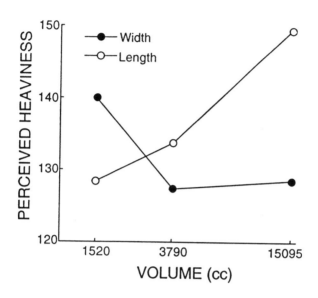

Figure 1. Perceived heaviness as a function of volume and the style of volume change.

heaviness, $R^2(18) = .99$, $p = .0001$, and produced a power law consistent with the size-weight illusion, perceived heaviness $\propto m^{1.15}I_1^{0.1}I_3^{-0.04}$ (all parameters significant, $p < .05$). Perceived heaviness scaled positively to I_1 and negatively to I_3.

Discussion

The present experiment showed that an increase in volume can produce either an increase or a decrease in perceived heaviness. Although it is traditionally assumed that an increase in volume will produce a decrease in perceived heaviness, the inertial model predicted the primary result that a given increase in volume will produce either an increase or a decrease in perceived heaviness depending on how that variation in volume is brought about. When the increase in volume produced an increase in I_3 (through an increase in width), a decrease in heaviness consistent with the size-weight illusion was observed. Conversely, when the same increase in volume was due to an increase in length, I_1 increased (instead of I_3) resulting in an increase in perceived heaviness.

Acknowledgments. This research was conducted at the Center for the Ecological Study of Perception and Action, University of Connecticut. The author acknowledges the contributions of Claudia Carello and M. T. Turvey. Support was provided by a Doctoral Dissertation Fellowship from University of Connecticut and by NSF grant SBR #93-09371 awarded to M. T. Turvey.

References

Amazeen, E. L., & Turvey, M. T. (1996). Weight perception and the haptic size-weight illusion are functions of the inertia tensor. *Journal of Experimental Psychology: Human Perception and Performance, 22,* 213 - 232.

Studies in Perception and Action IV
M. A. Schmuckler & J. M. Kennedy (Eds.)
© *Lawrence Erlbaum Associates, Inc.*

Haptic Perception Of Block Letters In The Horizontal Plane

Giuseppe Mirabella

Department of Psychology, University of Toronto, Toronto, Canada

Vision and touch establish the apparent orientation of an object in three-dimensional space (Kennedy, 1993, 1997). Vision, for instance, has criteria for determining whether an object, like a letter, has maintained its apparent orientation after being moved to a new position. For example, a page of text, to be "upright" and readable, must be placed on a table so that its "front" is facing up to the observer, and its "top" is far from them. However, if the page is to be read while fastened to a ceiling, its front must be facing "down", with its top near the observer. Evidently, so long as the top of the letter is highest in the visual field, the letter is upright.

Of course, criteria for the apparent orientation of pages are not used for all objects. A cup must be positioned differently than a page when moved upwards, to maintain its affordances as a container for liquid. The "top" and "base" positions of the cup are maintained vertically with respect to gravity.

The present study investigates how subjects perceive the apparent orientation of tactile letters placed on the "ceiling"—above their heads, in the horizontal plane. Does touch apply vision's criteria to letters? Or are criteria akin to those of objects that are manipulated, such as cups?

Experiment 1

Method

Seventeen subjects (14 females, 3 males; age range = 19-30) participated. Each was blindfolded.

Wooden block letters, "J" and "P", were placed on a device so that they could be easily presented horizontally above subjects' heads. Letters were approximately 20.0 X 14.0 X 1.5 cm.

Subjects were asked to report whether a presented letter was upright or not. Each letter was positioned so that its "top" was either "near" or "far" from the subject, and its "front" was either "facing up" or "down". Thus, letters were presented randomly in four positions: (a) Top: Near/Front: Up, (b) Top: Near/Front: Down, (c) Top: Far/Front: Up, and (d) Top: Far/Front: Down. The task involved 16 trials, 4 trials at each position. Orientation responses ("upright"/"not upright") were recorded.

Results

The mean proportion of "upright" responses for each letter position are shown in Table 1. Top: Far positions produced significantly more "upright" responses compared to Top: Near positions [$t(60) = 8.125$, $p < .001$]. The results indicate that subjects generally require the top of the letter to be far from them in order to assess a letter's orientation as "upright".

Of course, asking subjects to assess orientation is only one way of testing apparent orientation in touch. Another method is to have the subject identify the letter. In vision, an object is recognized fastest if it is presented the way it is customarily seen—in its standard, "upright" position. The same object in other positions will also be recognized, but it will take more time to do so. Is there one position in touch where an object is most easily identified? If so, is it the same position that would be found in vision? This is the focus of Experiment 2.

Experiment 2

Method

Twenty subjects (12 females, 8 males; age range = 18-31) participated.

The apparatus used in Experiment 1 was used again, except that, here, subjects were asked to identify the letters "F", "J", and "P".

The structure of the task was similar to the first experiment. Subjects were presented sixteen trials, four at each letter position. The task was constructed so that any letter had an equal probability of appearing on any one trial. The time taken to identify each letter was recorded.

Table 1
Mean Proportion of "Upright" Responses by Letter Position

"Front" of Letter	"Top" of Letter	
	"Near"	"Far"
"Up"	.34 (.34)	.75 (.29)
"Down"	.39 (.42)	.64 (.39)

Note. Standard deviations are in parentheses.

Results

Mean response times (RT) for each letter position are shown in Table 2. The Top: Near/ Front: Down position (the one that corresponds to the upright letter position in vision) was significantly faster (2.3 sec) than all other positions. Post hoc analyses found that this position was faster than the Top: Far/ Front: Down position (2.7 sec; Tukey's HSD, $p < .05$), which was assessed as upright in Experiment 1. The results suggest the position in which subjects identify letters the fastest in touch is also the position where the fastest identification in vision would be expected.

Discussion

This study focused on how the apparent orientation of objects, placed horizontally above the head, is perceived in touch, and whether these perceptions are comparable to those in vision. In Experiment 1, when asked to assess the orientation of a letter, subjects favored a letter with its top positioned farthest from them as "upright". This position is not upright in vision. This may be because, in touch, an object must be raised vertically, like a cup, for it to remain upright. A letter, when positioned horizontally, is typically encountered on a table with its top "far" and its front facing "up". Subjects may treat most situations where this position is maintained, with respect to gravity, as "upright".

In Experiment 2, subjects identified letters in touch fastest when the top was near the subject, and the front faced down. This agrees with what is expected in vision.

Table 2

Mean Response Times for Letter Identification by Letter Position

"Front" of Letter	"Top" of Letter	
	"Near"	"Far"
"Up"	2.4 (.5)	2.5 (.6)
"Down"	2.3 (.4)	2.7 (.6)

Note. Standard deviations are in parentheses.

How can we account for these different results? It seems that, when asked to assess orientation in touch, subjects may apply criteria based on affordances of containers. Hence, assessments of letters may be different from those in vision. However, identification of letters may be influenced by directions of parts of the stimulus from the observer as they are in vision, ignoring affordances of containers.

References

Kennedy, J. M. (1993). *Drawing & the blind: Pictures to touch.* New York: Yale University Press.

Kennedy, J. M. (1997). How the blind draw. *Scientific American, 276,* 76-81.

Section II: *Perception - Action Coupling*

II.A: *Affordances*

Studies in Perception and Action IV
M. A. Schmuckler & J. M. Kennedy (Eds.)
© *Lawrence Erlbaum Associates, Inc.*

Kinematic Specification Of Affordances

Thomas A. Stoffregen[1], Kathleen Gorday[1], Yang-Yi Sheng[1], & Steven B. Flynn[2]

[1] Department of Psychology, University of Cincinnati, Cinncinnati, OH, U.S.A.
[2] Department of Psychology, Northeast Lousiana University, LA, U.S.A.

Researchers have been scrupulous in motivating studies of affordances on the basis of the physics of animal-environment relations (e.g., Mark, 1987; Warren, 1984). Through such studies we are beginning to understand the physics that define affordances. Yet understanding of the causal physics is not sufficient for an ecological theory of perception. A tenet of the ecological approach is that affordances are specified; that the physical relations exist in 1:1 correspondence to structures in energy arrays. This should motivate studies of patterns in stimulus arrays that may specify affordances. However, this issue has received little attention.

The information that specifies affordances for another person's actions must be public (Rochat, 1995; Stoffregen, Sheng, & Gorday, 1995). That is, it must be available at distal points of observation. Thus, patterns in the optic array may specify affordances for others. This could provide a convenient opportunity to investigate the specification of at least one class of affordances; affordances for the actions of others. Our study constitutes a qualitative step in this direction. We reasoned that relations between actor and environment might be perceived on the basis of relational movement trajectories (kinematics) of actor and environment. This lead to the hypothesis that observers should be able to perceive affordances for actors from displays that preserve only these relational kinematics. We studied perception of affordances for sitting (Mark, 1987).

Experiment 1

Method

One tall (195 cm) and one short (153 cm) actor were filmed against a dark background, while wearing reflectors on major body joints. Actors were filmed at different distances so that they had the same on-screen height. Each actor engaged in three behaviors; 1) marching in place, 2) squatting and returning to an upright stance, and 3) sitting down and standing up from an unseen stool, which was covered in black velvet. Behaviors were executed next to an experimental chair which had a height-adjustable seat pan (Mark, 1987); reflectors were attached to the corners of the chair, and to the seat pan. The seat pan was moved continuously up and down as the actors behaved. Sixteen observers made nine judgments of each actor's maximum sitting height. On each trial O adjusted the video display (by instructing E to pause the tape) so that it was at what they judged to be the actor's maximum sitting height. Each of sixteen participants made 36 judgments of each actor, half with the seat pan ascending and half with it descending.

Results

The results are summarized in Figure 1, which presents mean judgments across trials and observers. The judgments for each actor were scaled in three ways: in centimeters, as a proportion of each observer's own leg length, and as

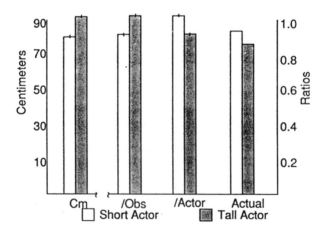

Figure 1. Results of Experiment 1.

a proportion of each actor's leg length. Judgments reflected the actors' actual sitting capabilities (right hand columns in Figure 1) only when scaled in terms of actor leg length.

Experiment 2

In Experiment 1 Os might have adjusted the seat pan until it was at the same height as the reflector on the actor's hip. Another possible problem was the constant relation between the on-screen size of the "image" of the chair and that of the actors, which resulted from the fact that the actors' behaviors were carried out in a fixed location. In Experiment 2 there was not a constant relation between the on-screen position of the actors and the chair.

Method

New tapes were made. The actors walked to and fro along the camera's line of sight, so that their images expanded and contracted relative to the chair.

Results

The data are summarized in Figure 2. The results were essentially identical to those of Experiment 1. Judgments reflected the actors' actual sitting capabilities (right hand columns in Figure 2) only when scaled in terms of actor leg length.

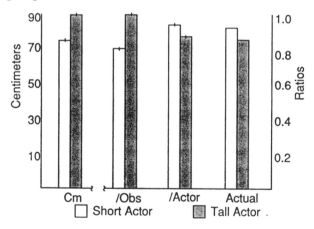

Figure 2. Results of Experiment 2.

Discussion

In both experiments, observers differentiated the kinematic displays for the two actors. This was true despite the fact that the two actors' images were the same size on the monitor. From Experiment 1 we can conclude that judgments were based on some property of the displays that was super-ordinate to image size (or, more precisely, that was super-ordinate to the vertical extent of the group of white spots that corresponded to each actor). The results of Experiment 2 suggest that judgments of affordances for the actors are possible even when there were dramatic and continuous changes in relative image sizes of actor and chair. These experiments indicate that kinematic patterns in the optic array can be sufficient for the perception of affordances for other people.

References

Mark, L. M. (1987). Eyeheight-scaled information about affordances: A study of sitting and stair climbing. *Journal of Experimental Psychology: Human Perception and Performance, 13,* 361-370.

Rochat, P. (1995). Perceived reachability for self and for others by 3- to 5-year-old children and adults. *Journal of Experimental Child Psychology, 59,* 317-333.

Stoffregen, T. A., Sheng, Y-Y., & Gorday, K. M. (1995, July). Perceiving affordances for another person's action. In B. G. Bardy, R. B. Bootsma, & Y. Guiard (Eds.), *Studies in perception and action III* (pp. 153-156). Mahwah, NJ: Lawrence Erlbaum Associates, Inc.

Warren, W. H. (1984). Perceiving affordances: Visual guidance of stair climbing. *Journal of Experimental Psychology: Human Perception & Performance, 10,* 683-703.

Studies in Perception and Action IV
M. A. Schmuckler & J. M. Kennedy (Eds.)
© *1997 Lawrence Erlbaum Associates, Inc.*

Perceiving Action Boundaries In The Volleyball Block

Gert-Jan Pepping & François-Xavier Li

University of Birmingham, School of Sport and Exercise Sciences, Edgbaston, Birmingham, U.K.

Warren (1984) proposed to analyze affordances in terms of the dynamics of the actor-environment system. An affordance is determined by the fit between the material properties of the environment and those of the actor, yielding critical points at which a phase transition to another mode of action occurs. Contemporary affordance studies have mainly concentrated on anthropometric action-related properties of the actor. In the task under investigation (stair climbing, walking through apertures) anthropometric properties were found to be important for the realization of the affordance. It is clear however that the actor's potential ability to generate forces influences the action, hence should influence the perception. So far little work has been done on the importance of kinetic properties of the actor in the perception of affordances (Konczak et al., 1992). To address this problem kinetic properties should play an important role in the task used.

When a ball approaches the net in volleyball, the defender has to decide what action to undertake: To jump and block or to retreat and dig the ball to prevent it from falling on his side of the field. It is thus highly important for the volleyball player to know at which height a ball is *blockable* and at which it is not, for the critical height at which the ball is no longer blockable corresponds to a phase transition in behavior. Performing a volleyball block involves both kinematic demands (reach height of the actor) and kinetic demands (the actors jumping ability).

This study addresses two questions: i) Are subjects able to perceive their action boundaries in blockability, and if so: ii) What actor-related property can account for their faculty to perceive blockability? The first question requires a positive answer otherwise blockability is not an affordance. With respect to the second question, kinetic properties like impulse should play an significant role in the perception of the affordance of blockability.

Method

Eleven male subjects were asked to indicate whether they thought a volley-ball (diameter 21 cm) hanging from the ceiling was blockable or not. 'Blockable' was defined as the height where the subject could jump and reach for the mid-line of the ball (a black strip of 1 cm wide) with both hands. Using the simple up-down method (Levitt, 1970) perceived maximum blockable height (PBH) for each subject was established. Maximum block height (BH) was measured by asking the subject to perform a maximum block. Both assessments were held in different rooms so subjects were never able to see whether their PBH matched BH. Furthermore the subject's mass and height were measured. From the height jumped impulse could be calculated. All data collection was done three times on three consecutive days.

Results

Our first question was: Are subjects able to perceive blockability? The data reveal that subjects are highly accurate in their perception of maximum block height ($\underline{M}$ = 2.78 m, SD = 0.11 m) compared to their achieved block height ($\underline{M}$ = 2.70 m, SD = 0.10 m). Subjects slightly overestimate PBH by less then 3%. Regression analysis (Figure 1) indicates a direct linear relation between PBH and BH (R^2 = .598; $p < .0053$). The correlation coefficient of PBH and BH is .77 ($p < .01$), underlining this linear relationship.

What property can account for the subject's ability to perceive the height he can block? Correlation coefficients were established for the different anthropometric and kinetic properties measured. This shows that PBH is correlated to impulse (correlation coefficient = 0.71; $p < .05$). No relationship can be found between either the subject's mass and PBH (correlation coefficient = .24; ns) or between the subject's height and PBH (correlation coefficient = .20; ns). Regression analysis on the association of impulse and block height perceived emphasizes their relationship (R^2 = .51; $p < .014$).

Conclusion

The aim of this study was to answer the following two questions: i) Can subjects perceive blockability and if so, ii) what property can account for this? Considering the first question it can be concluded that subjects are accurate in their perception of blockability. The 3% overestimate is less than half the volleyball's diameter and within the range of successful behavior.

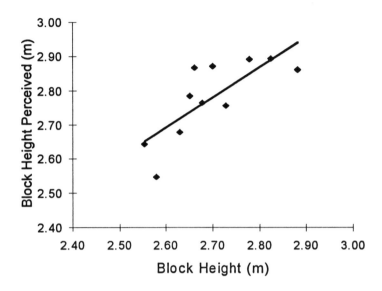

Figure 1. Average block height versus block height perceived.

Perceiving a volleyball at a certain height is to perceive it in terms of one's body and capacity for action. For a volleyball to be blockable it must be at a height within range to jump and reach for. In establishing perceived maximum blockable height, anthropometric properties such as the subject's height and mass play a non-significant role. Moreover, impulse appears to have an influence on the the perceived maximum blockable height. The results support the hypothesis that kinetic properties of the actor play an important role in perceiving blockability.

The volleyball block seems to be an appropriate task in order to investigate the importance of kinetic properties on the perception of affordances. Manipulation of both the kinetics and kinematics of the actor-environment system in the task of blocking a ball should contribute to our understanding of affordances.

References

Konczak, J., Meeuwsen, H. J., & Cress, M. E. (1992). Changing affordances in stair climbing: The perception of maximum climbability in young and older adults. *Journal of Experimental Psychology: Human Perception and Performance, 18,* 691-697.

Levitt, H. (1970). Transformed up-down methods in psychoacoustics. *The Journal of the Acoustic Society of America, 49,* 467-477.

Warren, W. H. (1984). Perceiving affordances: Visual guidance of stair climbing. *Journal of Experimental Psychology: Human Perception and Performance, 10,* 683-703.

Studies in Perception and Action IV
M. A. Schmuckler & J. M. Kennedy (Eds.)
© *1997 Lawrence Erlbaum Associates, Inc.*

Perceiving Action Capabilities Of Others: Age Effects

Kathleen M. Gorday

Department of Psychology, University of Cincinnati, Cincinnatti, OH, U.S.A.

People are able to perceive affordances for their own behaviors. Mark and Voegele (1987) demonstrated that people are able to perceive their own maximum sitting height. Observers made judgments about their own maximum sitting height while looking at a height-adjustable chair. When the judgments were scaled in centimeters, the taller subjects had higher maximum sitting heights than the shorter subjects. However, when the judgments were scaled in leg length, the difference in maximum sitting height between tall and short subjects disappeared.

Perceiving affordances for one's own behaviors is arguably the most common case for the perception of affordances. However, other situations exist in which a person must be able to perceive the affordances for another person's behavior, as any parent of a small child knows.

Stoffregen et al. (1996) investigated whether people could perceive the affordances for others. In their study, subjects judged the maximum sitting height of actors (one tall, one short) standing next to a height adjustable chair. The results showed that the subjects were able to perceive the maximum sitting height of the actors. When scaled in centimeters, the perceived maximum sitting height was higher for the tall actor than the short actor. When scaled in subject leg length, the judgments for the tall actor were higher than judgments for the short actor. However, when scaled in actor leg length, differences between the tall and short actor disappeared. These findings suggest that people are able to perceive the affordances for the behavior of others. Stoffregen et al. (1996) had young subjects judging other young people. However, action capabilities change as we age. Thus, affordances change as we age. Konczak et al. (1992) showed that older adults were able to judge accurately their own reduced stair climbing abilities. Older people have lower maximum sitting heights than young people of the same height. Yet they have the same leg length as these younger people. The differences are in soft tissues, such as muscles and tendons. These properties of the body are not as obvious as skeletal leg length. This raises an empirical question: Are we sensitive to these subtle, age-related changes in affordances? The present study attempted to answer this question.

Method

Four males were selected as actors. The tall, young actor was 25 years old (182 cm tall); the short, young actor was 25 years old (168 cm); the tall, older actor was 67 years old (179 cm); and the short, older actor was 62 years old (163.5). Each of the four actors was videotaped standing sideways next to a height adjustable, experimental chair. In addition, each actor was filmed walking, sitting down in an ordinary chair, and standing back up; the experimental chair did not appear in these latter recordings.

Before the experimental trials, observers were shown the videotapes of each of the actors moving around. They were then shown the tapes of the actors standing next to the experimental chair. In the videotapes, the seat pan was raised (and lowered) as each actor stood next to it. Observers told the experimenter to pause the tape when they judged the seat pan to be at the actor's maximum sitting height (SHmax). Sixteen observers made judgments of the older actors and 16 observers made judgments of the young actors. In both groups, each of the 16 observers made 18 judgments of each of the two actors.

Results

The judgments were expressed (and analyzed) in three ways; 1) in centimeters, 2) as a proportion of each observer's height, and 3) as a proportion of the actors' height. For the centimeter data, an ANOVA revealed a main effect for actor age (accounting for 29% of the variance), a main effect for actor height (accounting for 22% of the variance), and an interaction of actor age and height (accounting for 1% of the variance). For the observer-scaled data, an ANOVA revealed a main effect for actor age (40%), a main effect for actor height (18%), and an interaction of actor age and height (1%). For the actor-scaled data, an ANOVA revealed a main effect for actor age (31%), a main effect for actor height (4%), and an interaction of actor age and height (3%) (Figure 1).

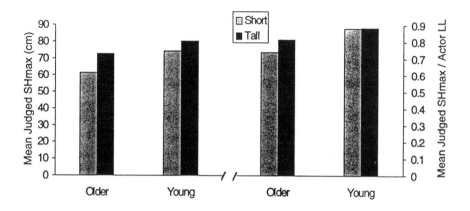

Figure 1. Mean judgments of maximum sitting height expressed in cm and as a proportion of leg length.

Discussion

When judging other young adults, the judgments scaled in centimeters revealed that people are capable of accurately judging relative differences in sitting capabilities for actors of varying heights. This suggests that it is possible for people to perceive the affordances for the behavior of other young adults. Second, when the SHmax judgments of the young actors were scaled as a proportion of observer leg length, there was also a difference between the tall and short young actors. This result suggests that people are indeed judging the affordances for other young adults, and not themselves. Third, judgments scaled in actor leg length revealed a constant proportion for tall and short young actors. This finding suggests that for young actors, the observers were basing their judgments on the height of the seat as a constant proportion of leg length. A constant proportion was used to judge the maximum sitting height of young actors of different heights.

As for maximum sitting judgments of older adults, the judgments scaled in centimeters suggest that the observers were able to perceive relative differences in sitting capabilities for older actors of different heights. The lower SHmax judgments for older adults suggest that the observers were able to perceive accurately the reduced capabilities of the older actors. The judgments scaled in observer leg length and actor leg length confirmed these findings. However, the judgments scaled in actor leg length revealed that observers were not making judgments of the older adults based on a constant proportion of leg length. Rather, the data suggest that the observers are using different means to perceive the maximum sitting height of tall, older adults and short, older adults.

References

Konczak, J., Meeuwsen, H. J., & Cress, E. M. (1992). Changing affordances in stair climbing: The perception of maximum climbability in young and old adults. *Journal of Experimental Psychology: Human Perception and Performance, 18,* 691-697.

Mark, L. S., & Vogele, D. (1987). A biodynamic basis for perceived categories of action: A study of sitting and stair climbing. *Journal of Motor Behavior, 19,* 367-384.

Stoffregen, T. A., Gorday, K. M., Sheng, Y. Y., & Flynn, S. B. (1996). Perceiving affordances for another person's actions. Manuscript submitted for publication.

Studies in Perception and Action IV
M. A. Schmuckler & J. M. Kennedy (Eds.)
© *1997 Lawrence Erlbaum Associates, Inc.*

Fatigue And Reachability

J. R. (Rob) Pijpers, Frank C. Bakker, & Floris Holsheimer

Institute for Fundamental and Clinical Human Movement Sciences, Faculty of Human Movement Sciences, Vrije Universiteit, Amsterdam, The Netherlands

Although subject to vivid debate, the concept of affordance is part and parcel of the ecological psychology. In 1984 Warren proposed a way to investigate affordances by means of a so-called intrinsic method in which variables of the environment (e.g., height of a step) and variables of a person's action system (e.g., leg length) are scaled resulting in dimensionless body-scaled ratio's: the pi-numbers. These pi-numbers are an indication of the fit between actor and his or her environment. Warren's method has successfully been followed by several investigators on a variety of tasks (for example, Mark, 1987). In the early nineties, Konczak, Meeuwsen, and Cress (1992) showed that the perception of maximum climbability is not only dependent on leg length relative to step height, but that also the flexibility of the hip is a deciding factor.

In the above-mentioned examples, the capacities of actors are seen as being stable (at least during the experiment). However, in many daily life situations, the capacities of actors are changing. This study attempts to demonstrate the effect of a person's changing capacity - i.e., fatigue - on the perception of reachability of a grip on a climbing wall.

Method

Subjects. Sixteen female subjects, little or no experience in climbing, were tested individually.

Materials. Estimates of the upper limit that subjects thought they were able to reach (PMRH: perceived maximum reaching height) were made on a specially constructed artificial climbing wall (3.5 m wide, 7.0 m high, inclination of 3 degrees) placed in a large experimentation room. At the wall a horizontal route (traverse) was prepared consisting of 12 grips of varying size: 7 hand grips and 5 feet grips. The mean height of the 5 lower grips was 0.3 m above the floor. An additional grip was movable in vertical direction. This grip was used for making the assessments of PMRH and for determining the actual reaching distance (see below).

Subjects' perception of exertion was measured during climbing using a Dutch version of the 15-point RPE-scale (Ratings of Perceived Exertion; Borg, 1970), rating the task from "no exertion at all (score 6) to "maximal exertion" (score 20).

Procedure. On two separate days, subjects were asked to make 4, 6, 8, and 10 traverses. A traverse was defined as climbing the horizontal route from the right to the left and back to the right again. The number of traverses subjects had to climb was randomly assigned. Subjects performed two series of traverses on each day, one in the morning, one in the evening. Beforehand, subjects were not informed about the number of traverses they had to perform that particular time.

Just before starting with a series of traverses, the PMRH was assessed twice. While subjects were standing in the wall the movable grip descended slowly. Subjects verbally indicated where on the wall the grip would be reachable for them. Subjects were carefully instructed about what was meant by reachable: right hand and both feet should be in contact with prescribed grips, and the left hand should grasp the movable grip in such a way that hanging on the grip would be possible. Immediately after these assessments, subjects indicated their rate of fatigue on Borg's RPE-scale. Then they started traversing. Each time after completing two traverses, subjects were asked to rate their exertion and make two estimates of the PMRH.

On a third day, subjects' actual maximum reaching height was measured. The procedure of day 3 was similar to that of the preceding two days but instead of making assessments of the PMRH, measurements of the actual maximum reaching height were made. Identical to the first two days of the experiment, subjects indicated their rate of fatigue. After ten traverses subjects were asked to continue traversing until "exhaustion"; from then on no measurements of the maximum reaching height were made, except one more time, namely: When subjects rated the task as "extremely hard" (Borg, 1970), they had to traverse for another two times whereupon the actual maximum reach was determined.

Results and Discussion

Table 1 shows the results of the PMRH before and after traversing 2, 4, 6, 8, and 10 times. Differences between PMRH before climbing, after 2, 4, or more traverses were analyzed by within-subjects ANOVAs. These ANOVAs were performed separately for the PMRH-values when subjects climbed 4 traverses, 6 traverses, 8 traverses, and 10 traverses. All analyses resulted in F-values indicating differences between means at at least the $p < .05$ level. Post hoc analyses (Newman-Keuls, $p < .05$) showed that, for all four analyses, differences between the PMRH-assessments before traversing and after 2 traverses were not significant. The PMRH after 4 or more traverses were significantly lower than those before traversing.

Table 2 shows the ratings of perceived exertion. These ratings were also subjected to within-subject ANOVAs just like the PMRH-values above. Again significant main effects were found resulting in F-values, which indicated differences between means at at least the $p < .001$ level. Post hoc analyses showed that the Borg score increased significantly after any two traverses.

Up to 10 traverses, the actual maximum reaching height did not significantly decline (varying between 213.2 and 214.6 cm). When traversing "to exhaustion" there was a small, but significant decline of the actual maximum reaching height (212.6 cm).

Table 1

Perceived Maximum Reaching Height (PHRH) (cm) Before Traversing and After 2, 4, 6, 8 and 10 Traverses (SD in Parentheses).

	Perceived maximum reaching height (in cm) when completing traverses			
	4	6	8	10
Before traversing	219.4	221.3	220.7	221.5
	(10.65)	(12.63)	(14.95)	(13.91)
After 2 traverses	218.6	218.6	218.6	219.6
	(11.48)	(12.53)	(15.29)	(14.10)
After 4 traverses	215.9	217.0	216.6	217.6
	(11.84)	(14.11)	(13.18)	(13.37)
After 6 traverses	-	215.8	215.8	216.6
		(14.41)	(16.00)	(14.23)
After 8 traverses	-	-	216.4	216.1
			(14.49)	(14.99)
After 10 traverses	-	-	-	216.2
				(14.61)

Table 2

Ratings of Perceived Exertion (Borg, 1970) Before Traversing and After 2, 4, 6, 8, and 10 Traverses (SD in Parentheses).

	Perceived exertion when completing:			
	4	6	8	10
Before traversing	8.9 (2.06)	8.4 (1.82)	8.6 (2.00)	8.6 (1.86)
After 2 traverses	10.6 (1.79)	10.4 (1.86)	10.3 (1.89)	10.3 (1.57)
After 4 traverses	12.5 (1.79)	12.1 (1.65)	12.3 (1.48)	12.0 (1.37)
After 6 traverses	-	13.4 (1.41)	13.6 (1.75)	13.5 (1.03)
After 8 traverses	-	-	14.9 (1.54)	14.4 (0.89)
After 10 traverses	-	-	-	15.4 (1.21)

In conclusion, due to fatigue, a different fit between actor and environment seems to emerge: what is maximal reachable changes if subjects are extremely fatigued. Subjects are sensitive to the changing fit between themselves and their environment. They assess their maximum reaching height lower after traversing a few times. However, the decline in PMRH is not exactly following the decrease in actual reaching height, nor is it purely reflecting the increase in subjectively experienced fatigue. It is as if subjects are anticipating their changing capacities, which should be a safe strategy.

References

Borg, G. (1970). Perceived exertion as an indicator of somatic stress. *Scandinavian Journal of Rehabilitation Medicine, 2-3,* 92-98.

Konczak, J., Meeuwsen, H. J., & Cress, M. E. (1992). Changing affordances in stair climbing: The perception of maximum climbability in young and older adults. *Journal of Experimental Psychology: Human Perception and Performance, 18,* 691-697.

Mark, L. S. (1987). Eyeheight-scaled information about affordances: A study of sitting and climbing. *Journal of Experimental Psychology: Human Perception and Performance, 13,* 361-370.

Warren, W. H. (1984). Perceiving affordances: Visual guidance of stair climbing. *Journal of Experimental Psychology: Human Perception and Performance, 10,* 683-703.

Studies in Perception and Action IV
M. A. Schmuckler & J. M. Kennedy (Eds.)
© *1997 Lawrence Erlbaum Associates, Inc.*

Perceiving What Is Reachable During Rapid Growth In Adolescence

Dorothy Heffernan & James A. Thomson

Department of Psychology, University of Strathclyde, Glasgow, Scotland

People are normally very good at matching their bodily characteristics with properties of their environment to produce accurate goal-directed movements (e.g., Warren, 1984; Warren & Whang, 1987; Carello, Grosofsky, Reichel, Solomon, & Turvey, 1989). Presumably, this calibration must be kept in tune as the organism develops and ages. However, physical educators often observe that adolescents experience a phase when they are relatively clumsy. What factors might cause these temporary problems in selecting the appropriate movement for a particular situation?

The present research investigates the possibility that these problems are related to a phase of rapid growth occurring during early adolescence. During this phase, children's physical proportions change over a relatively short span of time (Marshall & Tanner, 1986). This growth spurt is most noticeable in adolescent males aged 12 or 13. If the correct relationship between perception and action is to be maintained, some re-calibration will be required during this period, otherwise there will be a phase where previously possible movements are attempted unsuccessfully. Our specific prediction was these adolescents would be less successful at predicting their ability to perform goal-directed movements than older or younger boys.

Method

Carello et al. (1989) investigated the ability of adults to predict the limits of their movement abilities in a number of reaching tests. Since it was proposed to investigate the ability of adolescents to predict their reaching capabilities, it was decided that a test similar to one described by Carello et al. (1989) would be appropriate. As our experiment differed in some respects, however, the protocol will now be described.

   The experimental design compared children's prediction of their maximum reach while standing with their subsequent reaching performance. Subjects were instructed that they would be required to estimate the furthest distance at which they could *place* a small target object at each of four surface heights (20, 40, 60 and 80cm above ground level). There were four trials at each height and surface heights were presented in randomized order. Subjects were instructed that they should not cross the start line by placing either their hand or foot on the floor or surfaces and that their reach could involve bending at the knees or standing on one leg, provided that they could regain an upright position following the reach. All estimates were recorded in advance of any reach. Following the estimates, subjects performed the reach, and again there were four trials at each height. If a subject crossed the start line, either with a foot or by placing a hand on the floor to maintain balance, this was recorded as a mistrial, and they were asked to try again.

   75 participants were divided into three groups: Group 1 were aged 10-11; Group 2 were aged 12-13, and Group 3 were aged 14-15. The mean heights of the groups were 1.48m, 1.53m, and 1.70m, respectively. Group 2 represented boys during the rapid growth phase: the younger and older groups were controls.

Results and Discussion

   Means for the estimated and actual reaches were calculated for each subject. Figure 1 illustrates the increase in both distance estimated and distance reached as surface height increased [$F(3,216) = 2.92, p < .05$]. There was also a difference between the age groups [$F(2,72) = 26.82, p < .001$], related to the difference in height between the children. These differences were similar to the results obtained by Carello et al. (1989), who observed that both estimate and reach were greater for tall subjects than for short subjects, and that subjects were sensitive to the different reaching possibilities afforded by different surface heights.

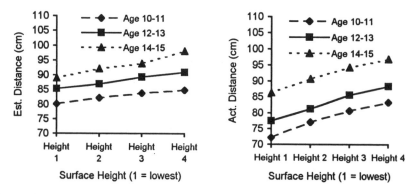

Figure 1. Mean estimate (left) and actual (right) reach at each of the four surface heights.

Since the focus of the study was on perceived reach during rapid growth, the correspondence between subjects' estimates of their reaching potential and their actual reaches was also examined. Figure 2 (left) plots the constant error in subjects' estimates for each age group at each surface height. It can be seen that the oldest group were relatively accurate in their predictions, especially at surface height 3. Thus, the two younger groups overestimated more, with the 12-13 group recording the highest overestimates at three of the four heights. This Age Group by Surface Height interaction was significant [$F(6,216) = 2.43$, $p < .05$).

A further analysis was carried out on the number of mistrials for each subject and this is illustrated in Figure 2 (right). The 12-13 age group had more than twice as many mistrials than either the younger or the older group. This difference was significant [$F(2,64) = 7.26$, $p < .001$]. The number of mistrials illustrates the difficulty experienced by this group in complying with the instructions: they frequently lost balance and fell forward while attempting to perform their maximum reach. Mistrials, where the subjects could not maintain balance, show that the 12-13 age group were least successful in identifying the region of muscular reversibility for forward reaching actions, and had difficulty regaining an upright position following the reach. This, taken together with the fact that they tended to overestimate their reaching ability more than the other two groups, suggests that they may have been using a perception-action coupling which had previously been effective, but which had been rendered inappropriate following the recent changes in limb length and centre of body mass which they had experienced.

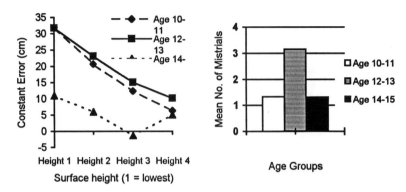

Figure 2. Mean constant error at each of the four surface heights (on left) and mean number of mistrials for each age group (on right).

References

Carello, C., Grosofsky, A., Reichel, F., Solomon, H. Y., & Turvey, M. T. (1989). Visually perceiving what is reachable. *Ecological Psychology, 1,* 27-54.

Marshall, W. A., & Tanner, J. M. (1986). Puberty. In F. Falkner & J. M. Tanner (Eds.), *Human Growth: A Comprehensive Treatise, Vol. 2* (pp. 171-209). New York: Plenum Press.

Warren, W. H. (1984). Perceiving affordances: Visual guidance of stair climbing. *Journal of Experimental Psychology: Human Perception and Performance, 10,* 683-703.

Warren, W. H. & Whang, S. (1987). Visual guidance of walking through apertures: Body-scaled information for affordances. *Journal of Experimental Psychology: Human Perception and Performance, 13,* 371-383.

Studies in Perception and Action IV
M. A. Schmuckler & J. M. Kennedy (Eds.)
© *1997 Lawrence Erlbaum Associates, Inc.*

Using An Object As If It Were Another: The Perception And Use Of Affordances In Pretend Object Play

Agnes Szokolszky

Department of Psychology, Attila József University, Szeged, Hungary

Pretend object play traditionally has seized attention because it appears to involve the increasing symbolic capacity to liberate meaning from the dominance of "perceptual cues". Ecological realism suggests, however, that perceptual factors should have a more influential and perpetual role in pretense than usually assumed.

The present approach frames object pretend play as the coupling of the goal-specific affordances of the substitute object with the intention-specific effectivities of the child. The central assumption is that the affordance-based fitness of the substitute objects influences children's pretend object choices as well as the quality of their pretend actions.

Sixty-four 3- to 5-year-old children played in three play episodes with three respective sets of substitute objects. Each set contained one target object and three substitute objects. Substitute objects differed in their affordance-based fitness. Each set contained one highly-fit substitute object with a clear identity, one less fit substitute object without a clear identity, and one least-fit substitute object with a clear identity. Half of the children used the objects in the realistic condition and half in the schematic condition (Table 1).

In each session the experimenter modeled the action with the target object, the child repeated the modeled action, then the experimenter put the target object away and introduced a two-minute free play with the substitute objects. After free play the experimenter put the three substitutes in front of the child and asked him/her to rank order the objects, justify the ranking, and show how the object could be used in place of the target object.

Target use actions were categorized as follows: *Integrated actions* typically were focused and accurate actions that fully exploited the task-relevant affordances of the substitute objects (e.g., carefully places the head of the doll on the flat front of the car); *Discrepant actions* reflected a misfit between the demands of the task and the affordances of the substitute objects (e.g., puts the

Table 1
Objects and Pretend Tasks

Object Sets	Task and Materials Conditions	
	Schematic	Realistic

Target: *pillow*
Substitutes:
    stuffed lamb (Highly fit definite)
    wedge (Made of paper; less fit ambiguous)
    car (Least fit definite)
	Put <u>doll</u> to bed; bed has a dollsized sheet and a blanket.	Put <u>oneself</u> to bed; bed has a childsized sheet and blanket.

Target: *broom*
Substitutes:
    bunch of artificial flowers (Highly fit definite)
    tassel (Less fit ambiguous)
    fork (Least fit definite)
	Sweep up the "messy kitchen floor"; *mess* is fictitious.	Sweep up the "messy kitchen floor"; *mess* is sugar spilled on the floor.

Target: *boat*
Substitutes:
    wooden shoe (Highly fit definite)
    basket-like container (Full of holes; less fit ambiguous)
    toy skate board (Least fit definite)
	Give the doll a "boat ride on the lake"; *lake* is a blue *vinyl mat*.	Give the doll a "boat ride on the lake"; *lake* is a *tub of water*.

head of the doll on the top of the car, the neck is in an uncomfortable position); *Bridging actions* displayed a special effort on the part of the actor to bridge the gap between the demands of the task and the affordances of the object (e.g., turns the car upside down, covers it with the sheet and puts her head down on it.)

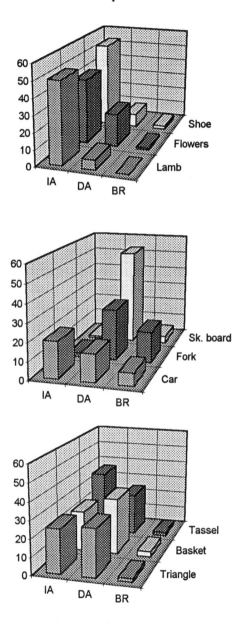

Figure 1. Actions with "Fit Definite" (top), "Unfit Definite" (middle), and "Ambiguous" (bottom) objects in the ranking task.

Children's perceptual judgments reflected affordance-based fitness to a reasonable degree. Justifications typically referred to the affordance properties of the objects; very few referred to appearance or to category membership. Adapted actions reflected affordance-based fitness more consistently than judgments. Highly fit objects were dominantly used in an "integrated" manner while least fit definite objects were used dominantly in a "discrepant" manner. Objects that were in-between regarding their fitness were used both in integrated and discrepant ways, with "bridging" actions also present (see Figure 1).

Results show that actions were adapted to the qualities of the objects at a fine grain and this adaptation was not necessarily a reflective process. Traditional approaches to pretend object use do not have the conceptual means to interpret these findings. In pretense the child is dynamically relating the affordances of the object to the demands of the pretend task. S/he is re-contextualizing, not de-contextualizing reality. Pretend object play can be conceived of in analogy to unconventional tool use, when, for example, a wooden shoe is used to hammer in a nail. They both involve the pragmatically motivated unconventional use of an object in place of another object in order to achieve a goal. Substitute objects help focus pretend acts by presenting opportunities for affordance-effectivity couplings.

Studies in Perception and Action IV
M. A. Schmuckler & J. M. Kennedy (Eds.)
© *1997 Lawrence Erlbaum Associates, Inc.*

Words Are Not Enough: How Educating Effectivities And Affordances Fosters The Early Lexicon

Patricia Zukow-Goldring

Center for the Study of Women, University of California, Los Angeles, U.S.A.

Infants comprehend what others say, before they produce speech themselves (Bates, Bretherton, & Snyder, 1988). Although the lexicon must be learned, the implications of this pervasive finding has sparked little research into the perceptual and social origins of speech comprehension during the prelinguistic period. Research proposing the potential importance of social interaction for lexical development almost exclusively studies how caregivers' verbal messages affect the language production of children during the one-word period and beyond (Nelson, 1985). Hypothesized innate and acquired cognitive processes within the child explain what is noticed and eventually learned.

Logically, however, words cannot explain unless a person already knows what words mean. Yet learning what words mean is what the infant "means" to learn.

Wittgenstein (1961) discussed the problem of teaching what is meant with words. He asserted that people cannot "say" or "explain" in language what a meaning relation might be. If words cannot explain something new, how do people see what is meant? Wittgenstein (1961, p. 4.1212) answered this seeming dilemma by arguing cryptically that "what *can* be shown, *cannot* be said." That is, individuals receiving messages can directly grasp meaning only through the "saying and showing" of the person expressing the message. Thus, caregivers can assist infants in perceiving what is meant by routinely providing examples of behavior in context, rather than by expressing more explicit linguistic messages.

I argue that caregivers make themselves understood by educating their infants' attention to the relation between what is happening and what is being said (Zukow-Goldring, 1997). Caregivers and infants engage in cycles of perceiving and acting that promote the comprehension of speech and infants' subsequent production. As events unfold, caregivers make prominent the inseparable reciprocity of effectivities of the body and the perceptual structure that affords embodied action. As a matter of course, they relate speech to ongoing events by making what they say perceptually available.

To test this position, this study focuses on how caregivers reduce ambiguity when infants do not initially understand the caregivers' message. To achieve a practical consensus or mutual understanding of events, I propose that caregivers modify their messages as a function of infants' level of participation in ongoing activities. Given the foregoing arguments, I predict that providing infants with more perceptual structure will assist caregivers and infants in reaching a working consensus. In contrast, additional or more specific verbal messages should not enhance the understanding of infants during either the prelinguistic or one-word period.

Method

I examined monthly video data from a naturalistic, longitudinal study of five European-American caregiver-infant and six Latino dyads from the middle of the infants' first year through the one-word period.

Attention-directing interactions. The collection of interactions selected for investigation display situations in which caregivers direct infants to notice one specific element, relation, or event over the myriad other possibilities available at any one time in any one place (Zukow-Goldring, 1997). Attention-directing interactions consist of all instances of perceptual imperatives uttered by caregivers, such as *look!, listen!, touch!, smell!, taste!,* etc., their accompanying gestures, and the gestures alone.

Target of attention-directing. The target (topic) of attention, such as non-dynamic person/object (*Look at the doll.*), agent-action-object-recipient sequences (*Look, Brian throws the ball to Cathy.*), or possession (*Look at Brian's ball!*), location (*Look in the bucket!*), repetition (*Look, again!*), in the caregiver's speech is a step or two ahead of the semantic level expressed in the infant's speech.

Attention-directing gestures. Five attention-directing gestures that accompany caregivers' verbal messages were coded, including *act-on*s, *show*s, *demonstration*s, *point*s, and *look*s. These gestures vary on a continuum of caregiver- to infant-regulation of attention to the effectivities of the body and the affordances of the environment.

Sequences containing initially misunderstood caregiver messages. We searched the corpus of *attention-directing interactions* for sequences in which the initial message was misunderstood. We evaluated all subsequent messages which had the same target of attention to determine whether caregiver and child reached a practical consensus. We assessed the messages in these sequences on the basis of two continua: the relative amount of *perceptual structure* provided by attention-directing gestures and the degree of *linguistic specificity* expressed.

Infant's expressive level. We examined the revisions of caregiver messages at two levels of development: the prelinguistic and lexical levels.

Results

To demonstrate the interdependence of five variables - perceptual structure, linguistic specificity, consensus, expressive level of the infant, and subject - the observed frequencies were subjected to a multivariate frequency analysis, using log-linear methods. At both expressive levels, difference testing confirmed that increasing attention to perceptual structure overwhelmingly related to achieving a practical consensus, whereas failing to do so was associated with a lack of consensus. (See Figure 1 for the European-American findings.) Caregivers varied considerably in the amount of linguistic specificity they expressed and in provision of perceptual structure. However, all caregivers

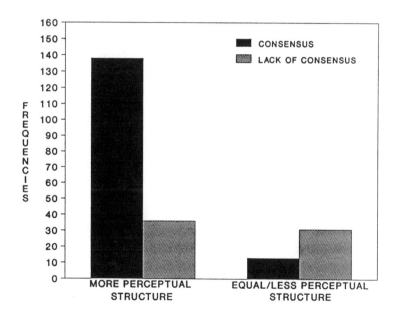

Figure 1. The relation between perceptual structure and consensus.

produced a preponderance of messages in which they made more perceptual structure available and prominent to infants, usually leading to a practical understanding of ongoing events.

Discussion

When caregivers resolve ambiguity for infants, gestures do "speak louder than words." This research documented that during the prelinguistic and one-word periods caregivers routinely provided additional perceptual structure to their infants following communicative breakdowns. As predicted by social ecological realism, this sensitive adjusting of subsequent messages to infants contributed significantly to reaching a common understanding. Caregivers also modified their verbal messages in subsequent turns by making them more specific. In contrast, however, these elaborations did not contribute to achieving a practical consensus regarding ongoing events. Instead, as caregivers educate attention, infants gradually learn to perceive, act, and know in culturally relevant ways.

References

Bates, E., Bretherton, I., & Snyder, L. (1988). *From first words to grammar: Individual differences and dissociable mechanism.* New York: Cambridge University Press.

Nelson, K. (1985). *Making sense: The acquisition of shared meaning.* New York: Academic Press.

Wittgenstein, L. (1961). *Tractatus logico-philosophicus* (D. Pears & B. McGuinness, Trans.) New York: Humanities Press.

Zukow-Goldring, P. G. (1997). A social ecological realist approach to the emergence of the lexicon: Educating attention to amodal invariants in gesture and speech. In C. Dent-Read & P. Zukow-Goldring (Eds.), *Evolving explanations of development: Ecological approaches to organism-environment systems* (pp. 199-247). Washington, DC: American Psychological Association.

Studies in Perception and Action IV
M. A. Schmuckler & J. M. Kennedy (Eds.)
© *1997 Lawrence Erlbaum Associates, Inc.*

Perceiving, Discovering And Constructing Affordances

Julie C. Rutkowska and Edward Baines

School of Cognitive and Computing Sciences, University of Sussex,
Brighton, U.K.

Preadapted perceiving

Gibson's (1979) extension of the theory of direct perception emphasized that the developmental origins of perceiving do not reside in discriminating objective qualities of things, such as substances and surfaces, then learning how these combine into objects. Rather, infants start out perceiving some of the meanings of things -- their affordances. Developmental research confirms that preadapted perception supports action with objects and persons. How does this support the acquisition of new knowledge of affordances? In particular: What is the role of three-way interaction between infant, adult and object?

Two candidates for social transmission of knowledge are considered: observation of a more able, adult model, which focuses on the infant learning role and is associated with "learning by seeing"; and social scaffolding, which focuses on the adult instructional role and is characterized by "learning by doing". Knowledge of novel affordances may not be fully explained by the theory of direct visual perception. Considering affordances from ecological psychology's perspective of the perceiving-acting cycle increases the complexity of analyzing how even simple instances of observing a more able model may affect learning. However, this perspective aids comparison of phenomena of model observation and social scaffolding, contributing to a pragmatic account of perceiving and knowing.

Can novel affordances be observed?

Observation of an adult model sometimes increases infants' tendency to perform modeled behaviors on objects. However, why some behavior-object pairings achieve this and others do not is unclear. For example, a study in which mothers modeled banging, shaking, moving and rubbing found a significant increase among 6-month-olds in banging and moving a ball and rattle, but also, rather oddly, in rubbing a doll against their body (von Hofsten & Siddiqui, 1993). By way of contrast, 12-month-olds increased banging the ball and moving the rattle, but none of the modeled behaviors with the doll.

It is difficult for such studies to clarify learning about affordances, to the extent that manipulatory behaviors are considered as forms of exploration rather than as significant in their own right. This treats the notion of affordances primarily in terms of properties of objects that are discovered/revealed as outcomes of behavior, coinciding with the traditional theory of direct visual perception's view of perceiving as an independent domain, and motor activity as unnecessary to making sense of what is seen. However, it downplays two related aspects of affordances.

Firstly, affordances are relative to the subject's capabilities for acting (for Gibson, neither objective nor subjective). In the case of manipulation, body-scaledness in terms of hand size partly determines whether something affords grasping for an adult or for infants of different ages. Modeling behaviors on objects that vary on multiple dimensions may obscure such relations. Only to the extent that a model's sensory-motor and physical capabilities coincide with the observer's own can they really demonstrate potential affordances for the other.

Secondly, object affordances and subject effectivities (potential purposive acts) are complementary dispositional properties of agent-environment systems (Shaw & McIntyre, 1974). Subject effectivities depend on object properties for their actualization. Hence, perceptual learning and action construction are opposite sides of a single coin. This phenomenon may be obscured if modelled behaviors already exist in the infant's repertoire, as they all do in the study noted above. Forefronting perceiving at the expense of acting contributes to an inappropriate tension between learning from observation in which infants (just) repeat acts that have interesting outcomes and learning "at a perceptual level" to detect affordances that specify those outcomes.

Emergent functionality through social scaffolding

Social scaffolding may be a more fundamental and significant form of social transmission than model observation. This involves adults engineering relations between infant sensory-motor capabilities and the environment so that they are enabled to achieve outcomes that they could neither attain nor envisage attaining if left to their own devices. Key features are reduction of degrees of freedom in a task, marking critical attributes to enhance attending and providing repeated experience of goal attainment. For example, an infant may learn to "wave bye-bye" through being turned to view someone leaving a room while their arm is repeatedly moved up and down.

Modeling likewise involves adults engineering environments so as to constrain degrees of freedom in the infant's experience. However, its direct interventions are restricted to sensory manipulations, such as object provision, without extending to the motor component of perceiving-acting. By way of contrast, Zukow-Goldring's (1997) observations confirm how physical, forceful and more reliable are the adult's scaffolding interventions in infant motor activity.

A central role is played by "emergent functionality," through which complex abilities can emerge from the independent interplay of seemingly simple sensory-motor components with the environment. Scaffolding may be considered as a form of supervised learning in which emergence of function is temporarily engineered, establishing the developmental space for more permanent adaptive change (Rutkowska, 1994). From the infant's perspective, serendipity -- unplanned, accidental but fortunate discovery -- is the primary form of learning in scaffolding contexts. Infants do not need their own pre-specified intentions and goals in order to acquire novel forms of activity for attaining them. Nor do they need to match the behaviors, intentions and goals of adults. Rather, it is through acting in ways that achieve comparable outcomes that infants construct adult goals for themselves. They may thus become able to appreciate commonalities between their own effectivities and those of adults, and between what objects afford them.

References

Gibson, J. J. (1979). *The ecological approach to visual perception.* Boston: Houghton-Mifflin.

Rutkowska, J. C. (1994) Scaling up sensorimotor systems: Constraints from human infancy. *Adaptive Behavior, 2,* 349-373.

von Hofsten, C., & Siddiqui, A. (1993) Using the mother's actions as a reference for object exploration in 6- and 12-month-old infants. *British Journal of Developmental Psychology, 11,* 61-74.

Shaw, R., & McIntyre, M. (1974) Algoristic foundations to cognitive psychology. In W. B. Weimer & D. S. Palermo (Eds.), *Cognition and the symbolic processes.* Hillsdale, NJ: Lawrence Erlbaum.

Zukow-Goldring, P. G. (1997) Educating attention: An ecological approach to achieving consensus. In C. Dent-Read & P. Zukow-Goldring (Eds.), *Changing ecological approaches to development: Organism-environment mutualities.* Washington, DC: American Psychological Association.

Studies in Perception and Action IV
M. A. Schmuckler & J. M. Kennedy (Eds.)
© 1997 Lawrence Erlbaum Associates, Inc.

Possible Informational Bases For The Perception Of Rapport

S. Stavros Valenti, Ken Wagner, & Marty Sobel

Department of Psychology, Hofstra University, Hempstead, NY, U.S.A.

One of the invariants of ecological psychology, it seems, is the lack of attention to face-to-face social interaction. Of course, we live in a material and populated environment, and the material aspects of this environment themselves (e.g., footpaths, dwellings, and artifacts) are the products of the history of their uses (Costall, 1995; Gaver, 1996). The thoroughly socialized material environment affords a vast range of actions, but the kinds of actions most on the minds and tongues of people are interactions: calling home, telling a story, seeking reassurance, discussing an idea. Face-to-face interaction may be one of the most difficult domains of study for an exact ecological science, but it clear that the problem will not become less difficult after solitary actions are better understood (e.g., Leudar, 1991).

Here we describe one domain of research which may interest students of social behavior as well as practitioners in mental health fields: the perception of rapport. People in all societies spend much of their work and leisure time in face-to-face interaction, an actively pursued interaction opportunity. Although not well understood, face-to-face interaction appears to be a ubiquitous and complex social affordance. These interaction opportunities are sometimes afforded by the material environment itself (e.g., a playground) or by specific individuals (e.g., one child appears more approachable than another). When an interaction is mutually satisfying, individuals have a range of cultural practices and materials for encouraging sustained interaction and planning the next encounter. But how does one know, firmly, that the interaction was satisfying for the self and *the other*? Our own research has focused on the possible informational bases of the awareness of rapport.

The nature of rapport

There is strong agreement among medical and mental health practitioners that the development of rapport is a key constituent of a therapeutic relationship. This position is consistent with observations of social developmental researchers who note that the absence of at least one close friend in childhood and adolescence, a possible partner for sharing thoughts and activities, is associated with high risk for disorders of mood and conduct. In the late 1980's Robert Rosenthal and colleagues proposed that rapport can be conceptualized as a constellation of qualities of focused and sustained interactions, where there are changing degrees of mutual attention and involvement, affective positivity, and coordination among participants (Bernieri & Rosenthal, 1991).

Face-to-face encounters create interaction possibilities, such as those for continued conversation, cooperation, giving and receiving assistance, and even for competition, although the specific social affordances may be "in formation" and not completely revealed. The experience of rapport, in our view, is the awareness of mutually-valued interaction possibilities. As is true for any perceived qualities of surfaces, objects, or events, the perception of rapport is based on informative structures in the ambient media sound or light or structures arising from dynamic and mutual touch. These socially informative, objective structures may include the kinds of rhythmic patterns observed in conversational turn taking, and coordinated gross body movements, body gestures, and expressions measured in research on interpersonal synchrony (Valenti & Good, 1991). Our research has focused on two aspects of rapport, nonverbal movement coordination (synchrony) and the coordination of verbalized affect.

Rapport and nonverbal movement coordination

Studies of movement synchrony have a long history in social and clinical psychology, and include *molecular* (moment-by-moment) analyses of discrete movements, coded for matching and complementarity of postures and gestures. These studies frequently encounter problems in identifying an appropriate unit of analysis, and molecular coding of interactions is quite labor intensive. More recently, some researchers demonstrated the value of using teams of trained judges serving as a kind of "culturally informed detection device" for synchrony, yielding subtle yet humanly meaningful *molar* judgments of movement coordination. Reviewing the literature, we noted that correlations between molar ratings of synchrony and self-reported ratings of interactional rapport range in the low to moderate range, with the highest correlations typically occurring for females (Valenti & Sobel, 1995). Movement synchrony, we reason, may be one possible structure underlying the perception of rapport. A more complete understanding of movement synchrony in conversations, however, would require that the verbal content be studied in relation to the coordination of gestures across time.

Rapport and the coordination of verbalized affect

Rapport, viewed as a co-constructed and mutually perceived quality of interaction, can be described with reference to its normative structural characteristics within particular social settings for particular participants. Here we describe some of the structures of coordination of verbalized affect in a recent study of adolescent conversations (Wagner & Valenti, 1997). Intimacy in adolescence is facilitated during conversations between friends. However, there is much we do not know about how adolescents listen and respond to one another, talk explicitly about their own private states and events, and the manner and extent of mutual reinforcement of self-disclosure in their conversations.

Our approach to this problem was to use sequential analysis of coded conversational turns which, in effect, uncovers particular varieties of transitions from one conversational turn to the next. Of principle interest was the content of one turn following a partner's explicit verbal labeling of affect -- a relatively rare event in the adolescent conversations we analyzed. The conversation was first represented as a stream of mutually exclusive and exhaustive content codes (e.g., self affect, partner affect, other affect, self no affect, etc.). The stream of codes was then examined for reliable sequential dependencies between explicit statements of experienced affect experienced by the self, the current partner, or some other person outside of the conversational context followed by the conversational partner's explicit statements of affect.

Of principle interest was the finding of a pattern of "matching" (Person 1 self affect followed by Person 2 self affect) as a better predictor of friendship quality and experienced rapport than either "reflection" (Person 1 self affect followed by Person 2 partner affect) or "disengagement" (Person 1 affect followed by Person 2 no affect). This finding is somewhat counterintuitive for students of clinical psychology because many approaches to counseling stress the importance of reflection for building rapport with clients, young and old alike. This finding underscores the importance of studying specific conversational structures, and not assuming the superiority or generality of one form of intimate discourse across settings or groups.

References

Bernieri, F., & Rosenthal, R. (1991). Interpersonal coordination: Behavior matching and interpersonal synchrony. In R. S. Feldman & B. Rime (Eds.), *Fundamentals of nonverbal behavior* (pp. 401-432). Cambridge, MA: Cambridge.

Costall, A. (1995). Socializing affordances. *Theory & Psychology, 5,* 467-481.

Gaver, W. W. (1996). Situated action II: Affordances for interaction: The social is material for design. *Ecological Psychology, 8,* 111-129

Leudar, I. (1991). Sociogenesis, coordination, and mutualism. *Journal for the Theory of Social Behaviour, 21,* 197-220.

Valenti, S. S., & Good, J. M. M. (1991). Social affordances and interaction I: Introduction. *Ecological Psychology, 3,* 77-98.

Valenti, S. S., & Sobel, M. (1995). *Rapport and interpersonal coordination.* Unpublished manuscript, Hofstra University.

Wagner, K. K., & Valenti, S. S. (1997, April). *Conversations of same-sex male and female adolescents: Relations between verbalized emotion sequences and friendship qualities.* Presentation to the biennial meeting of the Society for Research in Child Development, Washington, DC.

Section II: *Perception - Action Coupling*

II.B: *Visually-Guided Action*

Studies in Perception and Action IV
M. A. Schmuckler & J. M. Kennedy (Eds.)
© *1997 Lawrence Erlbaum Associates, Inc.*

The Functional Division Of Visual Information Under Induced Motion

Albert Yonas, Rocco Ross, and Molly Erdahl

Institute of Child Development, University of Minnesota,
Minneapolis, MN, U.S.A.

Neurophysiological evidence suggesting an anatomical separation of the cortical visual pathways in the primate cerebral cortex into two streams of visual processing was first presented by Ungerleider and Mishkin (1982). They proposed that information emanating from the visual cortex is separated into a dorsal stream for spatial vision and ventral stream for object vision. Milner and Goodale (1995) redefined this dissociation of visual information to represent a functional division of labor related to the development of two evolutionary significant systems. One, a perceptual system, allows the organism to identify and attach meaning to an object while the other, a visuomotor system, allows the organism to act on those objects. Although there is neurophysiological evidence to support the idea of two functional streams emanating from the visual cortex in the form of PET and MRI studies (Ungerleider & Haxby, 1994; Haxby et al., 1994), little behavioral evidence is available. This study was designed to find such evidence and to test the theory proposed by Milner and Goodale. In this induced motion study, subjects were asked to rapidly point at a stationary object that appeared to be moving. It was hypothesized that subjects would tend to point to the actual static rather than perceived moving location of the object.

Method

A 60 cm^2 frame centered within a 120 cm^2 frame was suspended from the ceiling so that the frame could swing freely in a pendular motion at 2.4 sec/cycle. The entire frame was painted with a luminescent lacquer. Centered within the plane of the frame, but not attached to it, was a luminescent dot 0.5 cm. in diameter. Studies with this apparatus showed that when the frame is set in horizontal motion in a darkened room, subjects reported seeing the luminescent dot move horizontally in the opposite phase of the frame's motion (see Figure 1) (Bridgeman et al., 1981; Reinhardt-Rutland, 1988).

Adult subjects with an LED attached to their right index finger were asked to point to the location of the dot by sliding their finger across a horizontal plane as fast as possible. This pointing occurred within the plane of the frame, 3.5 cm. below the dot. Pointing accuracy was tested under two conditions: the control condition, in which the dot and frame were stationary and the experimental condition, in which the dot was stationary, but the frame was moving. Subjects included in the statistical analysis reported induced motion throughout the experimental condition. The results of ten trials in each condition were recorded by a camera modified to interface with an IBM computer.

Results

In the condition in which subjects perceived induced motion of the dot, there was significantly greater variability in the pointing behavior ($M = 14.46$, $SD = 6.38$) than in the condition where there was no motion of the frame and therefore no perceived motion of the target. ($M = 8.41$, $SD = 3.69$, a sign-test revealed a $Z = 2.55$, $N = 26$, $p < .01$).

Five subjects reported no induced motion in the induced motion condition. Their data show no difference between the static condition and the induced motion condition.

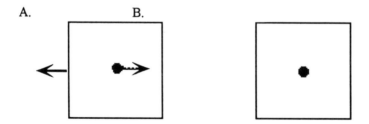

Figure 1. A. Drawing of induced motion display. Dot in center of frame is stationary but appears to move. Solid line indicates real motion. Dotted lines indicate perceived motion. B. Presents static frame and dot.

Conclusions

Because subjects showed higher variability in the location of pointing in the induced motion condition, it is likely that they pointed to the perceived rather than the actual location of the dot. Thus these results suggest that the hypothesis that perceptual and motor systems receive independent information does not fully describe information processing in perceptual and motor tasks.

These findings suggest that a great deal of cross-talk exists between the ventral system, processing perceptual information and the dorsal system, directing action. Separation of these systems may be most likely to occur in tasks requiring responsiveness to radial direction, such as the making of saccadic eye movements.

For most visually-directed actions, information for three-dimensional space and relational motion play a central role in the control of action.

References

Bridgeman, B., Kirch, M., & Sperling, A. (1981). Segregation of cognitive and motor aspects of visual function using induced motion. *Perception & Pychophysics, 29*, 336-342.

Haxby, J., Horowitz, B., Ungerleider, L. G., Maisong, J., Pietrini, P., & Grady, C. (1994). The functional organization of human extrastriate cortex: A PET-rCBF study of selective attention to faces and locations. *Journal of Neuroscience, 14*, 6336-6353.

Milner, D. A., & Goodale, M. A. (1995) *The visual brain in action*, Oxford Psychology Series #27. Oxford University Press.

Reinhardt-Rutland, A. H. (1988). Induced movement in the visual modality: An overview. *Psychological Bulletin*, 1988, 103, 57-71.

Ungerleider, L. G., & Mishkin, M. (1982). Two cortical visual systems. In. D. J. Ingle, M. A. Goodale, & R. J. W. Mansfield (Eds.), *Analysis of visual behavior* (pp. 549-586). Cambridge, MA: MIT Press.

Ungerleider, L. G., & Haxby, J. (1994). 'What' and 'where' in the human brain. *Current Opinion in Neurobiology, 4*, 157-165.

Studies in Perception and Action IV
M. A. Schmuckler & J. M. Kennedy (Eds.)
© *1997 Lawrence Erlbaum Associates, Inc.*

Preferred Critical Boundaries For Reaching In The Vertical Plane

Alana Blumental, Amy Rouse, Kelly Grandt & Leonard Mark

Department of Psychology, Miami University, Oxford, OH, U.S.A.

When actors are not restricted in how to reach, the transition between action (reach) modes is likely to occur not at the absolute limit of the actor's capability, but at a distance at which the relative comfort of two reach modes changes. Mark et al. (in press) identified preferred critical boundaries between different modes of seated reaching along a surface extending away from the observer. This study attempted to delineate preferred critical boundaries in the vertical plane (perpendicular to the surface of the table) among four reach modes (see Method). These data are needed to map reach envelopes that can be used in constructing ergonomic standards for the layout of workplace environments.

Method

Twenty-four students participated in this experiment for course credit. Two identical ergonomic chairs were used: One chair afforded an upright posture; its seatpan was flat (parallel to the floor) and its backrest was perpendicular to the seatpan. A second chair afforded a backward leaning posture (backrest set at a 14-deg angle to vertical with a flat seatpan). The chairs faced a height-adjustable workstation on which was placed a stack of twelve file bins that ranged in height from 0-88 cm with a difference between successive shelves of 8 cm. The position of chair and table were set to ensure that reach distances (in the transverse plane) were scaled relative to the actor's armlength. The stack of bins was placed at three distances: at the edge of the table; and at distances from the table edge equal to the actor's elbow-to-wrist and elbow-to-fingertip. The vertical cubicles were coded with color names. The actor was instructed to place a small lego block on the surface of the bin whose color name was called by the experimenter. Actors were told to reach in as natural as manner as possible. Actors performed two trials of this placing task for each of the three bin distances in each of the two chair positions. All reaches were videotaped.

Two experimenters categorized each reach into one of four reach modes: Reach mode 1 denoted a reach involving only arm extension; mode 2, a reach in which actors rotated their torso at the hip to extend the shoulder (but did not bend at the waist); mode 3, a reach in which actors leaned forward, but did not lift their body off the seat pan; mode 4 denoted actions in which actors shifted their weight off the chair's seatpan or stood.

Results and Discussion

Preferred critical boundaries between pairs of successive reach modes were determined for each actor by identifying the highest bin on each trial at which actors used each reach mode. If the highest bin used differed across trials, the two heights were averaged in order to determine the preferred critical boundary. The preferred critical boundaries for the upright and backward leaning postures were nearly identical. For distance 1 the transition between modes 1 and 2 occurred at 40 cm and between modes 2 and 3 at 72 cm; for distance 2, the transition between modes 2 and 3 occurred at 60 cm; for distance 3 the transition between modes 3 and 4 at 72 cm. (Where no transition between modes is given, one or both modes were not used at any height at that distance.) That the preferred critical boundary was unaffected by seated posture stands in contrast to Mark et al.'s (in press) findings for reaching in the transverse plane. This may be due to the fact that the postural difference between the two postures in this study was less dramatic than in the previous study. (The seat pan was not inclined as in the previous study to eliminate the need to reposition the chair when actors stood.) This pattern of change in action modes is illustrated in the figures, which show for each distance the percentage of reaches from an upright posture using each reach mode. These patterns are consistent with Mark et al.'s proposal – the transition between reach modes occurs at a preferred critical boundary, rather than at the absolute maximum distance for a given mode. Ergonomic standards for the layout of workplaces should be constructed with user preferences in mind, rather than the limits of users' action capabilities.

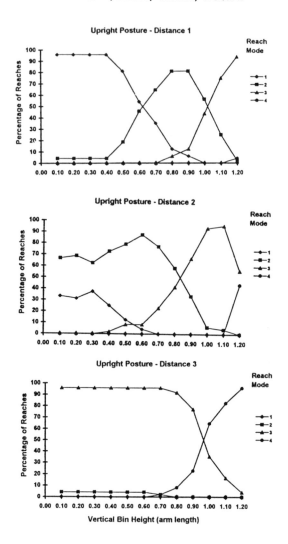

Figure 1. The percentage of reaches using each reach mode at each vertical bin height (measured in units of actors' mean arm length). The three graphs show the data for the three reach distances.

References

Mark, L. S. et al. (in press). Postural dynamics and the preferred critical boundary for visually-guided reaching. *Journal of Experimental Psychology: Human Perception and Performance.*

Studies in Perception and Action IV
M. A. Schmuckler & J. M. Kennedy (Eds.)
© 1997 Lawrence Erlbaum Associates, Inc.

A Haptic Perturbation To Visually-Guided Reaching

Christopher C. Pagano

Department of Psychology, Clemson University, Clemson, SC, U.S.A.

It has been demonstrated that in bringing the hand to a target, information obtained visually regarding target location must be coupled with kinesthetic information regarding the configuration of the limb both before (Pélisson et al., 1986) and during (Ghez et al., 1995) the reach. What sort of information regarding a limb's configuration and movement is available kinesthetically? Evidence suggests that sensitivity to limb position and movement originates in muscle and tendon receptors rather than in the joints themselves (e.g., Kelso, 1978). Further research indicates that perceived limb orientation corresponds to the orientation of the limb's mass distribution, which can be manipulated independently of the joint angles (Pagano & Turvey, 1995). Accordingly, the mass distribution of the limb may provide a quantification of kinesthetically perceived limb orientation during reaching. This possibility has been supported by preliminary findings regarding blind reaching with asymmetrical loadings (Pagano, 1995).

Method

Each trial began with the right hand holding a cross-shaped object in a launch-pad located at the hip. The object was held with the 'stem' oriented horizontally and the 'cross-piece' oriented vertically. The participant reached to bring the front of the stem as rapidly and accurately as possible to a target, while keeping the cross-piece oriented vertically. Participants were instructed not to collide with the target face at high speed. The target was viewed monocularly, with a patch placed over the left eye. During the first session, participants closed their right eye before each reach so as to receive no visual feedback concerning their performance during the reach. During a subsequent session the participants reached with the right eye open. Participants completed blocks of reaches with a 296 g metal cross-piece attached symmetrically, above the hand, and below the hand (see Figure 1). Each block

Pagano

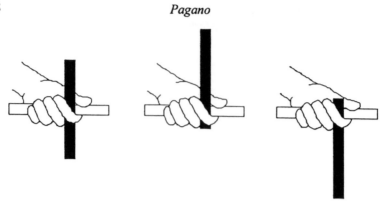

Figure 1. Participants completed reaches with a metal cross-piece attached to a hand-held object symmetrically, above the hand, and below the hand.

consisted of ten reaches separated by several seconds of rest. Reaches were recorded using a two-camera WATSMART system sampling an infrared diode (IRED) at 100 Hz. The IRED was placed on the knuckle of the right index finger.

Results

The target corresponded to a vertical z coordinate of zero. The mean z of the hand at the end of the fast phase of movement is given in Table 1 as a function of the mass and viewing conditions. With eyes closed some participants tended to reach lower when the mass of the hand-held object was distributed higher, and tended to reach higher when the mass was distributed lower. A 4 x 3 ANOVA on z with participant and mass condition as factors resulted in significant main effects for participant [$F(3,36) = 3.6, p < .05$] and mass condition [$F(2,36) = 10.3, p < .0001$]. The interaction was not significant ($p > .10$). A post hoc Tukey HSD test confirmed that z was higher with the mass below than with the mass above ($p < .01$). With vision some participants also tended to reach lower when the mass of the hand-held object was distributed higher, and tended to reach higher when the mass was distributed lower. A 4 x 3 ANOVA on z with participant and mass condition as factors resulted in a significant main effect for mass condition [$F(2,36) = 5.6, p < .01$], but not for participant [$F(3,36) = 1.9, p = .15$]. The participant x mass interaction was marginally significant [$F(6,72) = 2.1, p = .06$]. A post hoc Tukey HSD test confirmed that z was higher with the mass below than with the mass above ($p < .01$).

Table 1.
Mean Vertical Coordinate (cm) of the Hand Trajectory at the End of the Fast Phase of Movement.

	Mass Condition		
Participant	Mass Above	Symmetrical Mass	Mass Below
	Without Vision		
1	-1.70	-.75	-.39
2	-2.42	-.97	.05
3	-1.62	-2.00	-.60
4	-.64	-.65	-.31
Overall	-1.59	-1.09	-.31
	With Vision		
1	-.33	.43	.22
2	-.58	-.28	-.07
3	-.01	-.60	.02
4	-.54	-.11	.39
Overall	-.37	-.14	.14

Discussion

In both the presence and absence of vision, a perturbation to the trajectory of the limb was be produced by altering the limb's mass distribution. The observed effect was small. This may have been due to measurement limitations inherent in recording only a single IRED. The perturbation likely involved a rotation about one or more joints (see Pagano & Turvey, 1995), which could not be detected by a single IRED. The possibility remains that all participants were perturbed by the altered mass distribution, with this perturbation involving variations in orientation. In future experiments, multiple IREDs will be used to detect systematic variations in limb orientation.

A previous procedure ensured that the perturbation was in fact perceptual. Pagano (1995) observed a reliable perturbation when participants brought the distal tip of the hand-held object as close as possible to the target without making contact. This ruled out kinesthetic feedback regarding the endpoint of the trajectory, provided a target whose effect on the limb trajectory is through vision only, and ensured that the experimental effect reflects perceived arm position. Thus what was perturbed in these experiments was the perceived spatial configuration of the limb during reaching.

Acknowledgments. This work was supported in part by U.S. PHS NRSA 1FS32NS09575-01. The author gratefully acknowledges the assistance of Geoffrey Bingham and Michael Stassen.

References

Ghez, C., Gordon, J., Ghilardi, M. F., & Sainburg, R. (1995). Contributions of vision and proprioception to accuracy in limb movements. In M. S. Gazzaniga (Ed.), *The cognitive neurosciences.* Cambridge, MA: MIT Press.

Kelso, J. A. S. (1978). Joint receptors do not provide a satisfactory basis for motor timing and positioning. *Psychological Review, 85*, 474-481.

Pagano, C. C. (1995). *Haptic perturbation in targeted reaching.* Poster presented at the 8th International Conference on Perception and Action, Marseille, France.

Pagano, C. C., & Turvey, M. T. (1995). The inertia tensor as a basis for the perception of limb orientation. *Journal of Experimental Psychology: Human Perception and Performance, 21*, 1070-1087.

Pélisson, D., Prablanc, C., Goodale, M. A., & Jeannerod, M. (1986). Visual control of reaching movements without vision of the limb II. *Experimental Brain Research, 62*, 303-311.

Studies in Perception and Action IV
M. A. Schmuckler & J. M. Kennedy (Eds.)
© *1997 Lawrence Erlbaum Associates, Inc.*

The Effect Of Temporal Delay On Pointing Accuracy In Adults And Children

Joanna K. Graham, Mark F. Bradshaw and Alyson M. Davis

Department of Psychology, University of Surrey, Guildford, Surrey, U.K.

Clinical neurological evidence suggests that visual information may be processed in different streams: one to control visuo-perceptual judgments and tasks, and the other to control visuo-motor tasks (e.g., Goodale et al., 1991). The temporal nature of these different streams may differ. Whereas the former may have no time-constraints the latter must compute the relative distances of scene structures and body-parts continuously (to 'keep up' with, for example, a moving arm). The accuracy of reaching movements may therefore be vulnerable to induced error with the introduction of a temporal delay between the visual location of a target and the beginning of movement (see Thomson, 1983). We report an experiment which introduces a delay between stimulus presentation and reach onset in open-loop conditions. Previous 'aiming studies' have established that children differ from adults and from each other, with largest aiming errors reported for 8 year olds (Hay et al., 1986). We expect that error will increase with increasing delays for both adults and children but improvement with age may not be monotonic.

Method

Targets were laser-projected for 5 seconds onto a featureless table-top at 4 different positions relative to subject. Distance of each target was computed for subjects individually (2 were on the midline at 33% and 66% of arm-length and 2 were 45° eccentric at 50% arm-length) so all data were comparable. The reference light was projected centrally. Order of target, time delay and conditions were randomized and were within-subject. Thus, each of the 6 adult subjects made 36 judgments for each time-delay (0, 5 and 10 secs) in each condition (absolute/reference). For practical reasons, the experiment was modified for the children. The reference condition was not included and the number of trials was reduced. Responses were recorded by placing a sandwich of carbon and graph paper below the table surface. Subjects reached and left an indentation on the paper whilst the surface remained unmarked. The experiment was conducted in complete darkness.

Results and Discussion

Figure 1 shows that for total unsigned errors there was no appreciable deterioration in performance with respect to either time delay or condition.

Figure 2 presents total error for children aged 6 and 9 years (absolute condition only). A monotonic developmental trend is apparent whereby larger errors are made at 6 compared to performance at 9 years which is near adult-like.

Total signed errors for adults were then analyzed separately for directional (left-right) and amplitude (under-overshoot) signed errors for each condition (see Figure 3).

Figure 3 indicates a marked difference in performance between the two conditions and across time delays. In the absolute condition only, irrespective of target position, subjects made considerable undershooting errors. However, this effect only emerges in the 5 and 10 second delay conditions. The tendency to produce amplitude errors which undershoot was also noted in the children tested.   Reference condition errors were in terms of direction rather than amplitude, particularly for lateral targets. This may well reflect subjects' ability to align their aim when both reference and target are in the midline.

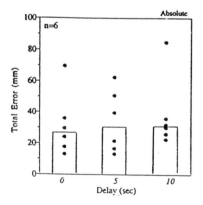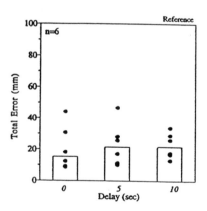

Figure 1. Distribution of mean pointing errors for all adult subjects.

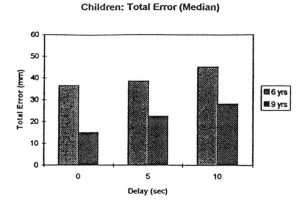

Children: Total Error (Median)

Figure 2. Distribution of total error scores for children

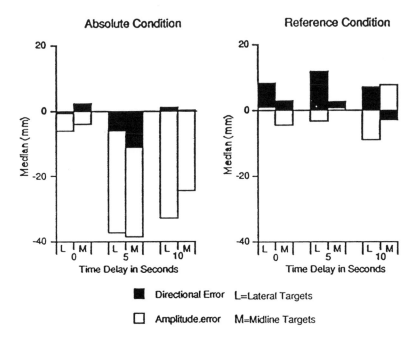

Figure 3. Error type by time delay and target position

Taken together our data show effects of increasing time delay when error type is taken into account. This is in accordance with the proposal of a rapidly-updated mechanism controlling visuo-motor tasks. Interestingly, our findings from children contradict Hay et al's (1986) result despite both tasks being open-loop. However, the two studies differ in the way visual feedback was prevented and ours involved aiming and pointing rather than aiming alone. Further experimental work is underway to explore these differences.

References

Goodale, M. A, Milner, A. D, Jakobson, L. S., & Carey, D. P. (1991). A neurological dissociation between perceiving objects and grasping them. *Nature* 349, 154-156.

Hay, L., Bard, C., & Fleury, M. (1986). Visuo-manual coordination from 6 to 10: Specification, control and evaluation of direction and amplitude parameters of movement. In M. G. Wade & H. T. A. Whiting (Eds.), *Motor development in children: Aspects of coordination and control.* NATO Series D: Behaviour and Social Sciences No 34.

Thomson, J. A. (1983). Is continuous visual monitoring necessary in visually guided locomotion? *Journal of Experimental Psychology: Human Perception and Performance, 9,* 3, 427-443

Studies in Perception and Action IV
M. A. Schmuckler & J. M. Kennedy (Eds.)
© *1997 Lawrence Erlbaum Associates, Inc.*

The Influence Of Visual Context On Movement Accuracy Is Dependent On Its Location In The Environment

Pierre Magne & Yann Coello

Laboratoire de Psychologie Cognitive, Département de Psychologie, Université Lille-3, Villeneuce d'Ascq, France

In aiming tasks, visuo-motor control has been shown to greatly improve when contextual information is available. Erkelens et al. (1989) observed that as a target moves along a sagittal axis, the accuracy of convergence eye movements was highly improved by the presence of a visual scene surrounding the moving target. Similar outcomes were observed for arm movements. Conti and Beaubaton (1980) showed that subjects had greater spatial accuracy when pointing to a target within a context, than when they pointed to an isolated target without background, despite the lack of visibility of the moving hand. The advantage provided by visual context was observed when the latter was available prior to the movement onset, or during the unfolding of the action (Velay & Beaubaton, 1986). In a previous study investigating the effect of the structure of the visual scene on movement accuracy, we noted that the size of the context influenced primarily target location, while the contour of the visual scene was rather used for on-line adjustments of hand path (Coello & Grealy, in press). Although the role of contextual information was well supported by numerous data, the nature of the relevant visual information involved in visuo-motor control has to be clarified. The aim of this experiment was to further explore this issue to test the effect of the location of contextual information on movement accuracy. For a sagittal movement, the hypothesis was that contextual information located on a sagittal or horizontal axis should improve respectively amplitude and azimuth control.

Method

Participants (N = 7) sat in front of a box divided horizontally by a reflecting mirror (see Figure 1a). With the head fixed on the upper part of the box, subjects could see looking in the mirror a virtual target displayed on the lower part. Twenty-five leds (Ø: 5mm) were used as stimuli, but only five of them were used as target (see Figure 1b). The center one was at a distance of 35cm from the starting point. Each target was displayed in an otherwise dark environment, or within a visual context (2 or 4 stimuli) forming a typical configuration (horizontal, sagittal or orthogonal axes, see Figure 1c). To test the effect of the amount versus the location of contextual information, two control conditions were added in which the visual context (2 or 4 stimuli) was grouped at different distances from the target (see Figure 1c). Experimental conditions (blocked trials) were randomly presented. Vision of the external environment was prevented during the whole experiment.

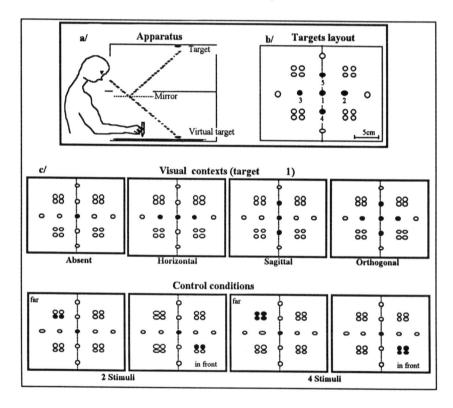

Figure 1. (a) Apparatus, (b) targets layout (black dots), (c) experimental conditions (presented for the target 1 only) as a function of the visual context (absent, horizontal, sagittal or orthogonal axes, control-2-stimuli, control-4-stimuli).

Sagittal pointing movements were performed on a digitiser tablet (Wacom UD-1825), which allowed the recording of (x,y) coordinates of an electromagnetic stylus held by the subject's right hand. Hand position was delivered to the subjects during inter-trial period only. Endpoint positions of individual movements were used to compute error parameters. Constant error was decomposed into radial error (the distance between movement vector length and target vector length) and angular error (the angle between the start-to-target-point vector and the start-to-end-point of movement vector). Statistical investigations were carried out on mean results regarding targets 1, 2, 3, 4, and 5.

Results

1. *Radial accuracy* (amplitude performance)

A one way ANOVA (visual context [6]) with repeated measures demonstrated a significant variation in the radial error as a function of the visual context (Absent, Horizontal, Sagittal, Orthogonal, Control-2-stimuli, Control-4-stimuli; $F(5,30) = 6.17$, $p < .001$). Figure 2a pointed out that radial error was smaller when a context was added to the target but only for the 'Sagittal' and 'Orthogonal' conditions as shown by Newman-Keuls comparisons (-43.54mm, $q(6,30) = 7.01$ and -42.77mm, $q(5,30) = 5.59$, $p < .01$ in both cases). No differences between these two conditions were observed and the other contexts did not differ from the 'Context absent' condition (-9.78mm).

These results suggest that sagittal movements were more accurate when contextual information was present, but only when it was oriented in the same direction as the movement's path. To better understand the effect of the position of the visual context according to the target, an analysis of the radial error was carried out for targets (1, 2, 3) only, in the 'Context absent' and 'Sagittal' conditions, and in the conditions where the context was farther versus in front of the target (these control conditions were grouped in the first analysis).

As predicted, statistical analysis (ANOVA: visual context [4]) indicated that radial error varied as a function of the visual context (Absent, Sagittal, Control-2-stimuli-far, Control-2-stimuli-in-front; $F(3,18) = 6.22$, $p < .01$). As shown in Figure 2c, the radial error was smaller for the 'Sagittal' (-32.27mm) and the 'Control-2-stimuli-in-front' (-32.50mm) than for the 'Context absent' condition (-39.75mm; $q(3,18) = 3.76$ and $q(2,18) = 3.64$, $p < 0.05$ in both cases). The 'Control-2-stimuli-far' condition (-41.93mm) did not statistically differ from the 'Context absent' condition.

2. *Angular accuracy* (azimuth performance)

In the 'Context absent' condition, the movement ended slightly to the left of the target (-1.54deg) as shown in figure 2b, but this error was not influenced by the addition of a visual context (Horizontal: -1.52deg, Sagittal: -1.52deg, Orthogonal: -1.53deg, Control-2-stimuli: -1.66deg, and Control-4-stimuli: -1.67deg; $F(5,30) = 0.53$, $p > .05$).

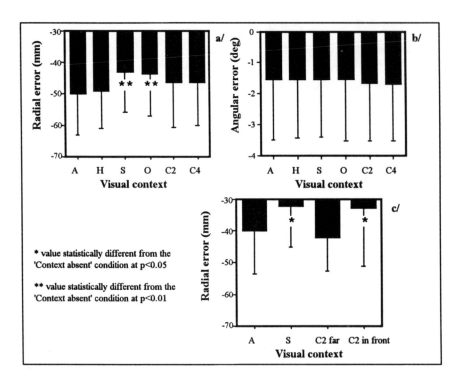

Figure 2. Mean radial (a) and angular error (b) as a function of the visual context (absent, horizontal, sagittal or orthogonal axes, control 2 stimuli, control 4 stimuli). In (c) is represented mean radial error (for targets 1, 2, 3 only) as a function of the visual context (absent, sagittal, control-2-stimuli-far, control-2-stimuli-in-front).

Discussion

The aim of this study was to test the influence of the location of contextual information on the accuracy of a pointing movement. The main outcome was that perceiving the target within a context seemed to have more influences on distancing than azimuth control of hand displacement. The visual appearance of the target might then provide the crucial information necessary for the control of movement azimuth, since varying the visual context did not influence angular accuracy. However, movement amplitude was sharply affected by the availability of contextual information. Initial undershoot was reduced when visual context was provided between the initial and the final position of hand path. Overall, these results suggest that in open-loop tasks amplitude control is more affected by a weakening of the visual signal than azimuth control, which is supported by a large body of data (Foley, 1980; Coello & Favereaux, 1996; Coello & Grealy, in press). Surprisingly, the advantage of background visual cues seems to be dependent on their location in the action field. In conclusion, visuo-motor coordinations may be understood as an interaction between sensory information relating to the target, the effector, as well as the whole elements in the structured visual scene being spatially relevant for the motor task.

Acknowledgments. We acknowledge Yves Rossetti, Jean-Pierre Orliaguet and Séverine Samson for their comments on this work. The study was supported by grants from the University Charles de Gaulle (Lille-3).

References

Coello, Y., & Favereaux, J. S. (1996). Effect of size and orientation of visual context on movement accuracy. *International Journal of Psychology, 3-4,* 11.

Coello, Y., & Grealy, M. (in press). Effect of size and frame of visual field on the accuracy of an aiming movement. *Perception.*

Conti, P., & Beaubaton, D. (1980). Role of structured visual field and visual reafference in accuracy of pointing movements. *Perceptual and Motor Skills, 50,* 239-244.

Erkelens, C. J., Steinman, R. M., & Collewijn, H. (1989). Ocular vergence under natural conditions. II: Gaze-shifts between real targets differing in distance and direction. *Proceedings of the Royal Society of London, 236,* 441-465.

Foley, J. M. (1980). Stereoscopic distance perception. In S. R. Ellis (Ed.), *Pictorial communication* (pp. 558-566). New York: Taylor Francis.

Velay, J. L., & Beaubaton, D. (1986). Influence of visual context on pointing movement accuracy. *Cahiers de Psychologie Cognitive European Bulletin of Cognitive Psychology, 6,* 447-456.

Studies in Perception and Action IV
M. A. Schmuckler & J. M. Kennedy (Eds.)
© *1997 Lawrence Erlbaum Associates, Inc.*

Measuring Shape And Egocentric Distance Perception Through Reaching

Ittai Flascher, Frank Zaal, & Geoffrey Bingham

Perception-Action Laboratory, Indiana University, Bloomington, IN, U.S.A.

In many studies, both visual and haptic perception of egocentric distances and objects' shapes have been shown to be different from Euclidean (e.g., Norman, Todd, Perotti, & Tittle, 1996; Todd, Tittle, & Norman, 1995; Kay, Hogan, & Fasse, 1996). Participants' judgments in these studies were usually given verbally or in the form of matching test stimuli to standards. In contrast, experiments investigating targeted locomotion have not found perception to be distorted (Loomis, DaSilva, Fujita, & Fukusima, 1992). Nevertheless, distortions of egocentric distance have been found for reaching with monocular vision (Bingham & Pagano, in press). Would distortions in shape perception be found in visually guided reaching? In the experiment reported below we use reaching to investigate the role of haptic feedback from contact with objects in the binocular and monocular perception of egocentric distance and shape.

Method

Two volunteers participated in the experiment. Participants were seated in a chair and grasped a stylus in their right hand such that 4.0 cm extended beyond the thumb. The task was to place the tip of the stylus in required locations near a white target sphere 5cm in diameter.

Procedure: Participants reached to one of three distances (.015 of maximum reach ≈ 1.4cm, .03 mr ≈ 2.5cm, .045 mr ≈ 3.2cm) in one of three directions from the target surface (front, side, back). Targets were either near (.5 of maximum reach) or far (.8 of maximum reach). The target sphere was held in position in the sagittal plane at eye height by a rod which extended from the upper left rear quadrant of the sphere to an axle. The axle allowed an experimenter to raise the target above reaching range. Distances from the surface were specified prior to the experimental session by showing them to the participant drawn on paper. For each trial, the experimenter named the location and distance to which the participant should reach (e.g., "Front-Far"). Participants then viewed the target sphere while moving their head back and forth three times to generate optic flow. Participants then shut their eyes and the sphere was removed beyond their reaching range. Then, participants removed the back end of the stylus from the launch platform next to their hip, and reached.

Data collection was triggered by the extraction of the stylus from the launch platform and was terminated by the experimenter after the participants indicated that they had positioned the stylus. In feedback trials the sphere was replaced in the target location so that participants could move to contact the surface. Eyes remained closed throughout the feedback phase.

Data Collection: An IRED (infrared emitting diode) was attached to the tip of the stylus and its position was recorded by a two-camera WATSMART kinematic measurement system. The location of the sphere's center was recorded prior to each session, and a gauge figure was recorded to confirm that measurements were isotropic.

Design: There were five independent variables: 1. Viewing conditions (Binocular or Monocular), 2. Haptic feedback (Feedback or No-feedback), 3. Distance of the target from the observer (Far, Near), 4. Direction from the target surface (Front, Side, or Back), 5. Distance from the target surface (Close, Middle, Far). Randomized trials were blocked by target distance with 10 trials per cell. A total of 180 trials (3 x 3 x 2 x 10) were performed in separate sessions for each of the viewing and feedback conditions.

Results and Discussion

Multiple regressions were performed regressing required distances from the target surface on reach distances from the surface. In separate analyses, we compared front to back and front to side. (1) Without feedback, reaches reproduced previous visual shape perception results. Distances to the front were expanded with respect to distances to the side by 30% for both binocular and monocular viewing [$r^2 = .73$, $p < .001$, $F(3,36) = 214.1$]. The mean slope was 2.71, $p < .01$, partial $F = 6.8$). This distortion did not vary with target distance in either viewing condition. (2) With haptic feedback, the relative expansion was eliminated. Slope difference was not significant in either front versus back or front versus side analyses. Partial F values were near 0 and $p > .5$ in all cases. Mean slopes were significant (all p's $< .001$) and equal to about 2.0 for monocular viewing and to about 2.46 for binocular viewing. (3) To estimate egocentric distance perception we computed the centroids of the distributions of reaches for each distance and direction from the target surface for each target distance and participant. Next we fitted a line to the front and back centroids by regressing the x on y coordinates (see Figure 1). We fitted a line to the side centroids by regressing y on x coordinates. We used the intersection of these two lines as an estimate of the perceived target location and used the x coordinate (distance in the sagittal plane) of this point as a measure of perceived egocentric distance. The egocentric distance of the entire distribution of reaches was expanded both with binocular (by 2.41 cm. at near target distance, and 0.86 cm. for far) and monocular viewing (near = 4.64 cm, far = 1.36 cm), without feedback. Egocentric distances became more accurate with feedback (binocular: near = 0.98 cm, far = 2.48 cm; monocular: near = 1.81 cm, far = 1.28 cm). (4) X distances of reaches to the side of the target yield the best trial by trial measure of perception of egocentric target distance. We examined these values over trial order (that is, in time). Without haptic feedback from contact with object surfaces, visually guided reaching is unstable and drifts. With this feedback, it becomes stable, therefore, more precise as well as more accurate. (5) We found in the multiple regression analyses that reach distances expanded required distances from the target surface by a factor of 2 or more. This expansion was reduced with haptic feedback, but not below the factor of 2.

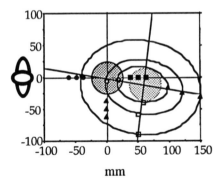

Figure 1. A top view (x, y plane) of target (dark disk) and "reached" target (faded disk) as determined by the crossing of the fitted lines. Target positions = filled symbols; reaching means = empty symbols.

References

Bingham, G. P., & Pagano, C. C. (in press). The necessity of a perception/action approach to definite distance perception: Monocular distance perception for reaching. *Journal of Experimental Psychology: Human Perception and Performance.*

Kay, B. A., Hogan, N., & Fasse, E. D. (1996). *The structure of haptic perceptual space is a function of the properties of the arm: On more time on the radial-tangential illusion.* Unpublished manuscript.

Loomis, J. M., DaSilva, J. A., Fujita, N., & Fukusima, S. S. (1992). Visual space perception and visually directed action. *Journal of Experimental Psychology: Human Perception and Performance, 18,* 906-921.

Norman, J. F., Todd, J. T., Perotti, V. J., & Tittle, J. S. (1996). The visual perception of three-dimensional length. *Journal of Experimental Psychology: Human Perception and Performance, 22,* 173-186.

Todd, J. T., Tittle, J. S., & Norman, J. F. (1995). Distortions of three-dimensional space in perceptual analysis of motion and stereo. *Perception, 24,* 75-86.

Studies in Perception and Action IV
M. A. Schmuckler & J. M. Kennedy (Eds.)
© *1997 Lawrence Erlbaum Associates, Inc.*

Task Constraints On The Preferred Critical Boundary For Visually-Guided Reaching

Douglas L. Gardner, Janina Paasche, Heather Edkins, Timothy Hirons, Leonard S. Mark, & Marvin J. Dainoff

Department of Psychology, Miami University, Oxford, OH, U.S.A.

Work by Mark et al. (in press) has shown that the transition between different styles of reaching occurs not at the absolute limit of the actor's capability (absolute critical boundary, ACB), but at closer distances, what they refer to as the preferred critical boundary (PCB). Mark et al. provided evidence that the PCB between two action modes reflects their relative comfort. Actors attempt to use the mode that maximizes the comfort associated with the goal directed action. The current study examines the role of the task in constraining the choice of action modes. For example, an actor picking up an object at their ACB may partially rise out of their seat (crouching) in order to pick it up rather than stretch as far as they can from a seated position. If required to manipulate the object at the same distance (ACB) for an extended period, the actor may stand.

Method

Materials and Procedure. Actors sat on a stool and were asked to pick up a yellow Lego block, pick up (or place) a 1" escutcheon pin from (in) a small hole, or pick up either a large or a small black bead with a needle. In the Block and Pickup conditions, actors simply had to pick up the block or take the pin from a hole. In the Place condition, actors were asked to place the pin in a particular hole, and in the Bead condition, actors had to pick up a small bead by sticking a needle through the hole in the bead.

Actors were asked to complete the reaching tasks at distances ranging from 60% to 120% of their maximum reach capability (ACB) for an arm and torso reach. Each reach made by the actor was coded by the experimenter as a "Type 1" if the actor leaned forward but did not get up, "Type 2" if the actor slid forward on the seat but did not get up, "Type 3" if the actor stood up partially,

"Type 4" if the actor stood up completely, or "Type 5" if the actor walked around to the side of the table to make the reach.

Results and Conclusions

Figure 1 shows the probability that a partial standing reach is used when picking up a block, a pin, a small bead with a needle, or placing a pin in a hole. Partial standing reaches are relatively unlikely to be used to pick up the small bead with a needle, but actors picking up a large block are likely to use a partial standing reach as the distance of the reach approaches their maximum seated reach capability. As the demand for fine manipulation decreases (from bead to block), the probability of a partial standing reach increases.

Figure 2 shows the progression through reach types (arm and torso to full standing) for the block condition. At approximately 95% of the ACB for a seated reach, actors make a transition to a partial standing reach, and at about 112% of the ACB, actors use a full standing reach.

Figure 3 shows that for the small bead condition, actors make a transition directly to a full standing reach, without the corresponding increase in partial standing reaches, and that the transition occurs at approximately 83% of the ACB, as opposed to 95% of the ACB, for the block condition.

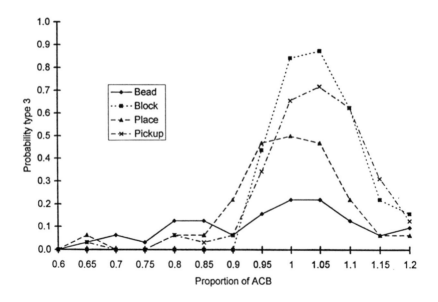

Figure 1. Probability of partial standing reaches by task.

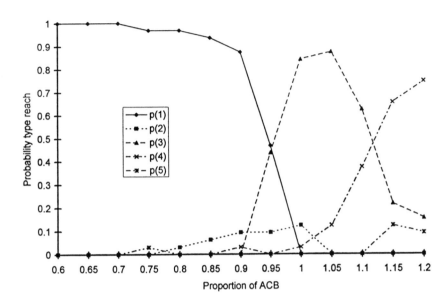

Figure 2. Probability of reach mode in the block condition.

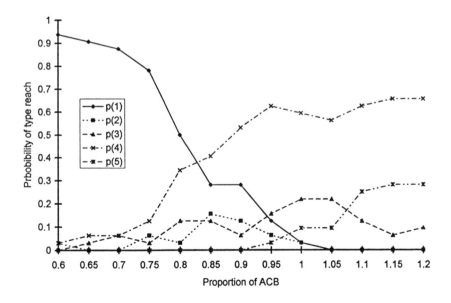

Figure 3. Probability of reach mode in the bead condition.

From this study, we can conclude that actors demonstrate a progression through different modes as distance increases, illustrating preferred boundaries for the various modes. Most importantly, actors change their mode of reaching to match characteristics of the task. In the bead condition, for example, actors generally made the transitions to the next mode at shorter distances and rarely used the partial standing mode.

References

Mark, L. S., Nemeth, K., Gardner, D., Dainoff, M. J., Paasche, J., Duffy, M., & Grandt, K. (in press). Postural dynamics and the preferred critical boundary for visually-guided reaching. *Journal of Experimental Psychology: Human Perception and Performance.*

Studies in Perception and Action IV
M. A. Schmuckler & J. M. Kennedy (Eds.)
© *1997 Lawrence Erlbaum Associates, Inc.*

Monocular Distance Perception Via Forward Versus Lateral Head Movements

Emily A. Wickelgren, Daniel S. McConnell, &
Geoffrey P. Bingham

Perception-Action Laboratory, Indiana University, Bloomington, IN, U.S.A.

The purpose of this study was to determine if targeted reaching is performed accurately using monocular distance information in optic flow generated by forward versus lateral head movements. We also investigated how accurate and precise performance would remain in each case either with or without haptically-experienced feedback from contact with targets. Bingham and Pagano (in press) investigated the use of optic flow generated by forward head movements with haptic feedback and found that reaches undershot the targets and did so increasingly as target distance increased. Ellard, Goodale and Timney (1984) found that monocular gerbils trained to jump over a gap employ larger up and down head movements than binocular gerbils, but no longer do so if allowed to approach the gap so as to generate optic flow from forward head motion (Marotta, Perrot, Nicolle, Servos, & Goodale, 1995). Marotta et al. (1995) have found that monocular people are more accurate in reaching to targets when they used head movements to judge distance, but both forward and lateral head movements were used and it remained unclear which was better.

Method

Four participants viewed a target disk monocularly via a head-mounted video display and camera (Bingham & Pagano, in press). Only the bright disk-shaped image appeared in an otherwise dark display. Target sizes co-varied with target distances to produce constant image sizes (before head movement). Participants reached to align a hand-held stylus with the target in four conditions: forward head movement with and without feedback, and lateral head movement with and without feedback. In each condition, participants reached 5 times to targets at 5 distances in a random order. Distances were proportions of the maximum reach distance for each participant (.50, .58, .66, .76 and .86). Each trial, the participant oscillated his/her head through 4 cycles (either forward or lateral) while viewing the target and then reached from the hip to place a stylus directly under a target at eye height. Upon the initiation of the reach, the video display was shut off so that reaches were performed without vision. In the feedback conditions, the participant was allowed to move upwards to touch the target after having aligned the stylus under the target. Head and hand movements as well as target position were recorded using a WATSMART 2-camera system at a sampling rate of 100Hz. IREDs (Infrared emitting diode) were placed on the tip of the stylus, on the target, and on the head. Reach distance was measured as the position of the IRED on the stylus when held under the target.

Results and Discussion

The mean reach distances of the 4 participants are shown in Figure 1, where the data for the feedback and no feedback conditions are plotted for each type of head movement. For analysis, we combined the data in terms of maximum reach units, but transformed some of the results to centimeters by multiplying by the mean maximum reach distance. We tested for differences in reach distances as a function of either differences in head movement within feedback conditions, or differences in feedback within head movement conditions. We performed multiple regressions on reach distances by regressing the actual target distances together with a vector coding either type of head movement or feedback (as +/-1) and an interaction vector. The interaction vector tests for a slope difference while the categorical variable tests for an intercept difference between the respective conditions. The test of feedback within the forward head movement condition was significant [r^2 = .74, $F(3,194) = 75.6$, $p < .001$]. The slope difference was significant ($p < .001$, partial $F = 10.9$). The test of feedback within the lateral head movement condition was significant [$r^2 = .52$, $F(3,198) = 24.6$, $p < .001$]. However, there were no slope or intercept differences. The multiple regression comparing types of head movement within the no feedback condition was significant [$r^2 = .58$, $F(3,194) = 33.1$, $p < .001$]. The y-intercept difference was significant ($p < .001$, partial $F = 19.6$). The mean slope was .61, and the separation between the curves was about 4.5 cm. The test of type of head movement within the feedback condition also was significant [$r^2 = .71$, $F(3,198) = 64.6$, $p < .001$].

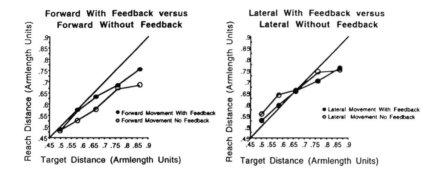

Figure 1. Mean reach distances as a function of target distance for the four conditions.

Again, the intercept difference was significant ($p < .01$, partial $F = 6.8$). The mean slope was .64 and the separation between the curves was about 2 cm.

The mean absolute error was calculated for each condition, and found to be greater for the forward head movement conditions (Forward with feedback = 4.7 cm, forward without feedback = 9.0 cm, lateral with feedback = 2.6 cm, lateral without feedback = 5.8 cm). As shown in Figure 1, forward head movement curves exhibit consistent undershooting although less with feedback than without feedback. With lateral head movement, participants tended to overshoot at the near distances and undershoot at the far distances. While reaches with lateral head movements were more accurate, they were less precise (that is, more variable). We computed coefficients of variation (CV) for each distance and participant. The mean CVs for forward head movement with and without feedback were 2.1 cm and 2.5 cm respectively, while those for lateral head movement were 5.2 cm and 8.8 cm respectively.

The underestimation of forward head movements could have resulted from distance having been estimated when the head was closest to the target during the head oscillation. This bird-like head motion was awkward and unnatural. Natural movement toward a target during a reach moves both the head and arm, in which case reaches might be more accurate. If so, forward head movement would be both more accurate and more precise. If not, then one is left with a choice between precision and accuracy. However, the low slopes ($\approx .70$) limit the possible accuracy for either type of head movement even with haptic feedback from contact with targets. The results confirm the conclusion of Bingham and Pagano (in press) that haptic feedback does not eliminate visual errors in distance perception.

References

Bingham, G. P., & Pagano, C. C. (in press). The necessity of a perception/action approach to definite distance perception: Monocular distance perception to guide reaching. *Journal of Experimental Psychology: Human Perception and Performance.*

Ellard, C. G., Goodale, M. A., & Timney, B. (1984). Distance estimation in the Mongolian gerbil: The role of dynamic depth cues. *Behavioral Brain Research, 14,* 29-39.

Marotta, J. J., Perrot, T. S., Nicolle, D., Servos, P., & Goodale, M. A. (1995). Adapting to monocular vision: Grasping with one eye. *Experimental Brain Research, 104,* 107-114.

Studies in Perception and Action IV
M. A. Schmuckler & J. M. Kennedy (Eds.)
© *1997 Lawrence Erlbaum Associates, Inc.*

Timing Of Interceptive Action In Children

John van der Kamp[1,2] Tjasa Planinsek[3], & Geert Savelsbergh[1,2]

[1] Research Institute for Fundamental and Clinical Human Movement Sciences,
Amsterdam/Nijmegen, The Netherlands
[2] Faculty of Human Movement Sciences, Free University,
Amsterdam, The Netherlands
[3] Faculty of Education, University of Ljubljana, Slovenia

Most interceptive actions, like a simple one-hand catch, develop during childhood. To ensure catching success, children not only have to learn to position the hand at the interception point, but also have to initiate and complete the grasp within a restricted time-window. Previous research (e.g., Isaacs, 1983; Shea et al., 1982) sought to explain the development of anticipatory timing in interceptive actions in terms of speed differences in information processing. To this end, a Bassin Anticipation Timer was utilised where children attempted to anticipate the illumination of a target lamp. Results suggested a change from a non-constant to a constant time-to-contact strategy from 5 to 12 years, i.e., effects of approach velocity on timing accuracy disappeared with age.

However, since the available information from a sequence of illuminating lights differs vastly from that of an approaching ball, translating these findings to simple one-handed catching might be hazardous. The more so, because from an ecological approach development or learning can be considered as becoming sensitive to different or additional information sources. The development of catching, therefore, might (partly) result from the involvement of different information sources guiding the timing of the grasp action.

A first step to uncover this developmental process is to examine whether timing strategies change during development. Furthermore, by manipulating the available informational constraints insight can be acquired into what specific information sources are involved (Van der Kamp et al., 1996, 1997). Therefore, 4 to 11 year old children were required to catch balls with different diameters under both monocular and binocular vision.

In sum, the purpose is to examine whether the catching performance is actually hampered by the inability of the children to time their catch accurately, and whether throughout childhood, there is a change in the information sources contributing to the control of the temporal properties of the grasp phase in catching.

Method

Nine young children (4 - 7 years) and eleven older children (8 - 11 years) were required to catch a total of 30 balls in a completely dark room. Three different sized balls were transported by a specially devised Ball Transport Apparatus (BallTrAp) and approached the subjects with a constant deceleration (average velocity 1.5 m/s). The balls were transported into the hand from a spatially fixed trajectory such that only temporal judgements were necessary. After contacting the hand, the ball immediately returned to its starting position giving rise to a time window of about 350 ms. Half of the balls were presented under monocular and the other half under binocular vision.

Results and Discussion

Analyses of variance for the percentage of unsuccessful catches showed an interaction of Ball by Vision [$F(2,32) = 6.4$, $p < .01$], indicating that the smallest ball was missed more often under monocular than under binocular vision (Figure 1).

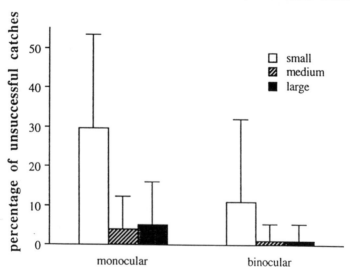

Figure 1. Percentage of catching failures. The data are grouped over age.

No significant differences were found for the percentage of misses, as well as for the kinematics of the timing of the grasp between the younger and older children. However, significant interactions of Ball by Vision were found for the moment of opening of the hand [$F(2,22) = 4.6$; $p < .05$], the moment of closing of the hand [$F(2,30) = 7.3$; $p < .01$], and the moment of completion of the catch [$F(2,30) = 9.0$; $p < .001$]. That is, children from both age groups behaved in accordance with a constant time-to-contact strategy only when provided with binocular vision. In contrast, in the monocular viewing condition, the grasp was initiated and completed later for the smaller balls, that is, a constant time-to-contact strategy was not present (Figure 2).

Unlike earlier observations in anticipatory timing, when children were actually catching balls no change in timing could be discerned during childhood. Hence, what seems to be learned in the development of catching is not so much control over the timing of the grasp, but control over the positioning of the hand. Moreover, like in adults (Van der Kamp et al., 1997), different viewing conditions led to different timing strategies, indicating the involvement of different information sources. That is, under binocular viewing a binocular information source, for instance the tau-function of disparity, is used, while in the monocular viewing condition probably

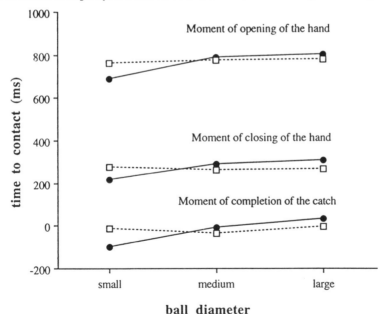

Figure 2. Kinematics of the grasp phase. The data are grouped over age. Note, negative values indicate occurrence after ball-hand contact.

a lower order information source like image size, but not the tau-function of visual angle, might be involved.

Acknowledgments. This paper was written while the first author was supported by the Foundation for Behavioural Sciences (575-59-055), which is funded by the Netherlands Organisation for Scientific Research (NWO), and the second author was supported by the Chancellor Fund of the University of Ljubljana.

References

Isaacs, L. D. (1983). Coincidence-anticipation in simple catching. *Journal of Human Movement Studies, 9,* 194-201.

Shea, C. H., Krampitz, J. B., Norham, C. C., & Asby, A. A. (1982). Information processing in coincident timing tasks: A developmental perspective. *Journal of Human Movement Studies, 8,* 73-83.

Van der Kamp, J., Savelsbergh, G., & Smeets, J. (1997). *Multiple information sources in interceptive timing.* Manuscript submitted for publication.

Van der Kamp, J., Vereijken, B., & Savelsbergh, G. (1996). Physical and informational constraints in the coordination and control of human movement. *Corpus, Psyche et Societas, 3,* 102-118.

Studies in Perception and Action IV
M. A. Schmuckler & J. M. Kennedy (Eds.)
© *1997 Lawrence Erlbaum Associates, Inc.*

The Focus Of Expansion Is Used To Control Walking

William H. Warren & Bruce A. Kay

Department of Cognitive and Linguistic Sciences, Brown University,
Providence, RI, U.S.A.

How do we steer toward a goal? Fifty years ago, James Gibson (1947, 1950, 1958) proposed that optic flow could be used to control steering by "keeping the focus of expansion in the direction one must go." For example, to walk through a doorway, one could detect the current visual angle between the FOE and the door and shift the direction of effector force through the same angle, thus shifting the FOE onto the door. One advantage of this FOE Hypothesis is that control is specified in a purely visual coordinate frame. However, to date Gibson's hypothesis has not been empirically tested.

An obvious alternative is simply to walk in the direction of the goal. The Visual Direction Hypothesis proposes that one detects the visual direction of the doorway and applies force in the opposite direction. This is only possible in legged locomotion, when the direction of force application (a) determines the direction of travel and (b) is known to the observer, which is not the case for flying, swimming, or vehicular travel. However, it requires a coordinate transformation from ocular to effector coordinates.

We tested these two hypotheses using a "virtual treadmill," in which the FOE in the display was offset by 5 deg from the actual direction of walking (Figure 1). The task was to walk through a doorway, which by our count we do upwards of 200 times a day. The Visual Direction Hypothesis predicts that the angle between the walking direction and the door (beta) will go to zero as the door is approached. In contrast, the FOE Hypothesis predicts that the angle between the FOE and the door (alpha) will go to zero, such that the doorway expands symmetrically -- with the consequence that the participant is not walking directly toward the door!

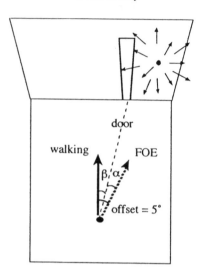

Figure 1. Schematic of virtual treadmill: Direction of FOE is offset from actual direction of walking.

Method

Ten participants walked on a wide-body treadmill in front of a closed-loop video display (112 x 95 deg) of a doorway approaching at the treadmill speed of 1 m/s. The display's center of projection was slaved to an electromagnetic sensor mounted on the participant's forehead, with a latency of 1 frame (33 ms at 30 Hz). Thus, the perspective view and optic flow on the screen was determined by the participant's movements on the treadmill. The "doorway" was a 5 cm slit in a texture-mapped frontal wall, with a texture-mapped floor, generated on an SGI Crimson RE. The initial distance of the doorway was 5 m, display duration was 5 s (Tc = 5 to 0 s). The last second was not analyzed, as slit width expanded beyond 5 deg. 3D head position was sampled at 30 Hz and filtered with a Butterworth filter (3.5 Hz cutoff). To reduce gait oscillations, time series of alpha and beta were ensemble averaged across trials and participants.

There were four basic conditions: FOE offset of 0 or 5 deg, crossed with initial door position of 0 or 5 deg. In the Control Condition (offset = 0 deg) we simulated normal locomotion, such that the FOE appeared in the direction of walking. Thus, when the initial position of the door was straight ahead at 0 deg, no steering adjustments were necessary; when it was 5 deg to the right (or left), a rightward (leftward) adjustment was required. In the Offset Condition (offset = 5 deg), we rotated the coordinate system of the motion sensor so that the FOE would appear 5 deg to the right (or left) of the actual direction of walking. Thus, when the initial position of the door was straight ahead at 0 deg, a leftward (rightward) steering adjustment would be necessary to shift the FOE onto the door; when the doorway was initially 5 deg to the right (or left), no adjustment would be needed.

Results

Mean alpha (angle between FOE and walking direction) tends to go to zero in all conditions, consistent with the FOE Hypothesis (Figure 2). When the doorway is straight ahead (0 deg), participants in the Offset Condition steadily shift the FOE over to the doorway in the first 2 s. With the doorway at 5 deg, participants initially walk in the visual direction of the door in the first 1.5 s, overshoot it in both the Offset and Control conditions, and then shift the FOE

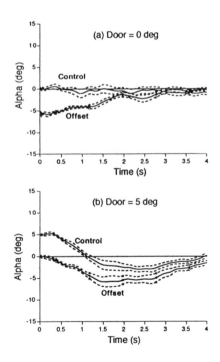

Figure 2. Mean time series of angle between FOE and doorway (alpha). Dotted curves indicate SE.

back to the door at 3-4 s -- presumably once the optical consequences of the initial move are detected. A second experiment, in which the offset angle was gradually increased during a trial, produced similar results.

Conclusion

The results are generally consistent with Gibson's FOE Hypothesis, although there is also an influence of the Visual Direction Hypothesis. Participants may initially move in the visual direction of a goal, but once anomalous optic flow is detected it appears to override visual direction. This nicely illustrates the role of active perception in visual control. As Gibson foresaw, optic flow appears to provide "the chief sensory guide for locomotion in space" when steering in legged locomotion.

References

Gibson, J. J. (1947). *Motion picture testing and research* (AAF Aviation Psychology Research Report 7). Washington, DC: US Government Printing Office.

Gibson, J. J. (1950). *Perception of the visual world.* Boston, MA: Houghton Mifflin.

Gibson, J. J. (1958). Visually controlled locomotion and visual orientation in animals. *British Journal of Psychology, 49*, 182-194.

Studies in Perception and Action IV
M. A. Schmuckler & J. M. Kennedy (Eds.)
© *1997 Lawrence Erlbaum Associates, Inc.*

An Ecological Approach To Mobile Robotics

Andrew P. Duchon & William H. Warren

Department of Cognitive and Linguistic Science, Brown University,
Providence, RI, U.S.A.

Although industrial robotics is now highly developed, mobile robotics has had limited success. A new field called behavior-based robotics has developed recently, spurred by the initial success of Brooks (1991). Its goal is the creation of robots that are 1) *situated* and so need to respond now to the environment; 2) *embodied*, having a constant dynamic relationship with the real world, and 3) *autonomous*, thus functioning without further input from the designer. Autonomy also implies that they are designed not so much to achieve predetermined goals, but rather are required simply to survive in the real world and in real-time.

The goal of real-time operation has also eliminated the use of computationally intensive symbolic operations for inferring the location and identity of objects and updating an internal world model. Instead, simple networks of individual behaviors are built such that there is no central model or controller. Complex behavior then emerges from the dynamic interaction between the agent and the environment, producing what appears to be goal-directed action.

Most work in robotics uses sensors which give metric distance information which the robot uses to place itself at a particular point in its world model. This information is combined with the goal location to plan a metric path to the goal. Visual information is traditionally used to create or augment this world model. Active control of the camera can make this task easier (Aloimonos and Rosenfeld, 1991), but purposive or animate vision goes one step further, asking "What is vision for?" (Ballard, 1991). If vision is used to obtain certain relationships between the robot and its environment, then the robot may not need to model the world at all before acting upon it.

All these views should sound familiar to ecological psychologists. Indeed, many papers in animate vision and behavior-based robotics make passing reference to the works of Gibson (e.g., 1979). However, we have tried to probe deeper into the relevance of ecological psychology for behavior-based robotics (Duchon and Warren, 1994; Duchon et al., 1995; see also: Pickering, 1992; Effken and Shaw, 1992): 1) Ecological psychology views animals and their environments as inseparable pairs. Behavior emerges out of the dynamic interaction between them. 2) Animals are equipped to directly perceive their environment, i.e., information is available in the environment which the animal can pick up in order to control its behavior, without inferential processing. 3) Thus, it is more important to put the animal in its environment than to model the environment in the animal. 4) These biological considerations transfer easily to mobile robots (so we can speak more generally of "agents"). We should be able to equip a robot with the sensors required to pick up a certain kind of information (e.g., optical flow) and use this information to modulate the robot's action parameters directly. 5) This idea is embodied in Warren's (1988) Laws of Control: changes in the forces produced by an agent's effectors (be they insect wings, human legs, or robot wheels) are a function of the changes detected in the optical flow.

Implementations

Since the most crucial aspect of behavior-based robotics is mobility, we began with control laws for obstacle avoidance (Duchon and Warren, 1994). This work used a small robot platform (30 cm in diameter, 75 cm high). The most successful control law was the Balance Strategy, in which the agent moves so as to balance the average amount of optical flow detected on either side of the optical axis (which is tied to the robot's heading). There is evidence that bees use a similar strategy (Srinivasan, 1992) and we are currently testing it in humans.

We have more recently implemented the Balance Strategy on a larger robot (60 cm in diameter, 120 cm high). Some obvious problems with implementing a control law used by 5g bees on a 100kg robot can be overcome without much work. Most can be solved simply by using a wide-angle lens, having the camera used to detect optical flow tilt down at a 45° angle, and weighting flow near the floor more than that on the walls. Running this strategy, the robot has wandered around an unmodified and restrictive office for up to 20 minutes without collision. Control laws for camera tilt and robot speed have also been developed, such that it will look up and move faster in open environments, and look down and move slower in cluttered environments.

We have also implemented a simple game of "tag" in both robots (Duchon et al., 1995). Control laws for escaping and chasing (common to predator-prey interactions) were developed using the optic variable of τ, or time-to-contact, to modulate the robot's behavior directly. With current hardware, motion measurements can be made at 10 Hz, allowing the robot to move at 30cm/sec-- fast enough for interaction with humans.

We are now working on adding higher-order behaviors, taking inspiration from another animal literature, namely cognitive mapping in rats (Duchon, 1996). By integrating neural networks (which will pick-up the dynamics of the agent's interactions with the environment) with control laws for obstacle avoidance, we hope to create autonomous robots with long-range navigational abilities.

Conclusion

We have briefly described the congruence between behavior-based robotics and ecological psychology. We have implemented ideas from the latter in a human-size mobile robot. The success of this shows that an ecological approach to visual control can be pursued regardless of the type of agent. Moreover, this approach is a two-way street. For example, we are currently running experiments on humans to see if they use similar strategies for controlling their locomotion.

References

Aloimonos, Y., & Rosenfeld, A. (1991). Computer vision. *Science, 253*, 1249-1254.

Ballard, D. (1991). Animate vision. *Artificial Intelligence, 48*, 57-86.

Brooks, R. A. (1991). New approaches to robotics. *Science, 253*, 1227-1232.

Duchon, A. P. (1996). Maze navigation using optical flow. In *From animals to animats 4* (pp. 224-232). Cambridge: MIT Press.

Duchon, A. P., & Warren, W. H. (1994). Robot navigation from a Gibsonian viewpoint. In *Proceedings of the IEEE International Conference on Systems, Man and Cybernetics* (pp. 2272-2277). Piscataway, NJ: IEEE.

Duchon, A. P., Warren, W. H., & Kaelbling, L. P. (1995). Ecological robotics: Controlling behavior with optical flow. In *Proceedings of the 17th Annual Conference of the Cognitive Science Society* (pp. 164-169). Mahwah, NJ: Lawrence Erlbaum.

Effken, J. A., & Shaw, R. E. (1992). Ecological perspectives on the new artificial intelligence. *Ecological Psychology, 4*, 247-270.

Gibson, J. J. (1979). *The ecological approach to visual perception*. Boston: Houghton Mifflin.

Pickering, J. (1992). The new artificial intelligence and biological plausibility. In *Studies in perception and action II* (pp. 126-129). Hillsdale, NJ: Lawrence Erlbaum.

Srinivasan, M. V. (1992). How bees exploit optic flow: Behavioural experiments and neural models. *Philosophical Transactions of the Royal Society of London B, 337*, 253-259.

Warren, W. H. (1988). Action modes and laws of control for the visual guidance of action. In O. G. Meier & H. Roth (Eds.), *Complex movement behaviour: The motor-action controversy* (pp. 339-380). North-Holland: Elsevier Science.

Studies in Perception and Action IV
M. A. Schmuckler & J. M. Kennedy (Eds.)
© *1997 Lawrence Erlbaum Associates, Inc.*

Social Expressions In Infant Locomotion: Vocalizations And Gestures On Slopes

Catherine S. Stergiou, Karen E. Adolph, Martha Wagner Alibali, Anthony M. Avolio, & Carly Cenedella

Department of Psychology, Carnegie Mellon University, Pittsburgh, PA, U.S.A.

Previous research on infant locomotion has focused on perceptual, motor, and cognitive aspects of crawling and walking. However, infants acquire locomotion in a social context. Infants' first steps are into the open arms of encouraging parents. Further, infants both interpret social expressions produced by others and produce such expressions themselves. Previous research showed that infants may gauge possibilities for locomotion by monitoring parents' facial expressions (Sorce et al., 1985). The current study shows that infants produce vocalizations or gestures in potentially risky situations. We expand on a previous longitudinal analysis of infants' exploratory activity and perceptual judgments as they coped with crawling and walking over slopes (Adolph, in press). Here, we report how infants' social behaviors reflect their ability to detect safe versus risky hills.

Method

We observed 29 infants longitudinally for a total of 219 test sessions. Fifteen experimental infants were tested once every three weeks from their first week of crawling until several weeks after walking onset. Fourteen control infants were tested at three matched sessions (first and tenth weeks of crawling and first week of walking) to control for experience on laboratory slopes. At each test session, infants encountered both safe and impossibly steep slopes ($0°$-$36°$) as determined with a psychophysical staircase procedure (Adolph, 1995).

Coders scored two types of social expressions on the starting platform: *vocalizations* (crying, babbling) and people-directed *gestures* (e.g., finger points, "gives", "pick-me-ups", head shakes). Coders also scored *anti-social* behavior when infants disengaged from social exchange (e.g., looking at ceiling

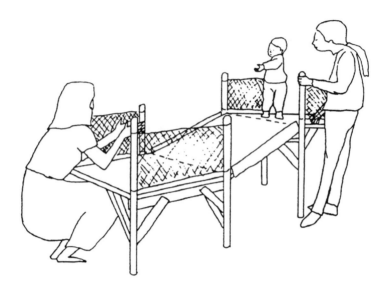

Figure 1. Parents stood at the far end of the adjustable ramp (0°-36°) and encouraged infants to come up or down, while an experimenter followed alongside infants to ensure their safety.

lights, playing with their clothes). A trial could include all types of social and anti-social behaviors.

Results and Discussion

Infants' social behaviors were discriminating from the start of independent mobility and became increasingly selective over weeks of crawling and walking (Figure 2a). At each session, infants exhibited more vocalizations and gestures when the consequences of falling were most aversive—on downhill, risky slopes. Across sessions, infants decreased their social expressions and limited them primarily to downhill, risky slopes. Repeated measures ANOVA collapsing across sessions confirmed that infants produced more social expressions (vocalizations and gestures combined) on downhill, risky slopes [$F(1,25) = 22.84$; $p < .001$]; experimental and control infants did not differ. Overall, 72% of social expressions included babbling with neutral or positive affect, 27% included crying, and 32% included gestures. Crawlers emitted

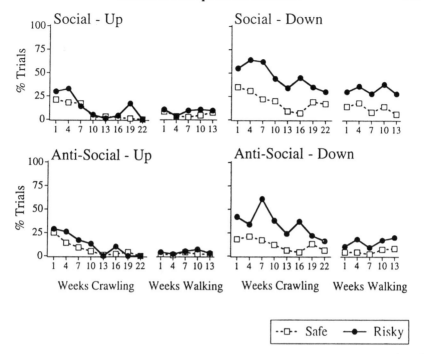

Figure 2. Social expressions (a) and anti-social behaviors (b) over weeks of crawling and walking.

more vocalizations than walkers [$F(1,25)$ = 5.80; p < .05], but crawlers gestured equally often as walkers [$F(1,25)$ = 0.36]. Apparently, crawling infants request more social support for locomotion than walkers, even though one means of social expression involves using the same limbs needed for balance.

Surprisingly, infants' anti-social behaviors showed a similar pattern to their social expressions (Figure 2b): high but discriminating levels of social disengagement in infants' first weeks of crawling and increasing selectivity over weeks of crawling and walking. Repeated measures ANOVA revealed more anti-social behavior on downhill, risky slopes [$F(1,25)$ = 4.00; p < .06], and during weeks of crawling [$F(1,25)$ = 11.62; p < .01]. Both social and anti-social behaviors parallel previous results for infants' exploratory looking and touching (Adolph, in press).

Even more surprising, despite social, anti-social, and exploratory behaviors that discriminated between safe and risky slopes on the starting platform, infants nonetheless plunged headfirst down impossibly risky slopes in their first

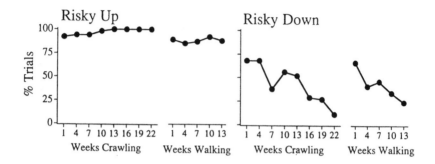

Figure 3. Errors on risky slopes over weeks of crawling and walking.

weeks of crawling and walking (Figure 3). Why might infants emit differential behaviors on the starting platform on the same trials when they show maladaptive judgments? If differential social expressions (or anti-social or exploratory behavior) reflected knowledge of potential consequences, infants should not have shown high error rates.

Rather, the data suggest that infants' social expressions may not have been wholly intentional in infants' first weeks of crawling. For example, vocalizations may result from high levels of arousal and the novelty of downward slanting surfaces. Regardless of intent, social expressions serve a useful function by alerting caregivers that infants are on the move. Later, when infants' social expressions are clearly intentional, infants may contribute to their own safety by appealing to adults for help in a potentially risky situation.

References

Adolph, K. E. (in press). Learning in the development of infant locomotion. *Monographs of the Society for Research in Child Development.*

Adolph, K. E. (1995). A psychophysical assessment of toddlers' ability to cope with slopes. *Journal of Experimental Psychology: Human Perception and Performance, 21,* 734-750.

Sorce, J., Emde, R., Campos, J., & Klinnert, M. (1985). Maternal emotional signaling: Its effect on the visual cliff behavior of 1-year-olds. *Developmental Psychology, 21,* 195-200.

Studies in Perception and Action IV
M. A. Schmuckler & J. M. Kennedy (Eds.)
© 1997 Lawrence Erlbaum Associates, Inc.

Infants' Responses To A Visual Cliff And Other Ground Surfaces

Marion Eppler, Tammy Satterwhite, Jeff Wendt, & Kotoe Bruce

Department of Psychology, East Carolina University, Greenville, NC, U.S.A.

As new motor skills emerge and mature, infants need to constantly update their understanding of their own changing abilities, and they also need to learn about features of the environment that have consequences for their actions. The purpose of this longitudinal study was to examine the developmental sequence and interrelationships for changing locomotor skills, attention, exploratory behavior, and adaptive action. As infants begin to crawl, do they notice differences in ground surfaces and do they understand how to use this information to appropriately guide action (avoiding an abrupt drop-off or insubstantial surface versus crossing along a safe path)? This study revisited the visual cliff and added three new visual ground surfaces (one continuous and substantial, one continuous and insubstantial, and one partial and substantial). Based on previous research with infants on slanting ground surfaces (see Eppler, Adolph, & Weiner, 1996), we expected infants to use exploratory activity to differentiate ground surfaces prior to relating this information to consequences for locomotion and acting adaptively.

Method

Nineteen infants were tested every three weeks from the first week of crawling through three months of crawling experience (1, 4, 7, 10, 13 weeks). They ranged in age from 6.8 to 10.6 months at their first test session (*M* age = 8.4 months). A cross-sectional control group (19 infants matched for age of crawling onset) was tested once at the same endpoint (13 weeks of crawling experience) to check for effects of repeated testing.

Infants were coaxed to crawl across a 4 ft square gap centered between starting and landing platforms (4 ft wide X 2 ft long, raised 30 in above the floor and covered with a continuous 4 ft X 8 ft sheet of sturdy 1/2 in thick Plexiglas). Four different visual patterns were presented to infants by placing materials in the gap directly underneath the Plexiglas: solid (substantial continuous surface) -- contrasting fabric that covered the entire gap; net (insubstantial continuous surface) -- volleyball net stretched across the entire gap with the floor visible below; bridge (substantial partial surface) -- 18 in wide board spanning diagonally across the gap; and cliff (no surface of support) -- no visible surface at the level of the platforms. The platforms, bridge, and ground beneath the Plexiglas gap were all covered in the same 1-in red and white checkerboard pattern. Infants were placed sitting on the center of the starting platform, and parents called to them from the opposite end. For the first and last trials, the entire Plexiglas surface was covered with a cloth to observe baseline behavior. The four test trials involved presentation of each of the four visual surfaces once, and infants received one of four counterbalanced presentation orders. Test trials were limited to two minutes.

Results and Discussion

The patterns for the two 13-week experience groups were very similar. Both groups clearly differentiated the four surfaces and acted adaptively. They showed the most avoidance and hesitation for the cliff, and least for the two continuous surfaces (solid and net); $F(3,37) = 10.44$, $p < .001$ (significant main effect for latency to cross the four surfaces; M latency to cross the cliff = 63.9 s, bridge = 37.5 s, net = 25.2 s, solid = 24.5 s). As comparison of these two groups demonstrates, this effect was attenuated somewhat by repeated testing; $F(1,37) = 4.68$, $p < .04$ (significant group difference for overall latency to cross; the interaction was not significant). Figures 1 and 2 illustrate how this effect is even stronger within a testing session than across testing sessions. Figure 1 shows greater differentiation of the surfaces at 13 weeks of experience when the cliff is presented on one of the first two test trials, while Figure 2 shows very little differentiation of the surfaces when the cliff is presented on the third or fourth trials. Apparently, infants are less likely to show hesitation and avoidance when they encounter the cliff on later trials. They cross all of the surfaces indiscriminately. This is in stark contrast to their behavior when they encounter the cliff on earlier trials. In Figure 2, the drop in latencies from week 1 to week 4 of crawling experience reflects increased crawling skill.

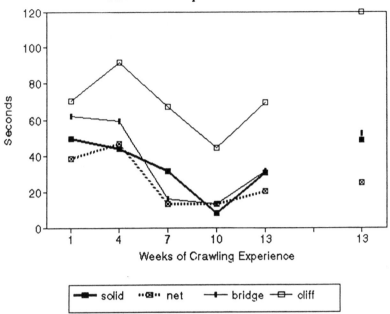

Figure 1. Time to cross (cliff on trial 1 or 2).

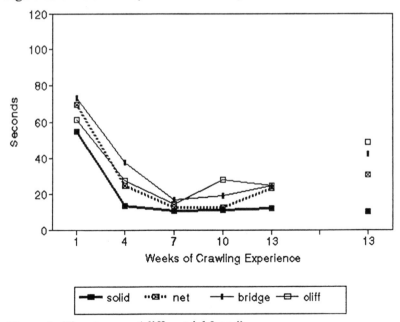

Figure 2. Time to cross (cliff on trial 3 or 4).

If we focus on infants who received the cliff on earlier trials (Figure 1), we see a developmental progression of increasing differentiation and adaptive action. By the fourth week of crawling experience, infants show greater avoidance on the cliff than for any of the other three surfaces, and this difference continues through 13 weeks of crawling experience. Overall, infants engaged in considerable exploratory behavior directed at the brink of the starting platform -- poking, rubbing, patting, and shifting their weight over a planted hand. They paused at the starting platform and peered over the edge during cliff and bridge trials, but not during net and solid trials. More detailed analyses of exploratory behavior are in progress. Preliminary findings indicate that infants use exploratory activity to differentiate surfaces of support prior to relating information about ground surfaces to consequences for locomotion.

References

Eppler, M. A., Adolph, K. E., & Weiner, T. (1996). The developmental relationship between infants' exploration and action on slanted surfaces. *Infant Behavior and Development, 19*, 261-266.

Studies in Perception and Action IV
M. A. Schmuckler & J. M. Kennedy (Eds.)
© *1997 Lawrence Erlbaum Associates, Inc.*

Infants' Ability To Detour Around Apertures And Obstacles

Jeff Wendt, Marion Eppler, & Kotoe Bruce

Department of Psychology, East Carolina University, Greenville, NC, U.S.A.

An important cognitive skill that develops during the latter portion of the first year is flexibility in problem solving, more specifically, the ability to generate alternate means to solve a problem (Piaget, 1952, 1954). One example involves blocking the direct path to a desired goal. Infants gradually shift from repeatedly taking the straight ahead path and failing to reach the goal to discovering and using alternative detour paths. In a longitudinal study of infants' ability to maneuver around a barrier, Lockman (1984) found that locomoting infants did not master crawling detours until several weeks after they had successfully solved reaching detours. This suggests that experience with a particular form of motor activity may facilitate the development of detour ability. The purpose of the present study was twofold: (1) to examine the role of locomotor experience in learning to solve detour problems; and (2) to compare infants' ability to solve two different kinds of crawling detour tasks with varying perceptual information. Nine-month-old infants with different amounts of crawling experience were encouraged to reach their parents by maneuvering around a large hole in the ground covered with clear Plexiglas (aperture detour) or around a small wall blocking the child's path (obstacle detour).

Method

Participants were 24 nine-month-old infants (M age = 279.4 days, range = 266-295) with an average of 59.9 days of crawling experience (range = 14-121).

The aperture task took place on a modified visual cliff which consisted of a 1/2 inch thick sheet of clear Plexiglas (4 ft wide X 8 ft long, raised 30 in above the floor) spanning a 4 ft square gap centered between two equally sized platforms (4 ft wide X 2 ft long). A bridge (1.5 ft wide X 4 ft long) was placed along one side stretching across the gap. All surfaces (except the gap) were covered with the same 1-in red and white checkerboard pattern. This task involved six 2-minute trials. On each trial, the experimenter placed the infant in a sitting position on one of the end platforms while the parent stood at the far end and used toys to coax the child across. The first and final trials were baselines where the entire Plexiglas surface was covered with a cloth. Two of the test trials involved presenting infants with only visual information for a drop-off (the platforms and bridge were situated underneath the Plexiglas). The two remaining test trials involved presenting infants with both visual and haptic information for a drop-off (1-in thick platforms and bridge were placed on top of the Plexiglas). For each pair of trials, the bridge was presented once to the right and once to the left.

The obstacle task took place in a small 4 ft wide X 8 ft long corridor built to parallel the aperture task. A small wall (2.5 ft wide X 2.5 ft tall) blocked the infants' path, with only a narrow 1.5 ft wide opening for the infant to pass through. This task also involved six 2-minute trials. On each trial, the experimenter placed the infant in a sitting position at one end of the corridor while the parent stood at the far end and used toys to coax the child across the floor. The first and final trials were used to establish baseline measures, so no barrier was present. On the four test trials when the small wall was in place, the opening was alternately positioned on the right and then the left.

For both tasks, parents were visible to the infant at all times. Both parent and child were positioned on the side opposite the detour path. Thus, if infants attempted to take a direct path to their parent, they encountered the aperture or obstacle. Solving the detour problem involved infants noticing and using the visible alternate path (i.e., bridge across the gap and opening in the corridor).

Results and Discussion

We attempted to create parallel scores for the two tasks. Degree of success at solving the two detour problems was coded with a rating scale ranging from 0 (total failure -- crossing the gap or clinging to the wall) to 4 (total success -- using the bridge or taking a diagonal path straight to the opening). Intermediate scores indicate partial success. Scores for the four trials were summed for each task, producing an overall degree of success score ranging from 0 to 16.

The infants were significantly more successful on the obstacle task (M score = 10.42, SD = 4.34) than on the aperture task (M score = 7.33, SD = 3.58); $t(24) = 2.79$, $p < .01$. The addition of haptic information in the aperture task also had a significant impact, apparently serving to draw infants' attention to the drop-off. Infants who began with the platforms and bridge on top of the Plexiglas (visual + haptic mean score = 8.75, *SD* = 3.33) were better at solving all four aperture trials than infants who began with the platforms and bridge underneath the Plexiglas (visual only mean score = 5.92, *SD* = 3.37); $F(1,22)$ = 4.29, $p < .05$. Figure 1 illustrates this difference on a trial-by-trial basis.

Surprisingly, the correlation between crawling experience and success was not significant for either the aperture (r^2 = .23) or obstacle (r^2 = .32) task. Overall, the infants performed at an intermediate level of success, but crawling experience did not contribute substantially to variability in the scores. We are in the process of conducting a more fine-grained analysis of exploratory activity. Various exploratory actions emerge in concert with developing motor skills (Gibson, 1988), and these actions should provide infants with the means to test out and discover alternative options for solving detour problems. Exploratory activity may be the key to understanding the developmental progression of detour ability. We are also in the process of collecting data from a comparison group of older 12-month-old infants.

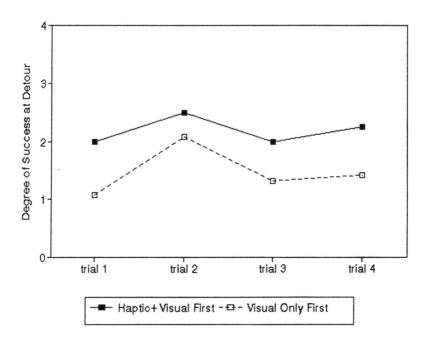

Figure 1. Aperture detours for two presentation orders.

References

Gibson, E. J. (1988). Exploratory behavior in the development of perceiving, acting, and the acquiring of knowledge. *Annual Review of Psychology, 39,* 1-41.

Lockman, J. J. (1984). The development of detour ability during infancy. *Child Development, 55,* 482-491.

Piaget, J. (1952). *The origins of intelligence in children.* New York: International Universities Press.

Piaget, J. (1954). *The construction of reality in the child.* New York: Basic Books.

Section II: *Perception - Action Coupling*

II.C: *Intermodal and Perceptual-Motor Coordination*

Studies in Perception and Action IV
M. A. Schmuckler & J. M. Kennedy (Eds.)
© *1997 Lawrence Erlbaum Associates, Inc.*

Gaze Inclination: A Source Of Oculomotor Information For Distance Perception

Richard P. Grutzmacher, Jeffrey T. Andre, & D. Alfred Owens

Whitely Psychology Laboratories, Franklin and Marshall College,
Lancaster, PA, U.S.A.

In the tradition of John Dewey (1896), J. J. Gibson (1966) stated that perceptual systems involve active exploration. A key process in visual exploration of primates is fixation (Owens & Reed, 1994), and it is this process that can inform us about an object's location. The present investigation provides evidence for new oculomotor "information" that supports perception of distance over a range of at least 20 m. By measuring participants' performance during a blind-walking task, we investigated how egocentric distance information is obtained, and used to guide locomotion in the absence of visual and auditory feedback. Rieser, Ashmead, Talor, and Youngquist (1990) showed that participants could view targets up to 21 meters away, and walk to them with their vision occluded. In the present study, participants viewed distant targets through 10 Diopter "base-up" or "base-down" prism glasses prior to walking towards the targets with their vision occluded. These prism glasses caused a vertical shift in participants' gaze inclination. The base-down prism glasses shifted the entire optical field up, while the base-up prism glasses shifted the entire optical field down. As a result, gaze inclination was systematically manipulated under natural conditions which left the structure of the retinal image unchanged. It was our hypothesis that viewing a target through prism glasses would result in anomalous oculomotor information, which would cause systematic errors in distance perception. Participants would walk consistently farther after viewing targets through base-down prism glasses, and shorter after viewing targets through base-up prism glasses.

Method

Participants. Eighteen undergraduate students (9 male, 9 female) with emmetropic or contact lens-corrected vision of at least 20/20 participated in the study. None reported any physical problems that would prevent them from walking while blindfolded.

Experimental Design. The study consisted of a three by three repeated measures design. Three different viewing conditions (base-up, base-down, and control) and three different target distances (10 m, 15 m, and 20 m) were used in the study. The order of viewing conditions were counter-balanced across participants, and the target distances were randomly ordered within each viewing condition.

Apparatus. The testing was conducted outdoors in a grassy field (50 m by 30 m). The target for the task was a 23 cm high, red-fluorescent cone. Participants viewed the target through 10 Diopter prism glasses that were worn underneath opaque, flip-up goggles. When the occlusion shield was up, the goggles provided a visual field 48° high and 126° wide. During the testing, participants were also required to wear a portable radio which played white noise (FM static) while they walked.

Procedure. Prior to testing, participants practiced walking with their vision occluded. Participants typically received three practice trials. During the practice trials, participants were given feedback about the accuracy of their performance. Following the practice session, participants completed 27 experimental trials. Each trial consisted of a five-second preview, followed immediately by visual occlusion, and blind-walking towards the target. Participants were instructed to stop when they felt that they had reached the target. After measuring the distance walked (in cm), participants were guided back to the starting line while blindfolded. No feedback was provided during the experimental trials. Performance was defined as the distance walked from the starting point. Distances were then subtracted from the cone distance for each trial. Distances walked that were shorter than cone distances were recorded as negative numbers; lateral deviations were not recorded.

Results

As illustrated in Figure 1, participants consistently walked farther after viewing targets with base-down prism glasses than when they viewed targets with no prism glasses. Furthermore, participants walked shorter when they viewed the target with base-up prism glasses than when they viewed targets

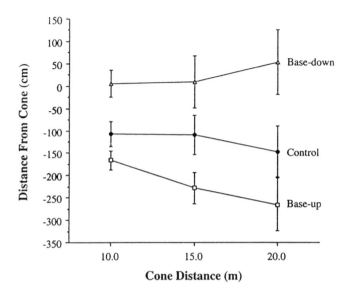

Figure 1. Mean distance walked from cone for each type of viewing condition as a function of cone distance.

with no prism glasses. ANOVA confirmed a significant main effect of viewing condition [$F(2,324) = 72.4$, $p < .0001$], and a significant interaction between viewing condition and target distance [$F(4,324) = 2.44$, $p < .05$]. As distance increased, the effect of the prism glasses became greater.

Discussion

Viewing a target through prism glasses, which caused a vertical shift in participants' gaze inclination without affecting other types of light-based distance information, produced systematic changes in distance perception. Figure 1 illustrates that participants consistently walked farther after viewing targets through base-down prism glasses, and shorter after viewing targets through base-up prism glasses. This can be attributed to the prism glasses which systematically manipulated oculomotor information, while preserving veridical retinal information. This previously unreported finding is important because it suggests that oculomotor adjustments provide useful information, even at relatively long distances of 10–20 m. Furthermore, this finding cannot be dismissed as laboratory artifact, because it was gathered under   natural conditions which preserved the texture gradient and structure of the light-based information.

While many studies have shown that distance perception is affected by accommodation and binocular convergence, it is generally agreed that these oculomotor "cues" are of no value for distances greater than 2–6 m (e.g., Sekuler & Blake, 1994). The present investigation, however, shows that egocentric distance perception is dependent upon the gaze-inclination of the eyes at distances well beyond the useful range of accommodation and binocular convergence. This type of oculomotor information results from the amount of effort that is required to fixate on the target, and may be related to the resting posture of the eyes (Owens & Reed, 1994). In the same way that the medial and lateral recti muscles are related to binocular convergence and near-distance perception, the inferior and superior recti muscles are related to gaze inclination and far-distance perception.   Therefore, the present study demonstrates that oculomotor information is not only important for near-distance perception when visual conditions are degraded, but that it is important for far-distance perception within stimulus-rich environments as well.

The type of oculomotor information discussed above is often overlooked, and may serve as an important ecological link between vision and the guidance of locomotion, especially under adverse conditions when optical/retinal information is less than optimal. To fully understand the interaction between oculomotor and optical information, we must begin to look at the retinal and oculomotor information that is obtained *prior to*, as well as during, the performance of visuomotor tasks.

References

Dewey, J. (1896). The reflex arc concept in psychology. *The Psychological Review, III*, 357-370.

Gibson, J. J. (1966). *The senses considered as perceptual systems* (1st ed.). Prospect Heights, IL: Waveland Press, Inc.

Owens D. A., & Reed, E. S. (1994). Seeing where we look: Fixation as extraretinal information. *Behavioral and Brain Sciences, 17,* 2.

Rieser, J. J., Ashmead, D. H., Talor, C. R., & Youngquist, G. A. (1990). Visual perception and the guidance of locomotion without vision to previously seen targets. *Perception, 19,* 675-689.

Sekuler, R., & Blake, R. (1994). *Perception* (3rd ed.). New York: McGraw Hill, Inc.

Studies in Perception and Action IV
M. A. Schmuckler & J. M. Kennedy (Eds.)
© *1997 Lawrence Erlbaum Associates, Inc.*

Visual-Movement Interaction In Infant Search

Mark A. Schmuckler & Hannah Y. Tsang

Division of Life Sciences, University of Toronto at Scarborough,
Scarborough, ON, Canada

One fascinating cognitive skill to emerge over the first few years of life involves the ability to orient one's self spatially within the environment. One example of this spatial skill is a child's ability to conceive of the existence of an object hidden from view, as well as to keep track of this hidden object's location in space. Piaget (1954) provided the classic example of this ability in his observation that young infants often search for a hidden object at a location at which it had previously been found, despite having seen the object being hidden at a different location; this error has been called the Stage IV, A $\overline{B}$ error (Bremner, 1985; Wellman, Cross, & Bartsch, 1986).

Piaget assumed that failures in finding such hidden objects indicated the limited nature of children's conceptions of objects, as well as children's problems in accurate spatial localization and updating of their position in the environment. Under normal circumstances, accurate spatial updating is accomplished using multiple sources of information. For example, movement of objects in the world is typically accompanied by visual and/or auditory information; similarly, self-movement typically produces visual information, as well as vestibular, proprioceptive, and kinaesthetic (e.g., body movement) inputs for such movement.

Recognition of the existence of multiple sources of information for spatial updating raises the issue of the importance of multiple information for spatial localization. Developmental research has operationalized this question by examining infant search behavior following either movement of objects in the world, or movement of the self through the world, and has found that infant search is more accurate following self-movement, as compared with object-movement (Bai & Bertenthal, 1992; Bremner, 1978a, 1978b; Bremner & Bryant, 1977). One key distinction between self- and object-movement is that self-movement gives rise to both visual and body movement information for spatial updating; in contrast, object-movement produces only visual information. Thus, it is possible that the superior search accuracy found after self-movement, relative to object-movement, results from the availability of multiple inputs for spatial updating. Unfortunately, no work has thoroughly explored the role of single versus multiple information sources on spatial orientation.

This study examined this issue by systematically combining visual and body movement information for spatial updating. This experiment employed a modified stage IV search task, in which infants saw a toy hidden in one of two locations on a table, and then searched for this hidden toy. Before beginning search, however, infants were either moved around the table to a new position ("infant displacement") or the table was moved relative to the infant ("table displacement"). Thus, infant vs. table displacements manipulate the presence of body movement information. Visual information was manipulated by either retaining or eliminating the lights within the room prior to infant/table displacement. Crossing body movement (infant vs. table displacement) and visual (light vs. dark) environment produces four conditions systematically varying the amount of information available for spatial updating.

Method

This study employed a total of 72 infants, consisting of 24 9.5-month-old infants, 24 14-month-old infants, and 24 18-month-old infants. Infants participated while seated on a parent's lap, in front of a table. On this table were two colored cups, in which small, brightly colored toys were hidden.

All infants received two body movement conditions. In the *infant displacement* condition, infants were rotated 180° around the table before beginning to search for the toy. Infant displacements were accomplished by having the experimenter roll the chair on which the parent/child sat around the table. In the *table displacement* condition, the table was rotated 180° in front of the infant before the infant was allowed to search for the hidden toy.

Body movement conditions occurred in one of two visual environments. In the *light* condition, displacements took place in a normally lit room. In the *dark* condition, the lights were turned off prior to all displacements, and were turned on prior to the infants' beginning to search. Half of the infants at each age were in each of the two visual environment conditions. Infants received four trials in both *infant* and *table displacement* conditions.

Results

Infant's search behavior was coded during the experimental session, and was ultimately characterized as "correct" or "incorrect". Correct search was defined as searching only in the cup in which the toy was hidden; all other responses were considered incorrect search.

Search accuracy was examined using a three-way ANOVA, with the factors of visual environment (light vs. dark), body movement condition (infant vs. table displacement), and age (9.5 vs. 14 vs. 18 months). This analysis revealed two significant effects. First, there was a main effect of body movement information, $F(1,66) = 6.14$, $p < .05$, with significantly more accurate search following infant displacement ($M = 1.83$ out of 4), relative to table displacement ($M = 1.40$). Second, and most critically, was the significant interaction between visual environment and body movement information, $F(1,66) = 6.96$, $p = .01$. This interaction appears in Figure 1, and demonstrates that search was best following infant displacement in the light; all other conditions lead to equivalent performance.

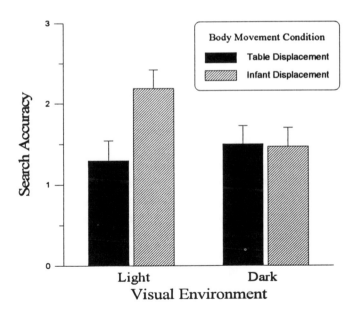

Figure 1. Search accuracy as a function of visual environment (light vs. dark) and body movement condition (table vs. infant displacement).

Discussion

This study replicates earlier work in spatial orientation in its finding that search following infant displacement was more accurate than search following table displacement (Bai & Bertenthal, 1992; Bremner, 1978a, 1978b; Bremner & Bryant, 1977). What is new in this study is the finding that multiple sources of information, as occurs following infant displacement in a lit environment, leads to superior search performance, relative to having only a single source of information, such as occurs following table displacement in a lit environment (providing visual information only), and infant displacement in a dark environment (providing body movement information only), or having no on-line information for spatial orientation, such as occurs following table displacement in a dark environment (providing no visual or body information). The fact that the two single source information conditions and the no information condition led to equivalent accuracy suggests that visual and body movement information interacts in infants' spatial orientation, with no single form of information sufficient for producing optimum search behavior.

References

Bai, D. L., & Bertenthal, B. I. (1992). Locomotor status and the development of spatial search skills. *Child Development, 63*, 215-226.

Bremner, J. G. (1978a). Spatial errors made by infants: Inadequate spatial cues or evidence of egocentrism? *British Journal of Psychology, 69*, 77-84.

Bremner, J. G. (1978b). Egocentric versus allocentric spatial coding in 9-month-old infants: Factors influencing the choice of code. *Developmental Psychology, 14*, 346-355.

Bremner, J. G. (1985). Object tracking and search in infancy: A review of data and a theoretical evaluation. *Developmental Review, 5*, 371-396.

Bremner, J. G., & Bryant, P. E. (1977). Place versus response as the basis of spatial errors made by young infants. *Journal of Experimental Child Psychology, 23*, 162-171.

Piaget, J. (1954). *The construction of reality in the child*. New York: Basic Books.

Wellman, H. M., Cross, D., & Bartsch, K. (1986). Infant search and object permanence: A meta-analysis of the A-not-B error. *Monographs of the Society for Research in Child Development, 51*, 1-51, 62-67.

Studies in Perception and Action IV
M. A. Schmuckler & J. M. Kennedy (Eds.)
© *1997 Lawrence Erlbaum Associates, Inc.*

Processing Specificity In Visual And Motor Imagery

Jennifer A. Stevens

Department of Psychology, Emory University, Atlanta, GA, U.S.A.

In visual imagery experiments, reaction time (RT) is a function of the movement extent (Kosslyn, Ball, & Reiser, 1978). However, time to complete imagined motor actions appears to be a function of the motor output required to complete the task (Decety & Michel, 1989). Jeannerod (1994) has asserted that visual and motor imagery behave differently because they are distinct imagery systems. Visual images are mental re-presentations of a visually perceived object or scene that can be consciously accessed and verbally described. In contrast, motor images cannot be verbally described or visually evaluated. These images are the precursors to real motor actions and as such are generated by weighing the environmental constraints of the task against the physical limits of the human motor control system. To the extent that an imagined motor action takes place within a visually represented space, the two imagery systems overlap. To conclude that there is a separation of processing channels for visual and motor imagery really requires an empirically based *direct* comparison which reveals a significant functional and/or anatomical difference between visual image processing and motor image processing. The present study was designed to make this direct comparison.

One established method for showing that two imagery processes are distinct is to test for selective interference effects (Brooks, 1967). If two tasks are processed in the same neural channel they will interfere with each other (i.e., result in significant increases in speed of processing) but not if they are generated by two different neural mechanisms. That is, simultaneous task processing only significantly impedes processing time when the two tasks are related.

The experimental hypotheses are as follows:

1) If visual and motor imagery are distinct, a visual interference task will impede speed of processing for visual images and not motor images. Likewise, a motor interference task will impede speed of processing motor (and not visual) images.

2) If visual and motor imagery operations overlap in cases of imagined motor actions completed within a visually represented environment, both visual and motor interference tasks should impede processing of such combination images.

Method

Participants. Eighteen undergraduates participated.

Apparatus. A wooden pathway consisting of five 2.44 m wood beam sections raised about 3.8 cm off the floor and bracketed together to form a length of 12.2m with a width of 27 cm was constructed.   A false wall encased a computer monitor (13 in) set at about eye level (approximately 1.7 m), both placed at the end of the path.

MacDraw was used to create visual stimuli; Superlab was used for stimulus presentation on a Macintosh IIci.

A stopwatch was used to make time measurements.

Design.   There were three blocks of imagery trials: visual (imagined DOT moving down the path), motor (imagined RUN in place 25 steps, and visual-motor (imagined WALK down the path). For each block, subjects completed two trials of the imagery task in a baseline and three different interference conditions:

- Baseline: Subject stands at ease while imagining movement.

- Fixate (Visual interference): Subject fixates on the computer screen at the end of the beam while imagining the movement. The computer screen flashed random block letters every 500 msec. To ensure that subjects were fixating, they were asked to report whether a specific letter had appeared in the array (e.g., Did you see the letter X?).

- Stand on one leg (Motor interference): Subject stands with knee bent, lower leg parallel to the floor while imagining the movement.

- Both together (Visual and motor interference): Subject fixates and stands with one leg raised while imagining the movement.

In the RUN in place and WALK path conditions subjects were also asked to complete two trials of an Actual condition, in which they physically performed the task.

Procedure.

Time measurements. Subjects timed their own imagined movements; they were told to start the watch as they imagined their movement beginning, stop the watch as their imagined movement was completed. Subjects never saw the times on the watch: the experimenter recorded from and cleared the stopwatch. The experimenter timed the actual condition times, starting and stopping the watch concurrently with subjects' movement.

Instructions. Subjects were instructed to imagine the movements occurring at a rate as quickly as possible. For <u>Actual</u> trials, subjects were asked to physically complete the task as quickly as possible.

Counterbalancing. Presentation of blocks was counterbalanced across subjects. However, order of the conditions in each block was standard: <u>Actual</u>, <u>No interference</u>, <u>Fixate</u>, <u>Stand on one leg</u>, <u>Combination</u>. (Note: there was no <u>Actual</u> condition for the DOT block.)

Results and Discussion

A within-subject repeated measures ANOVA revealed a main effect of task [$F(2,51) = 64$, $p < .001$]. Subjects imagined the DOT moving at tremendously quick speeds, and it took less time for imagined WALKs than RUNs in place (see Table 1).

Paired t-tests revealed patterns of interference effects that matched the hypotheses. Imagined DOT movement times were significantly slowed during visual interference conditions (<u>Fixate</u> and <u>Both together</u>); <u>Stand on one leg</u> did not interfere with subjects' ability to complete the imagined DOT movement. Imagined RUN movement times were significantly slowed in motor interference conditions (<u>Stand on one leg</u> and <u>Both together</u>); <u>Fixate</u> had no effect. For the imagined WALK, both visual (<u>Fixate</u>) and motor (<u>Stand on one</u>

Table 1
Imagined Movement Times (N = 18)

Task	Baseline	Fixate	Leg Up	Comb	Actual
			Condition		
Run					
M	7.58	7.78	8.23	8.19	6.16
SD	2.42	2.60	2.97	3.02	1.78
Walk					
M	4.74	5.26	5.14	5.53	6.34
SD	1.32	1.54	1.45	1.61	0.99
Dot					
M	3.14	3.83	3.09	3.84	
SD	1.91	2.30	2.02	2.36	

leg) interference conditions resulted in significant increases in imagined movement times. Further, in the <u>Both together</u> condition processing time was even more impaired than when just one interference task was completed suggesting the effect of the <u>both together</u> condition was additive for the WALK task.

Neurological studies show significant activation in the occipital and temporal regions during visual imagery (e.g., image scanning, Charlot, Tzourio, Zilbovicius, Mazoyer, & Denis, 1992), SMA activation in motor imagery (e.g. finger movement, Roland et al., 1980), and parietal and temporal activation in visual-motor imagery (e.g., imagined walking, Roland & Friberg, 1985). The brain appears to be selectively activated depending on the kind of imagery task. The behavioral results reported here are consistent with this neurological data. These results support a theory of the human imagery system with distinct visual and motor imagery processing channels. However, these results also indicate that the two kinds of processing channels can operate together. In fact, it is most likely the case that both play a vital role in most of our imagery operations.

References

Brooks, L. R. (1967). The suppression of visualization by reading. *Quarterly Journal of Experimental Psychology, 19,* 289-299.

Charlot, V., Tzourio, N., Zilbovicius, M., Mazoyer, B., & Denis, M. (1992). Different mental imagery abilities result in different regional cerebral blood flow activation patterns during cognitive tasks. *Neuropsychologia, 30,* 565-580.

Decety, J., & Michel, F. (1989). Comparative analysis of actual and mental movement times in two graphic tasks. *Brain and Cognition, 11,* 87-97.

Jeannerod, M. (1994). The representing brain: Neural correlates of motor intention and imagery. *Behavioral & Brain Sciences, 17,* 187- 245.

Kosslyn, S., Ball, T., & Reiser, B. (1978). Visual images preserve metric spatial information: Evidence from studies of image scanning. *Journal of Experimental Psychology: Human Perception & Performance, 4,* 47-60.

Roland, P. E., Larsen, B., Lassan, N. A., & Skinhøj, E. (1980). Supplementary motor area and other cortical areas in organization of voluntary movements in man. *Journal of Neurophysiology, 43,* 118-136.

Roland, P. E., & Friberg, L. (1985). Localization of cortical areas activated by thinking. *Journal of Neurophysiology, 53,* 1219-1243.

Studies in Perception and Action IV
M. A. Schmuckler & J. M. Kennedy (Eds.)
© *Lawrence Erlbaum Associates, Inc.*

Is Haptic Space Isotropic?

Matthew Butwill

CESPA, University of Connecticut, Storrs, CT, U.S.A.

James J. Gibson (1966) theorized that the members of the human skeletal system are arranged in a hierarchical manner, providing organization for lawful and structured perception. The members of this system make up a vector-like bone space which allows the detection of directions and distances of segments of the body over varied poses. Of special note is his conjecture (p. 119) that appreciation of distances between any two body parts is additive over the whole universe of bone postures, independent of direction. That is, haptic space is isotropic. Such a possibility may have important implications for perception theory given that much research in vision demonstrates that perception of extent is decidedly anisotropic (e.g., Norman, Todd, Perroti, & Tittle, 1996). In particular, judgment of distance depends on both object orientation and object distance. The critical comparison is between frontoparallel and longitudinal extents: participants report extents to increase with increasing distance from the observer, whereas extents along the line of sight decrease with increasing distance from the observer.

Are the systematic distortions with respect to orientation and distance that are found in visual research also to be found in cases of haptic perception, contrary to Gibson's intuitions? Previous research has examined this issue in terms of size perception of blocks spanned by the two hands. Isotropy holds for variations in grasp (between thumb and finger of one hand or across the thumbs or fingers of two hands), distance (from 0 to 25cm), and plane of support (0°, 40°, and 70°) (Butwill, Carello, & Turvey, 1996). The critical frontoparallel-longitudinal comparison is addressed here.

Experiment 1

Participants (n = 10) were to add together extents of objects grasped out of view on a tabletop. An edge of each object was held between the thumb and middle finger. The relevant extent of one object was in an orientation frontoparallel with respect to the body and the relevant extent of the other object was in an orientation longitudinal with respect to the body (Figure 1). Two such combinations of left and right are possible. Distance was fixed. The participant directed the experimenter to adjust a caliper-like report apparatus such that the combined extent would just fit through a produced gap. Objects of three widths (4, 6, and 8 cm) were cut from 10 x 1.9 cm lengths of wood.

Results

Subjects accurately reported the sum of the two held extents. A regression of perceived sum onto actual sum yielded a slope of about 1, (r^2 = .97). There was no difference between the two hands or the two configurations. As with previous manipulations of bone posture, haptic additivity was not systematically distorted, supporting isotropy.

Experiment 2

The objects in the haptic experiment differ from those typically used in vision experiments in that they are solid and supported by substantial surfaces. The anisotropy of visual space was therefore reassessed with these objects. Participants were again required to report the sum of two edges. Objects were

Longitudinal Extent   Frontoparallel Extent

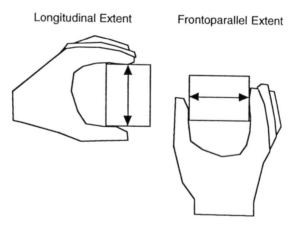

Figure 1. Top view of subject's hands (which were occluded under a hood; block orientation was counterbalanced).

mounted on a board in either of two orientations (Figure 2). A distance manipulation was also included, roughly corresponding to well within reach, just reachable, and beyond reach (see Norman et al., 1996).

Results

The numerical difference between frontoparallel (M = 13.00 cm) and longitudinal (M = 14.18 cm) was not significant, nor was there a significant effect of distance. The three sizes were significantly discriminated. Individual regressions again yielded slopes of about 1 (r^2 = .94 for frontoparallel and r^2 = .98 for longitudinal). The interaction of orientation and distance found by Norman et al. using LEDs against an undulating fabric surface was not replicated here. The contribution of distance was apparent however, in an interaction with object size (although only on the right). Importantly, this effect was the same for both orientations. Perceived size increased with distance. The distance effect is opposite to that found for visually perceived apertures located from 9 to 27 m away (Garrett, Barac-Cikoja, Carello, & Turvey, 1996). The role of scale remains to be explored for an adequate theory of perception of extent.

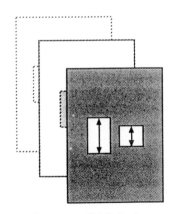
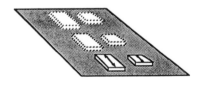

Frontoparallel Extents
(blocks were at chest level; the support
surface was placed at 3 distances)

Longitudinal Extents
(the support surface was at chest level;
blocks were placed at 3 distances)

Figure 2. Orientations of mounted objects.

Conclusion

Up to this point, simple manipulations of bone posture have not significantly distorted haptic additivity of hand-held objects, supporting Gibson's notion of an isotropic hierarchical vector space. However, in an extended haptic perception task (probing with a wooden rod) anisotropies have been found (Barac-Cikoja & Turvey, submitted). Perceived size of a lateral separation formed by two blocks separated in depth was found to depend on distance and gap orientation. These disparate findings suggest that different haptic functions may have different underlying mechanisms.

References

Barac-Cikoja, D., & Turvey, M. T. (submitted). *Anisotropy in the extended haptic perception of longitudinal distances.*

Butwill, M., Carello, C., & Turvey, M. T. (1996). *Additivity in haptic space.* Poster presented at International Society of Ecological Psychology, March 1996.

Garrett, S., Barac-Cikoja, D., Carello, C., & Turvey, M. T. (1996). A parallel between visual and haptic perception of size at a distance. *Ecological Psychology, 8,* 25-42.

Gibson, J. J. (1966). *The senses considered as perceptual systems.* Boston: Houghton-Mifflin.

Norman, J. F., Todd, J. T., Perotti, V. J., & Tittle, J. S. (1996). The visual perception of three-dimensional length. *Journal of Experimental Psychology: Human Perception and Performance, 22,* 173-186.

Studies in Perception and Action IV
M. A. Schmuckler & J. M. Kennedy (Eds.)
© *Lawrence Erlbaum Associates, Inc.*

Perceiving Lengths Of Rods Wielded In Different Media

Kerri G. Donahue & Christopher C. Pagano

Department of Psychology, Clemson University, Clemson, SC, U.S.A.

The rotation of an object requires time-varying torques producing time-varying motions with angular velocities w and angular accelerations $d\omega/dt$. The inconstant motions are coupled to the inconstant torques through the inertia tensor $\mathbf{I}$, an invariant structured array that quantifies an object's different resistances to rotational acceleration in different directions. In short, for a given axis of rotation, torque $N = I(d\omega/dt.)$. Experiments have shown that $\mathbf{I}$ comprises the relevant independent quantity in perceiving lengths of occluded rods by wielding rather than other potentially relevant quantities such as torque, kinetic energy, work, and mass (e.g., Solomon & Turvey, 1988).

The present experiment further explored the role of $\mathbf{I}$ by varying the medium in which rods were wielded. While resistances due to air are typically negligible, those offered by water are substantial. Thus the total torques required to rotate an object in water is considerably greater than those required to rotate in air, being a function of $I(d\omega/dt)$ plus the resistances offered by the water. As a result, it is much more difficult to wield a rod in water and more deformations and distortions of the body tissues are involved.

The resistances produced by the denser medium increase proportionately as rod length increases. This is because as rod lengths become longer, more surface area is exposed to the water, and more water must be displaced to rotate the rod. If participants are influenced by torques associated with the increased rod lengths, then we would expect an interaction between rod length and medium. That is, perceived length will increase with actual length in all media, but if participants pick up on torques, this increase will occur at a greater rate in water than in air. Alternatively, if participants rely solely upon $\mathbf{I}$, there should be no difference in perceived lengths of similar rods wielded in air and water, because $\mathbf{I}$ remains invariant over medium.

Methods

Ten undergraduate students at Clemson University participated. The objects were aluminum rods 20, 30, 40, 50, and 60 cm in length, with I_1s of 2381, 7856, 18374, 35976, and 62121 g·cm^2, respectively, and with radii of 0.635 cm. The seated participant placed the right arm through a narrow opening in a curtain. Two cylindrical containers, one filled with water and other empty, were positioned on side of the curtain opposite to the participant. The containers were 100 cm tall, 73 cm wide at the top, and 60 cm wide at the base. The participant's forearm rested on a flat surface positioned over one of the containers, with the wrist at the edge of the surface. With the water-filled container, the water was 6 cm from the participant's wrist. On the participant's side of the curtain was a visible 100 cm report-rod.

At the beginning of each trial, one of the rods was placed in the participant's right hand in the downward position. The rod was held in an enclosed fist with the top end of the rod even with the thumb, and the length of the rod extending downward into one of the containers. The participant's task was to wield the occluded rod using motions about the wrist, and use the left hand to position a marker on the report-rod so that the distance from the top of the report rod to the marker corresponded to the length of the wielded rod. Participants were instructed to avoid hitting the sides of the container during wielding. In half of the trials the rod was wielded in the container with water, in the remaining trials the rod was wielded in the empty container. The participants were told that the containers were used to restrict the amplitude of movement; they were not informed that wielding may occur in water. Ear mufflers were worn during the experiment.

Results & Discussion

Overall, the mean perceived reachable distances with the 20, 30, 40, 50, and 60 cm rods were 20.5, 31.3, 43.4, 59.4, and 73.1 cm, respectively. The mean perceived reachable distances with the rods wielded in water and air were 47.4 and 43.6 cm, respectively. A 5x2 ANOVA confirmed significant main effects for medium condition [$F(1,9) = 9.5, p < .05$] and rod length [$F(4,36) = 214.7, p < .0001$]. The interaction was not significant; $F(4,36) = 1.0, p = .40$.

To test the respective roles played by medium and I_1, a multiple regression was conducted predicting log mean perceived length from the continuous independent variable of log I_1, a categorical independent variable of medium (coded orthogonally), and a log I_1 x condition interaction term. The interaction term was not significant (partial $F < 1$). This result was identical for the individual data; the interaction term was insignificant for all ten participants ($p > .05$). The multiple regression was repeated without the interaction term, yielding an $r^2 = .997$, with both I_1 and medium significant in the mean data (partial Fs = 2004, $p < .0001$, and 16, $p < .01$, respectively). In the individual data the medium term was significant for only two of the ten participants (P4 & P5). A simple regression with log I_1 resulted in an $r^2 = .989$ for the mean data (see Figure 1), and .98, .93, .95, .93, .94, .99, .95, .96, .97, and .94, for P1 through P10, respectively.

The present results demonstrate that I is the major contributor to the perceived lengths of rods wielded in air or water, accounting for 98.9% of the variance in mean perceived length, while the medium condition accounted for only an additional 0.8% of the variance. Additionally, the contribution of medium failed to reach significance in the individual data for eight of the ten participants.

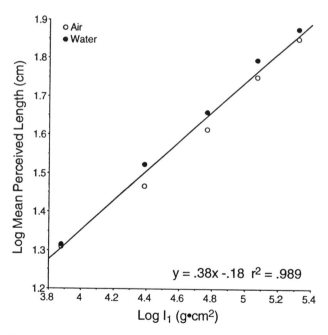

Figure 1. Log mean perceived length as a function of log I_1 for the two medium conditions.

These findings   add to the growing understanding that the basis for perception lies in invariants (e.g., Gibson, 1966). More specifically, these results underscore the significance of **I** in understanding the perception of spatial properties by dynamic touch.

Acknowledgments. We gratefully acknowledge suggestions by Ben Stevens and Eugene Galluscio. Correspondence should be addressed to CCP.

References

Gibson, J. J. (1966). *The senses considered as perceptual systems.* Boston: Houghton Mifflin.

Solomon, H. Y., & Turvey, M. T. (1988). Haptically perceiving the distances reachable with hand-held objects. *Journal of Experimental Psychology: Human Perception and Performance, 14,* 404-427.

Studies in Perception and Action IV
M. A. Schmuckler & J. M. Kennedy (Eds.)
© *Lawrence Erlbaum Associates, Inc.*

Object Visibility And The Inertia Tensor As Factors In The Size-Weight Illusion

Megan M. Burke[1] & Eric L. Amazeen[2]

[1] CESPA, University of Connecticut, Storrs, CT, U.S.A.
[2] Faculty of Human Movement Sciences, Vrije Universiteit,
Amsterdam, The Netherlands

Recently the size weight illusion has been demonstrated with objects that are fixed in mass and linear dimensions but which vary in the pattern of the eigenvalues of the inertia tensor (Amazeen & Turvey, 1996). The inertia tensor account of the size-weight illusion predicts that as cylindrical objects of constant mass increase in size via an increase in length, they will be perceived as heavier. Conversely, as the size of objects increases via an increase in width, they will be perceived as lighter. This account holds for occluded, wielded objects. When observers are allowed to view the objects, this differential effect disappears. (Amazeen, 1996). Studies done using objects other than cylindrical (e.g., cubes) have produced the size-weight illusion for both viewed and occluded hand held objects (Ellis & Lederman, 1993).

The present research sought to further the understanding of the role of optical information in the perception of heaviness. It was predicted that viewed objects would produce the pattern of the size-weight illusion and that occluded objects would conform to the inertia tensor predictions. It was further predicted that objects viewed before but not during wielding would yield a pattern similar to that of objects constantly occluded (Masin & Crestoni, 1988). Three experiments were conducted. Eighteen experimental objects were of three different masses, three different volumes, and two types of volume change (variation by length and width; see Figure 1). The cylindrical objects (constructed from styrofoam, lead shot and glue) were attached to a wooden dowel that extended 20 cm from the top of each cylinder.

In Experiment 1, the object was visible all the while it was wielded (though the full set of objects was kept hidden from the subject's view). Subjects were free to move about the wrist as much as they desired while the arm was supported by an armrest. The task was magnitude estimation and the subject received a "standard" object not from the experimental set before the presentation of each experimental object.

Experiments 2 and 3 proceeded in similar fashion. In Experiment 2, subjects were shown each object in stationary position immediately before wielding it occluded from view. They were not shown the standard object. In Experiment 3, subjects received no visual information about the objects before or during wielding.

Results

Experiment 1

With objects viewed while wielding, both changes by length and by width produced the size-weight illusion pattern (see Figure 2a). An ANOVA revealed significant main effects for weight [F (2,18) = 45.76, p < .0001] and size [F (2,18) = 6.40, p < .01] with no interactions.

Experiment 2

With objects viewed stationary before being wielded nonvisibly both changes in length and width produced the size-weight illusion (see Figure 2b). Weight [F(2,18) = 39.81, p < .0001] and size [F(2,18) = 12.48, p < .001] were significant. Also significant were the interactions for weight by size [F(4,36) = 3.02, p < .05] and type of volume change by size [F (2,18) = 4.18, p < .05].

Experiment 3

Subjects were given no visual information about the objects before or during the trials. An ANOVA revealed an effect for weight [F(2,20) = 31.29, p < .0001] but not of size (p > .6). A significant interaction was found for type of volume change by size [F(2,20) = 7.54, p < .01] (see Figure 2c).

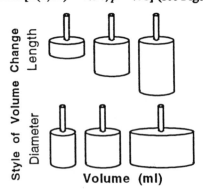

Figure 1. Experimental objects, varying by length and width.

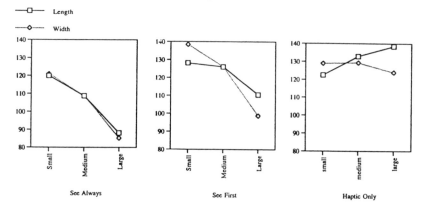

Figure 2. Results of Experiments 1 - 3.

Conclusion

The data of Experiment 3 are consistent with previous findings and the inertia tensor explanation of the size-weight illusion. Vision's influence on the perception of weight requires further investigation. The hypothesis that vision brings to weight perception a certain cognitive expectancy is pervasive throughout the literature. Although reliably demonstrated to have a sensory basis, it is conceivable that expectations also contribute to the size-weight illusion. The results of Experiment 2 might support a hybrid account; they were intermediate between concurrent visual and haptic information and visual information alone. Future research will examine the relation between an object's visible geometric symmetry and its dynamic symmetry as quantified by the inertia tensor.

References

Amazeen, E. L. (1996). *Are independent perceptions of weight and size possible by touch?* Doctoral dissertation, University of Connecticut, Storrs, CT.

Amazeen, E. L., & Turvey, M. T. (1996). Weight perception and the haptic size-weight are functions of the inertia tensor. *Journal of Experimental Psychology: Human Perception and Performance, 22,* 213-232.

Ellis, R. R., & Lederman, S. J. (1993). The role of haptic versus visual volume cues in the size-weight illusion. *Perception & Psychophysics, 53,* 315-324.

Masin, S. C., & Crestoni, L. (1988). Experimental demonstration of the sensory basis of the size-weight illusion. *Perception & Psychophysics, 44,* 309-312.

Studies in Perception and Action IV
M. A. Schmuckler & J. M. Kennedy (Eds.)
© *Lawrence Erlbaum Associates, Inc.*

Measuring Entropy In Cascade Juggling

Auke Post & Peter Beek

Institute for Fundamental and Clinical Human Movement Sciences,
Vrije Universiteit, Amsterdam, The Netherlands

The act of juggling can be described as a perception-based control system, in which visual and haptic information about task performance is used by the juggler (van Santvoord & Beek, 1994). Visual information is available in the form of (parts of) the ball trajectories, and haptic information is available in the form of ball-hand contact.

Van Santvoord and Beek (1994) reported that under spatiotemporally constrained conditions, the variability of the flight paths of the balls along the horizontal dimension (X) decreased significantly with decreasing juggling height (or increasing juggling frequency). The variability along the vertical dimension (Y) was significantly smaller than along X, but did not change significantly with height. This finding was interpreted as support of the notion of a 'spatial clock', according to which the juggling act is more tightly controlled in the vertical dimension than in the horizontal dimension. Following up on this line of research, which was restricted to static measures, we started to analyze the dynamic properties of the ball trajectories as a function of relevant task variables. In particular, using Kolmogorov entropy as a measure of information loss, we began to investigate how increase in juggling frequency affected the predictability of the trajectories of the balls in the X and Y dimension.

Method

Apparatus and Procedure. Four jugglers of intermediate skill participated in the experiment. Subjects were placed in front of a high speed camera (nominal frame rate 125 Hz; shutter revolutions were recorded for later determination of the actual frame rate) at a distance of about 5 m. The equipment consisted of three so-called 'stage' balls, which had to be juggled in cascade fashion.

Subjects were tested under two frequency constrained conditions: preferred juggling speed, and a (self-selected) speed that was markedly faster than the preferred juggling speed.

Before each trial, the subject was allowed a few practice cycles. When the subject reported that a stable performance was achieved, the camera was started. During each trial, at least 20 complete juggling cycles were recorded. Subjects were recorded twice per condition. In case a ball was dropped during an experimental run, it was repeated until an 'error-free' run was obtained.

Data acquisition and reduction. After development, the films were projected onto the opaque screen of a film motion analyzer. Frame by frame, the X- and Y-coordinates of the centers of the balls were digitized, fed into a computer, and stored for later analysis. The actual frame rate (and thus the sampling frequency) during a trial was determined by comparing the shutter data with a simultaneously recorded computer time base.

Results

Estimation of the Kolmogorov entropy as a measure of the rate of information loss along an attractor was done as follows (Hilborn, 1994; Schouten, Takens, & van den Bleek, 1994): Given a time series with a sampling frequency f_s, define time step τ_s as the time interval between two sample points ($1/f_s$). The separation of two adjacent points on different orbits of the attractor is characterized by an exponential cumulative distribution function:

$$C(b) = e^{-Kb\tau_s} \tag{1}$$

where b represents the number of sequential pairs of points on the attractor for the last pair of which the interpoint distance is for the first time bigger than a predefined maximum. Point pairs were randomly chosen, provided that the initial interpoint distance was smaller than the predefined maximum.

The rate of exponential decrease of $C(b)$ with increasing b is measured by the invariant entropy K. The maximum-likelihood estimate of the Kolmogorov entropy K_{ML}, expressed in bits/s, is:

$$K_{ML} = \frac{-\dfrac{1}{\tau_s}\ln\left[1-\dfrac{1}{\bar{b}}\right]}{\ln 2}, \qquad \text{with} \qquad \bar{b} = \frac{1}{M}\sum_{i=1}^{M} b_i, \tag{2}$$

where M is the sample size of interpoint distances, which should be large (at least 10^5) for reliable estimation.

The Kolmogorov entropy per trial was estimated with *RRChaos* (Schouten & van den Bleek, 1993) for X and Y of each ball in a trial. These values were averaged over identical conditions and balls.

Mean $K_{ML}(Y)$ was not statistically different from mean $K_{ML}(X)$ (0.60, resp. 0.67). Given the size of M, the theoretical mean maximal value of K_{ML} was about 1654, whereas the overall mean actual value of K_{ML} was 0.63.

To evaluate the effect of Speed (fast, preferred), two paired-samples two-tailed t-tests were performed on the Kolmogorov entropy results, one for X and one for Y. No significant effect was found for Speed on K_{ML} in X, whereas a significant effect was found for Speed on K_{ML} in Y ($t(3) = 3.31$, $p < .05$).

Conclusions and Discussion

Given the theoretical maximal value, all obtained values of K_{ML} were extremely small. This implies that the loss of information in the ball trajectories was marginal; they were, in other words, highly predictable. This result can be interpreted to reflect the fact that juggling is a highly periodic activity that capitalizes in part on the predictability of the laws of Newton that apply to the flight trajectories.

Nevertheless, the results of the analysis revealed that the rate of information loss in Y was significantly larger for higher movement frequency, whereas the rate of information loss in X remained (statistically) unaffected. This result can be interpreted to reflect a decrease in control with increasing frequency, which is mainly detectable in the vertical dimension along which the

Table 1

Values of K_{ML} in X- and Y-Dimension in Different Frequency Conditions.

subject	$K_{ML}(X)$ fast	preferred	$K_{ML}(Y)$ fast	preferred
1	0.49	0.42	0.50	0.36
2	0.60	0.77	0.87	0.71
3	1.15	0.65	0.88	0.41
4	0.60	0.66	0.66	0.41

juggling act is (by hypothesis) controlled predominantly. This interpretation is consistent with the notion of juggling as a sustained spatial clock, with the clock properties of space becoming less effective for higher juggling frequencies.

References

Hilborn, R. C. (1994). *Chaos and nonlinear dynamics*. New York: Oxford University Press.

Santvoord, A. A. M. van, & Beek, P. J. (1994). Phasing and the pickup of optical information in cascade juggling. *Ecological Psychology, 6,* 239-263.

Schouten, J. C., & van den Bleek, C. M. (1993). *RRCHAOS: A Menu-driven software package for chaotic time series analysis*. Delft: Reactor Research Foundation (unpublished).

Schouten, J. C., Takens, F., & van den Bleek, C. M. (1994). Maximum-likelihood estimation of the entropy of an attractor. *Physical Review E, Vol. 49,* 126-129.

Studies in Perception and Action IV
M. A. Schmuckler & J. M. Kennedy (Eds.)
© *Lawrence Erlbaum Associates, Inc.*

Motion Sickness Without Imposed Motion

L. J. Smart & Randy J. Pagulayan

Department of Psychology, University of Cincinnati, Cininnati, OH, U.S.A.

Motion sickness is associated with imposed motion, as on a ship or other vehicle. Motion sickness also occurs in some situations in which there is no imposed motion, such as weightlessness, or while wearing prism spectacles. Motion sickness can also be elicited during activities that involve sustained angular motion. Anecdotally, people can make themselves dizzy, and even ill, by vigorous twisting of the body or head. Similarly, sickness is known to result from a fast waltz, where it has been reported even among competitive ballroom dancers.

There have been few laboratory studies of self-induced motion sickness. In the present article we report the occurrence of motion sickness in standing participants who were not subjected to any imposed motion. Participants also were not subjected to any form of sensory distortion or rearrangement. Their behavior produced minimal angular motion, and included no vigorous activity. Our experiments (Stoffregen & Smart, 1997) were not intended to induce sickness; the appearance of symptoms came as a considerable surprise to us.

Method

The general method is described in Stoffregen and Smart (1997). Here we describe only aspects of the method differing from their report. A total of 42 undergraduates took part in four experiments. One of these (*Monocular*) was the second experiment reported by Stoffregen and Smart (1997), while another (*Varying Distance*) was a closely related variant. In the other two experiments (*26% Booth* and *100% Booth*), the standing position was enclosed with a small booth. The booth was a plexiglas construction, 2.27 m high, 1.0 m wide, and 0.77 m deep. The booth was placed so that the participant's head was 0.4 m from its front wall. In the 26% Booth experiment, small squares of granite-pattern contact paper were attached to the plexiglas, covering 26% of the area. In the 100% Booth experiment, the walls of the booth were completely covered with the contact paper, with only a small hole (35° by 31°) in the front wall that permitted viewing of the far and near targets. Conditions and the sequence of trials were the same as in Stoffregen and Smart (1997).

Participants were given no information regarding motion sickness. There was no indication on any of the experimental materials (sign-up sheets, letter of informed consent, etc.) that motion sickness might be expected. Participants were not instructed about the possibility of motion sickness, and they were not told that the experiment would be discontinued if they experienced symptoms. The primary measure of motion sickness was self-reports. Since we were not expecting motion sickness, the first participants reporting symptoms were not administered any formal measure of their symptoms. After four participants reported sickness, subsequent participants were asked to fill out the Simulator Sickness Questionare, or SSQ (Kennedy et al., 1993). The SSQ was used only by participants who spontaneously reported symptoms. We did not collect any data on the subjective state of participants who did not spontaneously report symptoms. Participants who did not report sickness completed all trials. Those who reported symptoms discontinued the experiment at the time of symptom report.

Results

Sickness. Across the four experiments nine participants reported symptoms of motion sickness (21%). A chi-square test indicated that incidence did not differ significantly across experiments. Participants reported a variety of symptoms, including tunnel vision, difficulty focusing, fatigue, difficulty concentrating, shakiness and headache, faintness, increased temperature/sweating, and nausea. One participant grayed out. The SSQ was administered to five participants. Scores were similar to those reported for seventeen Navy and Marine Corp flight simulators (Kennedy et al., 1993).

Postural motion. We analyzed the variability of spontaneous postural sway for sick and well participants. As a measure of postural motion we used the root mean square (RMS) of the position of the head-mounted Flock of Birds receiver. RMS position was analyzed separately for anterior-posterior (AP) and lateral motion. We conducted an analysis of variance on mean RMS sway for sick and well participants. Due to the differing number of trials completed by individual participants, the ANOVA was conducted on individual trials. For both AP and lateral motion, RMS sway was greater for the sick participants (AP: $F(1,546) = 37.36, p < .001$; Lateral: $F(1,543) = 108.71, p < .001$).

Discussion

Motion sickness was observed in nine individuals who were not subjected to imposed motion of any kind. The onset of motion sickness symptoms was rapid, occurring after less than twenty minutes of experimental participation (in five cases sickness was reported after less than ten minutes). Participants who reported sickness exhibited increased variability of postural motion in both the anterior-posterior and lateral axes.

The present findings do not fit comfortably within the sensory conflict theory of motion sickness. In this theory (e.g., Oman, 1982), motion sickness is associated with discrepancies between current sensory inputs and expected inputs (derived from an internal model of situation dynamics). Motion sickness is predicted to occur when the magnitude of sensory conflict exceeds some threshold value. According to Oman (1982), low-magnitude sensory conflict is a nearly constant feature of daily behavior. The existence of a magnitude threshold is needed to account for the fact that this conflict does not produce motion sickness.

The dynamics of our laboratory situation should have matched exactly any internal models in participants' memories. Accordingly, the magnitude of sensory conflict generated by visual fixation and postural sway in our laboratory should have been extremely small. Thus, any threshold whose purpose was to suppress conflict arising from ordinary behavior should have been effective in our experiments. Our findings pose a problem for any theory in which motion sickness is related to the magnitude of sensory conflict, or to thresholds that suppress low-magnitude conflict.

We do not know whether the increased postural sway occurred after the onset of symptoms, or before. Thus, the postural data cannot be related to the postural instability theory of motion sickness (Riccio & Stoffregen, 1991), which predicts that postural instability precedes symptoms.

The present data may be the most concrete documentation of terrestrial motion sickness in the absence of imposed motion. This may motivate further studies of similar phenomena. Under what circumstances can sickness be induced without externally-imposed motions? What is the relation between self-induced motion sickness in terrestrial and weightless environments? Would labyrinthine-defective persons be susceptible to self-induced motion sickness in unperturbed stance? Self-induced motion sickness is a rare and atypical phenomenon, but it may have important implications for theories of motion sickness etiology.

References

Kennedy, R. S., Lane, N. E., Berbaum, K. S., & Lilienthal, M. G. (1993). Simulator sickness questionnaire: An enhanced method for quantifying simulator sickness. *The International Journal of Aviation Psychology, 3,* 203-220.

Oman, C. M. (1982). A heuristic mathematical model for the dynamics of sensory conflict and motion sickness. *Acta Otolaryngologica, 44* (Suppl. 392).

Riccio, G. E., & Stoffregen, T. A. (1991). An ecological theory of motion sickness and postural instability. *Ecological Psychology, 3,* 195-240.

Stoffregen, T. A., & Smart., L. J. (1997). Postural stabilization of visual fixation. This volume.

Section III: *Action*

III.A: *Patterns of Coordination*

Studies in Perception and Action IV
M. A. Schmuckler & J. M. Kennedy (Eds.)
© *Lawrence Erlbaum Associates, Inc.*

Intention Determines Oscillatory Tracking Performance

John F. Stins & Claire F. Michaels

Faculty of Human Movement Sciences, Vrije Universiteit,
Amsterdam, The Netherlands

It has been repeatedly found that rhythmic movements involving in-phase coordination are more stable than movements involving anti-phase coordination. The patterns of differential stability obtained with in-phase and anti-phase coordination are not limited to interlimb coordination (e.g., Haken, Kelso, & Bunz, 1985) but also apply to coordination involving tracking a rhythmic moving visual stimulus (Wimmers, Beek, & van Wieringen, 1992).

An interesting situation occurs when one "aspect" of the bodily movement bears an in-phase relation with an oscillator (say, an external stimulus or another limb) and another aspect of the movement bears an anti-phase relation with the oscillator. In this article we investigate such a situation—a hand that oscillates in-phase with a rhythmic moving visual stimulus yields a motion of a response device that is anti-phase with the stimulus, and vice versa.

In this experiment participants performed an oscillatory tracking task with a steering wheel, using either a proximal or a distal hand placement (see Figure 1). With the distal hand position, we expect anti-phase coordination to be less stable than in-phase coordination. With the proximal hand position, however, hand movements that are in-phase with the stimulus (i.e., hand and stimulus are moving in the same direction) result in wheel rotations that are anti-phase with the stimulus, and vice versa. Our question was, which of the two phasing relations would be spontaneously exploited by the actor using a phase transition (bifurcation) paradigm.

Method

Nine participants were asked to unimanually grip the wheel either at the distal or the proximal position, and rotate the wheel back and forth at the same frequency as the stimulus in a predetermined phase relation. The frequency was

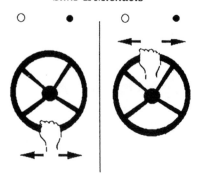

Proximal hand position   Distal hand position

Figure 1. The response device—a steering wheel—held proximally (left) and held distally (right).

increased from 1.2 Hz (the lowest frequency) to 2.8 Hz, in 0.2 Hz steps. Each frequency increment took place after 10 full cycles.

If participants felt that they were no longer able to keep the correct phase, they were asked not to resist, and continue moving in the way they felt was most comfortable. Participants received two mappings: A steering-*consistent* mapping, in which the distal part of the wheel moves in-phase with the stimulus, and a steering-*inconsistent* mapping, in which the distal part of the wheel moves anti-phase with the stimulus, irrespective of hand position. Each participant received 10 trials for each hand position and for each mapping.

Results

Separate ANOVAs were performed on the standard deviations of the relative phase (SD ϕ) for each participant and for each hand position. We also determined for each trial whether a bifurcation had occurred. Figure 2 shows the average SD ϕ and the number of bifurcations.

With the distal hand position, all participants were more variable and tended to have a larger number of bifurcations when they had to move the wheel/hand in the opposite direction to the stimulus, which suggests that anti-phase coordination was less stable than in-phase coordination. With the proximal hand position, six participants appeared more stable when they moved their hand in-phase with the stimulus, whereas three participants exhibited no preference for either mapping. In addition, fewer bifurcations were observed with the proximal hand placement than with the distal hand placement.

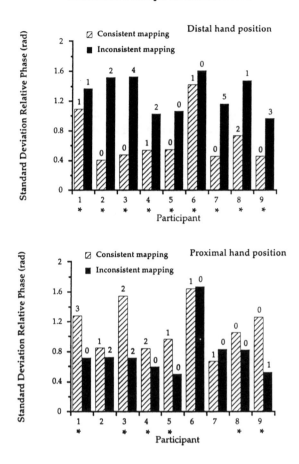

Figure 2. Mean SD ϕ (in rad) for each participant for each mapping. The presence of an asterisk (*) below a pair of bars indicates a significant ($p < .05$) main effect of mapping, for the distal hand placement (top) and the proximal hand placement (bottom). The number of bifurcations for each condition is shown above each bar.

Discussion

With the distal hand position, we found that anti-phase coordination was less stable than in-phase coordination. With the proximal hand position we found that performance appeared more stable when participants synchronized their *hand* with the stimulus than when they synchronized the *wheel* with the stimulus. However, in previous experiments, using the same wheel-turning paradigm, we found that some participants were more stable when they synchronized the *wheel* with the signal. These findings suggest that, what appears to be the "same" movement can reflect one of two different actions, viz., moving a hand versus rotating a wheel. Similar to Kelso, Delcolle, and Schöner (1990), we argue that the meaning of anti-phase and in-phase depends on the intentions of the actor which, in turn, may determine the dynamics of the perception-action pattern.

References

Haken, H., Kelso, J. A. S., & Bunz, H. (1985). A theoretical model of phase transitions in human hand movements. *Biological Cybernetics, 51*, 347-356.

Kelso, J. A. S., Delcolle, J. D., & Schöner, G. (1990). Action-perception as a pattern formation process. In M. Jeannerod (Ed.), *Attention and Performance XIII* (pp. 139-169). Hillsdale, NJ: Erlbaum.

Wimmers, R. H., Beek, P. J., & van Wieringen, P. C. W. (1992). Phase transitions in rhythmic tracking movements: A case of unilateral coupling. *Human Movement Science, 11*, 217-226.

Studies in Perception and Action IV
M. A. Schmuckler & J. M. Kennedy (Eds.)
© *1997 Lawrence Erlbaum Associates, Inc.*

The Role Of Amplitude In Frequency-Induced Transitions In Rhythmic Tracking

C. (Lieke) E. Peper & Peter J. Beek

Faculty of Human Movement Sciences, Vrije Universiteit,
Amsterdam, The Netherlands

Haken et al. (1985) modeled frequency-induced transitions from anti-phase to in-phase coordination in rhythmic hand and finger movements by means of two nonlinearly coupled oscillators (HKB-model). In this model the stability of the two coordination modes depends on the values attained by two coupling coefficients, which vary as a function of the real amplitude of the oscillations. Given the empirically observed inverse relation between movement frequency and amplitude (modeled by a Rayleigh term in the component oscillators), these amplitude-dependent coupling coefficients allowed for a theoretical understanding of the observed frequency-induced transitions. The postulated functional role of movement amplitude, mediating the influence of the control parameter movement frequency, was examined for a case of unilateral coupling. From the HKB-model, we predicted that larger movement amplitudes result in more stable coordination. According to this prediction, anti-phase coordination can be sustained at higher movement rates, resulting in higher critical frequencies.

Method

Subjects. So far, 4 right-handed male subjects participated (age: 24 - 34 years).

Setup. The subjects firmly grasped a vertical manipulandum connected to a rotatable horizontal lever resting on a vertical axle. A potentiometer attached to the axle registered the lever's angular position (sample frequency 200 Hz). An oscillating visual stimulus with adjustable amplitude and frequency could be presented on a LED-bow, positioned in front of the subject.

Procedure. The subjects oscillated their right hand (rotation about the wrist) in either in-phase or anti-phase to the visual stimulus, while tracking the amplitude of the stimulus. Frequency was scaled from 1.0 Hz to 2.8 Hz (0.2 Hz steps: 10 bins, 10 cycles per bin). Three amplitude conditions (5°, 15°, and 25°) were tested. Five trials were conducted per condition. The subjects performed 20 control trials with a preferred frequency for each amplitude condition, as well as without a prescribed amplitude (30 seconds, 5 trials per condition).

Results

Control trials. The mean amplitudes as obtained for the four amplitude conditions were all significantly different (means: 5.3°, 15.3°, 25.2°, preferred amplitude: 20.1°), $F(3,9) = 54.0$, $p < .0001$, in the absence of a statistically significant effect on preferred frequency.

Frequency-scaled trials. Constant errors (CE) for mean amplitude were determined per bin and tested in a Coordination Mode (CM) X Amplitude X Movement Frequency (MF) ANOVA. For anti-phase coordination no effects of movement frequency were observed. During in-phase coordination, amplitude decreased significantly over the frequency steps (Figure 1); interaction effect CM X MF, $F(9,27) = 3.8$, $p < .005$ [main effect of MF, $F(9,27) = 4.1$, $p < .005$]. In addition, the three-way interaction was significant, resulting mainly from a steady amplitude in the second half of the in-phase trials for the smallest amplitude, $F(18,54) = 2.0$, $p < .05$. Note that the CE's were small, implying adequate movement amplitudes in each condition.

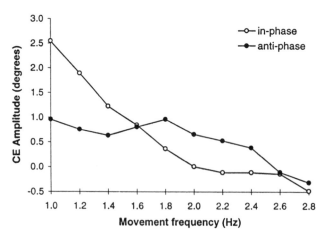

Figure 1. Constant error in movement amplitude as a function of movement frequency.

The critical frequency was defined as the frequency attained in the last stable bin for which the RP differed less than 30° from the initial or required RP and for which the inverse of transformed uniformity (ITU, measure of variability of directional data, Mardia, 1972) was smaller than .45.

Stability was lost in all anti-phase trials. In 58% of these trials a transition occurred to a RP that was shifted 180° with respect to the required or initial RP (determined on the basis of mean RP per bin, tolerance range 30°), with at least two successive bins being stably performed at this new RP (ITU < 0.45). In 62% of the in-phase trials stability was lost, without a transition to the anti-phase relation.

A one-way ANOVA with the factor Amplitude on the mean critical frequencies per condition as obtained for the anti-phase trials revealed no effects of amplitude on the critical frequency [$F(2,6) = 0.25$]; means per amplitude condition (5°, 15°, 25°): 1.42, 1.51, 1.46 Hz.

A CM X Amplitude X MF ANOVA on ITU revealed a steady increase in variability for in-phase coordination, while for anti-phase coordination a pronounced peak was observed at the 1.8 frequency bin (Figure 2), CM X MF interaction: $F(9,27) = 2.8$, $p < .05$ [main effects: CM, $F(1,3) = 10.4$, $p < .05$; MF, $F(9,27) = 4.8$, $p < .0001$]. This bin coincides with, on average, the first unstable bin (1.5 Hz [last stable bin] + 2 Hz [next bin] = 1.7 Hz). Future analyses will address these data when scaled around the transition point.

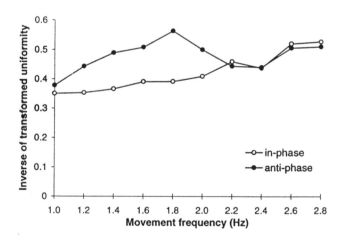

Figure 2. Variability in relative phase, indexed by the inverse of the transformed uniformity, as a function of movement frequency.

Discussion

Contrary to the predictions of the HKB-model, in the investigated tracking task no effects of amplitude on critical frequency or the degree of variability were observed. Moreover, although on average no frequency-induced decrease in amplitude was obtained for the anti-phase trials, transitions in coordination were observed in the majority of these trials. These preliminary results suggest that frequency-induced phase transitions are not necessarily caused by the drop in amplitude that generally accompanies an increase in movement frequency.

Acknowledgments. Lieke Peper holds a fellowship of the Royal Netherlands Academy of Arts and Sciences.

References

Haken, H., Kelso, J. A. S., & Bunz, H. (1985). A theoretical model of phase transitions in human hand movements. *Biological Cybernetics, 51*, 347-356.

Mardia, K. V. (1972). *Statistics of directional data.* London: Academic Press.

Studies in Perception and Action IV
M. A. Schmuckler & J. M. Kennedy (Eds.)
© *1997 Lawrence Erlbaum Associates, Inc.*

Continuous Frequency Modulation Of Symmetric And Asymmetric Coordination Dynamics

Hyeongsaeng Park

CESPA, University of Connecticut, Storrs, CT, U.S.A.

The dynamics of bimanual rhythmic coordination are given by a motion equation in relative phase (e.g., Kelso et al., 1990):

$$\dot{\phi} = \delta - a \sin \phi - 2b \sin 2\phi + \sqrt{Q}\, \zeta_t \tag{1}$$

The relative phase $\phi = \theta_{left} - \theta_{right}$ between the phase angles (θ_i) of the oscillating body segments is a collective variable (the overdot signifies first time derivative). The ratio, b/a, is a control parameter which determines the relative strengths of the attractors at 0 and π phase relations when $\delta = 0$ and the relative strengths of the attractors in the vicinity of 0 and π when $\delta \neq 0$. The quantity δ represents the detuning or imperfection parameter (Strogatz, 1994) often represented by the difference in the uncoupled frequencies of the contralateral segments, $\omega_{left} - \omega_{right}$. The final term in Eq. (1) represents a stochastic force of strength Q that arises from the subsystems behind the collective variable. Predictions about the equilibria of the 1:1 coordination pattern and their relative stabilities follow by setting the left hand side of Eq. (1) equal to zero, ignoring the noise term, and solving for ϕ given specific values of δ and b/a. Figure 1 shows the zero-crossings for a symmetric system $\delta = 0$ and an asymmetric system $\delta = 1$ for different values of b/a.

In the present research, bimanual rhythmic coordination of two hand-held pendulums in a plane parallel to the body's coronal plane (Mitra et al., 1997) was studied at different movement frequencies. (For movements parallel to the coronal plane, spatial inphase is muscular antiphase and vice versa.) The relation between pendulums determined δ and movement frequency determined b/a. At each of 7 values of δ (0, ±1, ±2, ±3), participants tried to produce

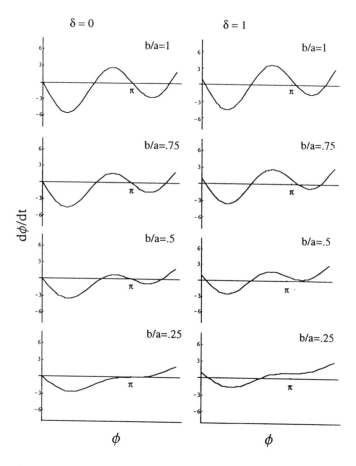

Figure 1. Evolution of a symmetric system and an asymmetric system with decreasing *b/a*. While the symmetric case, δ = 0 (left column) is unaffected by the changing *b/a* , the asymmetric case, δ = 1 (right column) reveals a shift in the equilibrium values of relative phase away from 0 and π. In respect to nonlinear dynamical models, the left column can be described as invariant fixed points before and after a subcritical pitchfork bifurcation that changes the attractor at π to a repeller, leaving only the attractor at 0. The right column can be described as a shifting of fixed points with *b/a* before a saddle-node bifurcation that is an initial coalescing of the attractor and repeller followed by the annihilation of both fixed points.

(without benefit of vision) 1:1 frequency locking in either inphase or antiphase as movement frequency increased every 3 s from 0.95 Hz to 1.93 Hz. Figure 1 indicates that relative phase should (a) be unaffected by frequency for the symmetric case, $\delta = 0$; (b) increase with frequency for $\delta \neq 0$; and (c) become destabilized in the muscularly antiphase mode at higher frequencies in ways dependent on δ. Figure 2 shows that (a) and (b) were essentially confirmed; Figure 3 shows loss of stability that differed for the different δ conditions.

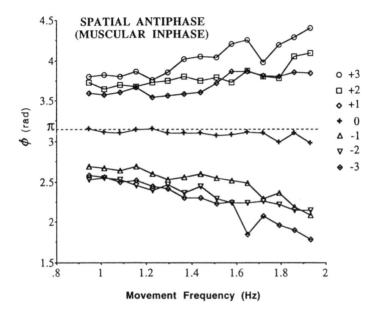

Figure 2. Interaction of two control parameters, movement frequency (b/a) and detuning (δ) in the inphase (spatially antiphase) condition. The legend identifies the δ conditions. In the symmetric case, $\delta = 0$, relative phase does not change with increasing movement frequency (that is, with decreasing b/a); in contrast, in the asymmetric cases, $\delta = \pm 1, \pm 2, \pm 3$, relative phase increases or decreases linearly ($p < .0001$). This interaction corresponds to the theoretical prediction shown in Figure 1.

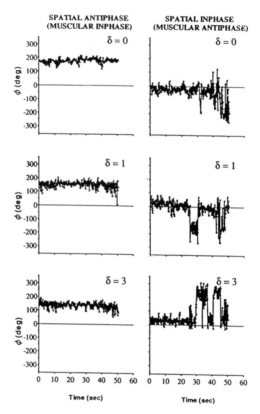

Figure 3. Examples of destabilization under the different δ conditions from one participant. The relative phases on the vertical axis are in spatial coordinates. As in Figure 2, movement frequency is increasing over the 50 s trial. The muscular antiphase mode shows more destabilization at higher movement frequencies than the muscular inphase mode, with the form of the coordination breakdown dependent on δ.

References

Kelso, J. A. S., Delcolle, J. D., & Schöner, G. (1990). Action-perception as a pattern formation process. In M. Jeannerod (Ed.), *Attention and Performance XIII*. Hillsdale, NJ: Erlbaum.

Mitra, S., Amazeen, P. G., & Turvey, M. T. (1997). Dynamics of bimanual rhythmic coordination in the coronal plane. *Motor Control, 1,* 44-71.

Strogatz, S. H. (1994). *Nonlinear dynamics and chaos.* Reading, MA: Addison-Wesley.

Studies in Perception and Action IV
M. A. Schmuckler & J. M. Kennedy (Eds.)
© *1997 Lawrence Erlbaum Associates, Inc.*

Scale-Invariant Memory During Functional Stabilization

Paul J. Treffner[1] & J. A. Scott Kelso[2]

[1] Department of Psychology, University of Southern Queensland,
Toowoomba, Australia.
[2] Center for Complex Systems, Florida Atlantic University,
Boca Raton, FL, U.S.A.

Current models of coordination typically exhibit dynamics that are restricted to *stable* states such as limit cycles and point attractors (e.g. Treffner & Turvey, 1996). Mode-locking, if present, means fixed phase- and frequency-locking. Recent experiments indicate that perception-action might also be construed as an open, self-organizing complex system that exhibits great flexibility by operating near by critical instabilities (Kelso, 1995). This provides the system with the possibility of generating appropriate control strategies across multiple spatial and/or temporal scales (Treffner & Kelso, 1995). In sum, complex systems exhibit scale-invariance by exploiting *unstable* dynamics. Complementary to the analysis of the local dynamics of nonlinear transition phenomena, one can inquire whether a global analysis focusing on the statistical properties of the ensemble of trials also yields signatures characteristic of a dynamical self-organized system. In order to investigate the harnessing of instability, we investigated the dynamics of balancing an inherently unstable, inverted pendulum in a functionally stable manner.

Method

Four right-handed graduate students attempted to balance an aluminum rod that was constrained to slide laterally along a 180 cm track positioned at waist level. The pivot housing at the base of the rod could be easily moved from side to side by the subject's right hand.

Six different lengths were tested: 30, 45, 60, 75, 90, and 105 cm, with corresponding eigenperiods of 1.10, 1.35, 1.56, 1.74, 1.90, and 2.06 s.

Beginning with the longest and ending with the shortest rod, each subject attempted to balance continuously for 300 s. Using an Optotrak, displacement data of the bottom of the rod (the hand) and the top, sampled at 100 Hz, provided a raw time series of 30,000 points from which the angle from vertical was also computed.

Since the trajectory of a balanced rod appears similar to a random walk, the Hurst exponent, H, was calculated. For purely random (Brownian) motion, $H = 0.5$, indicating that no correlation exists between a point and all other points. In contrast, with $H > 0.5$, the direction of past changes is preserved (global positive correlation called "persistence"), i.e., decreases (increases) in the past will be followed by decreases (increases) in the future. With $H < 0.5$, the direction of past changes is reversed (global negative correlation called "antipersistence"), i.e., decreases (increases) in the past will tend to be followed by increases (decreases) in the future (Bassingthwaighte et al, 1994). Processes with $H \neq .5$ are considered as random fractals due to such scale-invariance. Following Hurst's empirical relation ($R/S = DT^H$), scaling is revealed if a linear region exists in the log-log plot of R/S versus DT, where R is the range of the *raw* time series for a given window size (with DT a power of 2), S is the standard deviation of the *increments*, and a mean R/S is calculated for each window size.

Results

Figure 1 displays plots of the grand mean (over all subjects and lengths) of R/S for hand displacement, the purported action variable. Two linear scaling regions exist: a short-term, persistence region ($H = .95$), and a long-term, antipersistence region ($H = .29$). In addition, a crossover region exists between them at 2.6 s. The long-term scaling implies a kind of "memory" in the global perception-action dynamics for a duration of 80 seconds into the past. A similar result was revealed for the purported perception variable, angle of rod: short-term persistence ($H = .94$), and long-term antipersistence ($H = .15$). However, the crossover at 1.3 s occurred earlier for the angle than for the hand. This may be due to the much greater constraint placed on how far the rod can move from vertical in comparison to the much less constrained movement of the hand.

The crossover between persistence and antipersistence was also revealed by plotting the local slopes (local estimates of H) against DT. Figure 2 indicates that the transition between persistence and

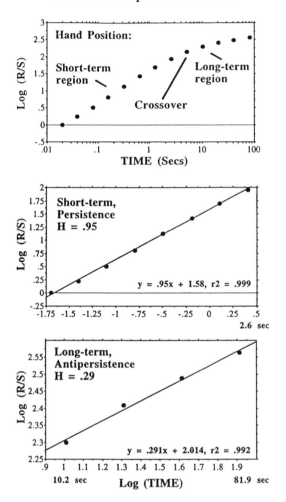

Figure 1. Top: Overall Hurst plot for the action variable (hand displacement) where R/S was collapsed across all subjects and all rod lengths. Two linear scaling regions are apparent. Middle: The short-term region from the top graph indicating persistence up to 2.6 s. Bottom: The long-term region from the top graph indicating an antipersistence memory of 80 s.

antipersistence occurred almost 6 s earlier for the rod angle than for the hand. Importantly, the rod's natural frequency (constrained by rod length) determined the crossover point for the angle variable in a consistent manner. Thus, shorter (difficult) rods led to earlier transitions to antipersistence than did longer (easier) rods.

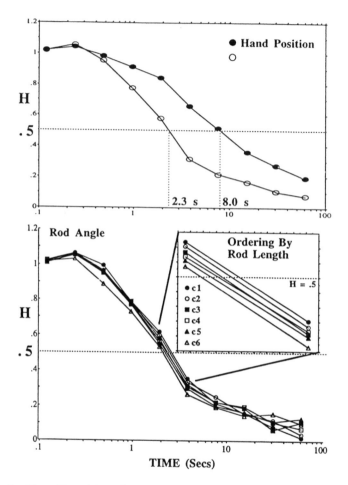

Figure 2. Top: Transition diagram for the collapsed data, showing that the switch in H from persistence (H > .5) to antipersistence (H < .5) occurs earlier for the perceptual variable (angle) than for the action variable (hand displacement). Bottom: Transition diagram for the angle, showing the influence of rod length on the angle's crossover point (inset). C1-C6 = long through short rod length conditions.

Since the extent of the estimated long-term "memory" is limited by the largest window of DT, a single, uninterrupted 30 minute trial was produced by an expert subject. Analysis revealed that for the hand, linear persistence (H = .87) switched at 3.2 s to antipersistence (H = .25), and this held for 3.4 mins into the past. For the angle, persistence (H = .86) switched at 1.6 s to antipersistence (H = .27), and also held for 3.4 mins. Interestingly, from 3.4 mins to 13.6 mins for the angle, H = .48, corresponding to purely random behavior. Thus, beyond 3.4 mins, all correlation was lost implying an upper bound on the system's memory.

We have shown that the dynamics of active stabilization may be characterized as a stochastic process. More than mere description, such characterization impels alternative notions of formative organizational mechanisms. Further, we have shown that the extrinsic mechanics (rod length) influences the stochastic dynamics in a principled manner. Finally, the long-term correlation inherent in the perception-action dynamics suggests that phenomena such as "memory" might be recast in terms of generic mechanisms of self-organization (Treffner & Kelso, 1996).

References

Bassingthwaighte, J. B., Liebovitch, L. S., & West, B. J. (1994). *Fractal physiology*. New York: Oxford University Press.

Kelso, J. A. S. (1995). *Dynamic patterns: The self-organization of brain and behavior*. Cambridge, MA: MIT Press.

Treffner, P. J., & Kelso, J. A. S. (1995). Functional stabilization of unstable fixed-points. In B. Bardy, R. Bootsma, & Y. Guiard (Eds.) *Studies in perception and action* (pp. 83-86). Mahwah, NJ: Erlbaum.

Treffner, P. J., & Kelso, J. A. S. (1996). Generic mechanisms of coordination in special populations. *Behavioral and Brain Sciences, 19*, 89.

Treffner, P. J., & Turvey, M. T. (1996). Symmetry, broken symmetry, and the dynamics of bimanual coordination. *Experimental Brain Research, 107*, 463-478.

Studies in Perception and Action IV
M. A. Schmuckler & J. M. Kennedy (Eds.)
© *1997 Lawrence Erlbaum Associates, Inc.*

Relative Coordination Reconsidered:
A Stochastic Account

David R. Collins

CESPA, University of Connecticut, Storrs, CT, U.S.A.

In his experiments with specially prepared fish, von Holst (1939/1973) came to distinguish two basic states of coordination, absolute coordination when two fins very rarely lost pace with each other, and relative coordination when one fin frequently lost a cycle relative to the other. An attempt to understand the distinction between these coordinations has been proposed by Kelso and colleagues (see Kelso, 1995), drawing upon bimanual coordination studies in which both relative and absolute coordination can be observed for antiphase coordination modes, but it is generally assumed that essentially just absolute coordination occurs for inphase. This follows from the observation that phase transitions can occur in finger coordination experiments from antiphase to inphase, but not inphase to antiphase (Kelso, 1995). Kelso and colleagues have argued that relative coordination can be explained by a mechanism of intermittency, from the chaotic literature (see Kelso, 1995).

In order for a set of equations to exhibit chaotic phenomenon, it must contain at least three continuous variables, or at least one iterative variable. Thus, for the standard coordination equation,

$$\dot{\phi} = d - a\cos\phi - 2b\cos2\phi + \sqrt{Q/2}\xi_t \tag{1}$$

to exhibit intermittency, the stochastic parameter Q must be set to zero, and the equation converted to an iterative map (Kelso, 1995). Kelso (1995) described how the iterative equation can exhibit intermittency, and achieve probability distributions about each of the attractive states of Eq. 1 similar to those he cites from von Holst (1939/1973).

An alternate interpretation of relative coordination is possible by noting that Eq. 1 can exhibit the same probability distributions by retaining the stochastic term as well as its continuous form. Collins and Turvey (in press) showed that experimental data and simulations of Eq. 1 can agree with predictions based on solutions to the Fokker-Planck equation using the potential form of Eq. 1

$$V = -d\phi - a\cos\phi - b\cos2\phi \tag{2}$$

The stationary probability distribution for the $d = 0$ case is

$$P = Ne^{-2V/Q} \tag{3}$$

It may be possible to find steady state solutions when d is not 0.

Figure 1 describes how probability distributions obtained from Eq. 3 (for $d = 0$) and from simulations (for $d = 0$ and $d = 2$) agree in form with the phenomenon of relative coordination, of which absolute coordination can be viewed as an idealization as $Q \rightarrow 0$. Figure 2 shows the predicted mean time between phase transitions, or Mean First Passage Times (MFPT), between each potential well via (Gilmore, 1981),

$$\text{MFPT} = \frac{2\pi}{\sqrt{\left|\dfrac{d^2V}{d\phi^2}\right|_{max} \dfrac{d^2V}{d\phi^2}\bigg|_{min}}} e^{2(V_{max}-V_{min})/Q} \tag{4}$$

Discussion

The paper indicated how a stochastic interpretation of relative coordination is possible to complement previous intermittency interpretations. Further predictions about expected probability distributions and phase transition times (alternately, probabilities of transitions in a given time) are available for many stochastic equations, while these problems remain intractable for most chaotic equations of interest. The stochastic variable is intended only to be an approximation of a more complicated process, possibly a first approximation of an underlying contribution from the remaining variables of a chaotic (continuous) system of equations. It may be too optimistic to consider relative coordination explained by an intermittency interpretation based solely upon a single iterative variable with no variance left to "noise" other than the inability to measure any state of a system to infinite precision.

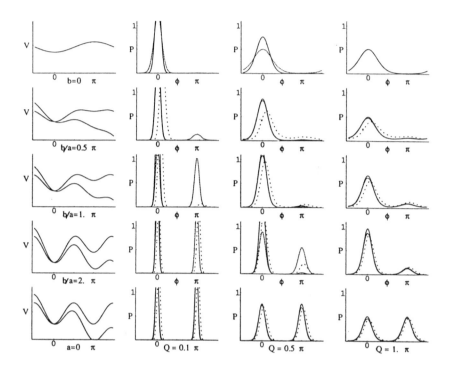

Figure 1. The potential (*V*) curves at the left depict Eq. 1 for the special cases of one attractor (top), two identical attractors (bottom), and three cases interpolating between these extremes, with detuning either present or not (positive *d* skews each curve clockwise). The three columns to the right show the corresponding predicted *P* for each *d* = 0 potential curve. The dashed curves in these columns show the results of stochastic simulations of Eq. 1 in the absence and presence of detuning (fine dashing for *d* = 0; wide dashing for *d* = 2). The strong dispersion effect of increasing *Q* is shown for each potential. The bias of phase transitions is exhibited by the shift of probability mass from the antiphase to inphase peak, particularly for large *Q*. *a* = 2 for each but the last, while *b*, *d* and *Q* were defined relative to *a* (or *b* for *a* = 0).

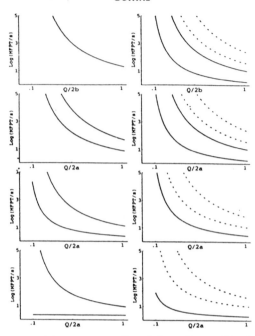

Figure 2. Phase transitions are predicted for all possible "paths" along the potential curves in Figure 1 (left column). One distinct transition is available for the single attractor case $b = 0$ due to the $2p$ modularity of Eq. 1, while four paths are possible when detuning is present. MFPT from Eq. 4 for each of the possible transition paths are depicted corresponding to the potentials in Figure 1, from *bottom* to *top* excluding the $b = 0$ case of Figure 1 (left column, $d = 0$; right column, $d = 2$; $a = 0$ at top, $b / a = 0.5$ at bottom). The curves are higher and more right-ward for inphase to antiphase (longer times) and for uphill transitions in the right column. For $b = 0$, MFPT for $Q = 1.0$, .5, and 0.1 was 23 s, 171 s and 10^9 s, respectively.

References

Collins, D. R., & Turvey, M. T. (in press). A stochastic analysis of superposed rhythmic synergies. *Human Movement Science.*

Kelso, J. A. S. (1995). *Dynamics patterns: The self-organization of brain and behavior.* Cambridge, MA: The MIT Press.

Gilmore, R. (1981). *Catastrophe theory for scientists and engineers.* New York: Wiley.

von Holst, E. (1939/1973). *The behavioral physiology of animal and man.* Coral Gables, FL: University of Miami Press.

Studies in Perception and Action IV
M. A. Schmuckler & J. M. Kennedy (Eds.)
© *1997 Lawrence Erlbaum Associates, Inc.*

Comparing Discrete And Cyclical Movement Coordination Of Prehension

Chris Button, Simon Bennett, & Keith Davids

Department of Exercise and Sport Science,
Manchester Metropolitan University, Alsager, U.K.

Recent theories of movement coordination have attempted to apply the principles of nonlinear oscillations to cyclical actions, such as gait, speech and juggling (see Beek, Peper & Stegeman, 1995; Kelso, 1995). Dynamical systems theory describes the complex interaction of a system's components in terms of regions of stability. However, whilst cyclical actions translate well into such dynamical accounts, there has been little work on discrete movements such as pointing or reaching and grasping (Beek et al., 1995). Theoretically, discrete movements should be amenable to a similar dynamical analysis if there are common principles at work. However, as Yates (1979) warns, "...mathematical truths are very different from physical truths and are not sufficient basis for modelling" (p. 57), further empirical work is needed. The study of Wallace, Stevenson, Spear & Weeks (1994) represents one attempt to apply a dynamical approach to interceptive and prehensile actions. However, the task required subjects to move in time to a metronome and therefore the generalisability of dynamical systems theory to discrete actions still remains unclear. Other studies have also sought to model prehension and interceptive actions such as ball catching from a dynamical systems perspective (e.g., Wimmers, Beek, Savelsbergh, & Hopkins, in press). In particular, non-linear phase transitions were shown to occur with babies as they develop from just reaching to reaching and grasping (Wimmers et al., in press). The aim of this study was to examine the efficacy of the scanning procedure in predicting a subject's most stable attractor. A second aim was to further examine the non-linear dynamical nature of coordination patterns in both cyclical and discrete grasping movements

Method

Eight adults volunteered as subjects. The task involved reaching for and grasping a dowel. To study an individual's dynamics a scanning procedure was used (see Wallace et al., 1994). This required the subjects to vary the Trfc according to markers placed at 10 equidistant points along the movement trajectory. It was shown that at the most stable point (the attractor), the constant error and variability of Trfc was least, with a systematic increase in these values further away from the attractor. Subjects practiced at each position until they felt comfortable. They then performed a further 10 experimental trials during which the displacements of the distal ends of the thumb and forefinger were recorded with an ELITE on-line motion analysis system. The first marker position (1) was 3.5 cm from the start position, the second a further 2.8 cm away, and so on until position 10 which was 3.5 cm from the target dowel. Pre- and post-tests were conducted in which subjects were free to grasp at whatever position they felt comfortable. This procedure was carried out in 2 conditions (discrete and cyclical). In the cyclical condition subjects moved in time to a metronome (frequency of 1.4Hz). In the discrete condition subjects were allowed to reach and grasp voluntarily within a movement time of 700ms.

Results and Discussion

The independent variables were trial block (pre-test, Trfc predicted by scanning, and post-test) and condition (cyclical and discrete). The dependent variables were: preferred Trfc and SD of Trfc. Two-way ANOVAs (condition x trial block) with repeated measures on both factors were performed on the group data. No significant differences were found. Further 2-way ANOVAs were performed on the individual-subject data. Significant condition and trial block differences were noted [e.g., for subject 7 on Trfc, $F(11,1) = 10.06$ and $F(22,2) = 15.16$, both $p < .01$]. For example, closer inspection of the individual data for one subject revealed a large increase in the preferred Trfc in the cyclical condition compared to the discrete condition. Further, the scanning procedure predicted a lower value of Trfc than both the pre-test and post-test revealed (see Figure 1). Various other individual differences were found between the conditions and the trial blocks.

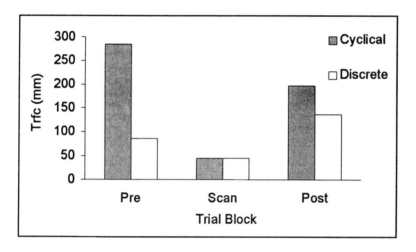

Figure 1. Mean preferred Trfc as a function of trial block and condition exemplified in one subject.

The variability in the pre-test, scanning and post-test data suggests that the scanning procedure may not predict the same position of lowest variability as shown by the subject when free from any constraints on their grasp position. These clear individual differences suggest a need for a change of emphasis in future studies away from the use of the scanning procedure to predict Trfc. Further, the data reinforces "...the methodological dangers involved in constructing dynamical (and other) models on the basis of data pooled across participants and emphasizes the need to construct models at the level of the individual participants" (Beek, Rikkert, and van Wieringen, 1996, p. 1092).

References

Beek, P. J., Peper, C. E., & Stegeman, D. F. (1995). Dynamical models of movement coordination. *Human Movement Science, 14,* 573-608.

Beek, P. J., Rikkert, W. E. I., & van Wieringen, P. C. W. (1996). Limit cycle properties of rhythmic forearm movements. *Journal of Experimental Psychology: Human Perception and Performance, 22,* 1077-1093.

Kelso, J. A. S. (1995). *Dynamic patterns: The self-organization of brain and behaviour.* London: MIT Press.

Wallace, S. A., Stevenson, E., Spear, A., & Weeks, D. L. (1994). Scanning the dynamics of reaching and grasping movements. *Human Movement Science, 13*, 255-289.

Wimmers, R. H., Beek, P. J., Savelsbergh, G. J. P., & Hopkins, B. (in press). Evidence for a phase transition in the early development of prehension. *Developmental Psychobiology.*

Yates, F. E. (1979). Physical biology: A basis for modeling living systems. *Journal of Cybernetics and Information Science, 2*, 57-70.

Studies in Perception and Action IV
M. A. Schmuckler & J. M. Kennedy (Eds.)
© *1997 Lawrence Erlbaum Associates, Inc.*

Expert-Novice Comparison Of Coordination Patterns In The Volley-Ball Serve.

J. Jacques Temprado, M. Della-Grasta, M. Farell, & M. Laurent

UMR "Movement and Perception", CNRS and University of the Mediterranean, Faculty of Sport Sciences, Marseille, France.

According to a dynamical perspective of movement coordination, topological invariants of the coordination can be characterized by one or several essential variables (Kugler et al., 1980), permitting the identification of stable states that constitute the "intrinsic dynamics" of the coordination. This intrinsic dynamics may then serve as a frame of reference for the evaluation of qualitative transformations in coordination during learning (Zanone & Kelso, 1992). There could, however, exist situations in which learning does not consist of the integration of a new stable state into a pre-existing intrinsic dynamic, but in overcoming the initial disorder to stabilize a specific coordination for the performance of the task (Beek & van Santvoort, 1992).

The goals of the present study were 1) to identify the essential variable(s) of the intra-limb coordination of the serving arm, and 2) to determine whether the development of expertise corresponded to an 'all or none' process (progressing from initial disorder to order) or to the successive stabilization of different coordination states.

Method

Subjects. An expert group (6 subjects) and a novice group (14 subjects) were compared.

Task Subjects had to perform overhand volley-ball services aiming to hit a cylindrical target placed 16 m away, on the other side of the net.

Figure 1. A global picture of the volley-ball serve.   Filled black circles represent the markers used for movement analysis.

Movement analysis. The subjects were filmed with a frequency of 50 Hz. Three markers were placed on the wrist, shoulder and elbow of the serving arm. The center of the ball was also digitized. The x and y coordinates of each marker were recorded, first digitized, then transformed to real-world coordinates. We analyzed the linear position of shoulder, elbow, and wrist in the front-back dimension.

Results

Task Performance.   Performances of the two groups were compared. ANOVAs carried out on the amplitude of the ball trajectory and on the variability of the ball trajectory confirmed that the two groups differed in their capacities to perform the task.

Type of coordination.   The coordination between shoulder, elbow, and wrist was analyzed using cross-correlations of the trajectory of the three joint-pairs (shoulder/elbow, elbow/wrist, shoulder/wrist).

The proportion of trials with a positive correlation was subjected to an arcsin transformation and then analyzed by a 2 (expertise) x 3 (joint-pair) mixed ANOVA with repeated measures on the last factor. Analysis of the frequency of trials performed with an in-phase relationship (i.e., a + sign of cross-correlation coefficient) of each joint-pair for each subject showed that expertise was manifested in a significant change - from positive to negative - of the sign of the correlation coefficient of the shoulder-wrist coupling (novices: 7% of + sign, experts: 72% of + sign).

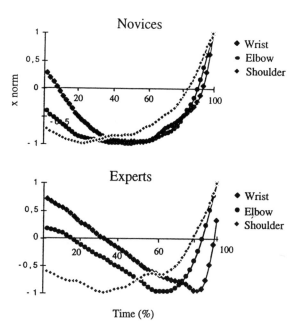

Figure 2. Time series of the shoulder, the elbow and the wrist of the striking arm for both the experts and the novices. Normalized coordinates on the x axis are plotted as a function of the normalized time.

Strength of relationships between the joints. A 2 (expertise) x 3 (joint-pair) mixed ANOVA with repeated measures on the last factor was carried out on the mean absolute values of the correlation coefficients. Results showed that the values of the correlation coefficients were lower among the experts than among the novices for the shoulder-elbow relationship and the elbow-wrist relationship, but not for the shoulder-wrist relationship. Moreover, the intensity of coupling of the wrist-elbow unit and of the shoulder-elbow unit was equivalent for the novices but not for the experts. For the experts, the intensity of coupling of each unit was different.

Analysis of different coordination patterns. Three patterns were identified in each sample of trials performed by the two groups:

1) an A pattern in which all the joint units were coupled in phase (+++). This pattern is the representative pattern of the novices.

2) a B pattern in which all the units except the shoulder-wrist unit were coupled in phase (++-). This pattern is the representative pattern of the experts.

3) a C pattern in which only the wrist-elbow unit was coupled in phase (+--). This pattern is observed with a small frequency in the two groups.

The frequency of these patterns was computed on the basis of all the trials performed in each group. For the novices we observed the A pattern in 75 % of the trials, the B pattern in 30 % of the trials and the C pattern in 5% of the trials. For the experts, we observed the A pattern in 7% of the trials, the B pattern in 75 % of the trials and the C pattern in 18% of the trials.

Discussion

Analysis of the nature of inter-joint coupling suggest that this variable summarizes a qualitative difference between the patterns of coordination of the experts and the novices. Thus, it could be considered as a good candidate as the essential variable of the intra-limb coordination of the serving arm. Moreover, the main feature of expertise was manifested in releasing of degrees of freedom of the motor system, that is in freeing the shoulder-elbow, shoulder-wrist and elbow-wrist units.

Analysis of the different pattern of coordination performed by each subject group suggests that the development of coordination is not an all-or-none process. Rather, it consists of a succession of at least two qualitatively different states of coordination. From a dynamical view of learning, one can assimilate the novice repertoire to the intrinsic dynamics from which expertise develops. The modification of the distribution of the coordination patterns corresponds to a change in their relative power of attraction in the repertoire of the subjects. Thus, expertise consists of the strengthening of a coordination pattern that exists intrinsically in the repertoire of the novice rather than in the creation of a completely new pattern.

References

Beek, P. J., & van Santvoord, A. A. M. (1992). Learning the cascade juggling: A dynamical systems analysis. *Journal of Motor Behavior, 24,* 85-94.

Kugler, P. N., Kelso, J. A. S., & Turvey, M. T. (1980). On the concept of coordinative structures as dissipative structures: 1. Theoretical lines of convergence. In G. E. Stelmach & J. Requin (Eds.), *Tutorials in motor behavior* (pp. 3-47). Amsterdam: North-Holland.

Zanone, P. G., & Kelso, J. A. S. (1992). Evolution of behavioral attractors with learning: Nonequilibrium phase transitions. *Journal of Experimental Psychology: Human Perception and Performance, 18,* 403-421.

Studies in Perception and Action IV
M. A. Schmuckler & J. M. Kennedy (Eds.)
© *1997 Lawrence Erlbaum Associates, Inc.*

Learning A New Phase Relation Modifies The Intrinsic Dynamics

Polemnia G. Amazeen

Faculty of Human Movement Sciences, Free University,
Amsterdam, The Netherlands

Monofrequency (1:1 frequency locked) coordination is characterized by two stable phase relations: in-phase ($\phi = 0$) and anti-phase ($\phi = \pi$). Because they are produced in the absence of any specific behavioral requirement, 0 and π have been referred to as *intrinsic dynamics* (Schöner & Kelso, 1988). New patterns are produced in the context of these already-acquired patterns. Intuitively, the resulting competition between old and new causes difficulties for the learner. Nonintuitive is the notion that acquisition of a new coordinative pattern causes a deformation of the attractor landscape of the intrinsic dynamics that could influence subsequent production of 0 and π (Schöner, Zanone, & Kelso, 1992).

In past experiments (e.g., Zanone & Kelso, 1992), a probe of all phase relations between 0 and π permitted an empirically-obtained approximation to the attractor layout of the evolving dynamics. For a number of learners, the strengthening of an attractor at $\pi/2$ was accompanied by a weakening of the attractor at π. In the present experiment, mean relative phase f and its standard deviation SDϕ provided a quantitative index of the degree of change in the intrinsically stable attractors. These more fine-grained dependent measures were used in place of the probing technique because research has shown reliable shifts in the location of attractors to be as small as $\phi = 0.06$ rad (Treffner & Turvey, 1995). In-phase and anti-phase are naturally shifted by variations in the timing differences $\Delta\omega$ between the component limb segments. In the present experiment, manipulation of $\Delta\omega$ allowed for observation of whether learning affects this fixed point shift.

Method

Twenty-four participants were divided evenly into three groups on the basis of experience: participants in the two learning groups had previously acquired either $-\pi/2$ (right hand leads left by ¼ cycle) or $-\pi/4$ (right hand leads left by ⅛ cycle); participants who had not acquired any new phase relation were placed in the control group. On any given 30-sec trial, participants produced an intended phase relation $\phi_{intended}$ of either 0 or π with one of five pairs of hand-held pendulums ($\Delta\omega = 0, \pm1, \pm2$ rad/s). Movement trajectories of the pendulums were collected using a Sonic 3-Space Digitizer and MASS digitizer software. ϕ was used as the estimate of the stable fixed point and SDϕ served as an estimate of its stability.

Results and Conclusion

Figure 1 depicts the significant effect of learning on the intrinsic dynamics as indexed by ϕ, $F(8,84) = 3.64$, $p < .01$. Fixed point shift was produced by $\Delta\omega$ in all three learning groups: $\phi - \phi_{intended}$ was nearest zero when $\Delta\omega = 0$, shifted in the positive direction for $\Delta\omega > 0$ and shifted in the negative direction for $\Delta\omega < 0$. The control group replicated the results of numerous studies on the intrinsic dynamics (e.g., Treffner & Turvey, 1995), with fixed point shift significantly amplified for π, $F(4,84) = 10.77$, $p < .0001$. The pattern for the $-\pi/4$ group was qualitatively different: $\phi - \phi_{intended}$ was uniformly more positive for π than for 0, $F(1,7) = 10.98$, $p < .05$. One consequence is that at $\Delta\omega = 0$, the production of anti-phase was more accurate than the production of in-phase. The pattern was somewhere in between for the $-\pi/2$ group: production of 0 and π was equivalent across all levels of $\Delta\omega$.

Figure 2 summarizes the effects of learning on the intrinsic dynamics as indexed by both dependent measures. Note that, with respect to ϕ, learning affected 0 but not π, $F(2,21) = 3.88$, $p < .05$. Specifically, the stabilization of a negative phase relation ($-\pi/2$ or $-\pi/4$) caused a small but significant negative shift of the in-phase attractor, a change that was not witnessed in previous experiments (e.g., Zanone & Kelso, 1992). Conversely, with respect to SDϕ, learning affected π but not 0, $F(2,21) = 4.17$, $p < .05$. Although SDϕ was higher for π than for 0 across all three groups, learning served to lower the variability of π only. The implication is that stabilization of a new phase relation increases the attractiveness of π, causing the two fixed points of the intrinsic dynamics, in-phase and anti-phase, to become more equally attractive.

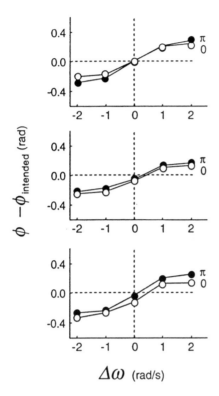

Figure 1. The shift of mean relative phase ϕ from an intended phase ϕ_{intended} of either 0 or π as a function of timing differences $\Delta\omega$ between the pendulums in the (top) control group, (middle) $-\pi/2$ learning group, and (bottom) $-\pi/4$ learning group.

This result stands in contrast to previous findings that indicate that the attractor at anti-phase may disappear as a result of learning (e.g., Zanone & Kelso, 1992). The last finding should be interpreted cautiously, however, because increased exposure to the pendulum task by learners may have caused greater stabilization of anti-phase. Nevertheless, the evidence points to a modification of the intrinsic dynamics by learning.

Acknowledgments. Support was provided by a University of Connecticut dissertation fellowship awarded to P. G. Amazeen and NSF Grant #SBR 94-22650 awarded to M. T. Turvey.

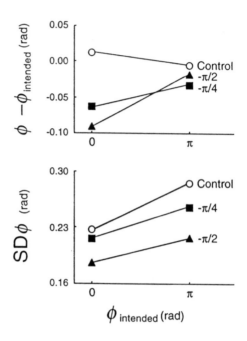

Figure 2. The effect of learning on the production of in-phase ($\phi_{intended} = 0$) and antiphase ($\phi_{intended} = \pi$), as indexed by the two dependent measures, (top) $\phi - \phi_{intended}$ and (bottom) SDϕ

References

Schöner, G., & Kelso, J. A. S. (1988). Dynamic patterns of biological coordination: Theoretical strategy and new results. In J. A. S. Kelso, A. J. Mandell, & M. F. Shlesinger (Eds.), *Dynamic patterns in complex systems.* Singapore: World Scientific.

Schöner, G., Zanone, P. G., & Kelso, J. A. S. (1992). Learning as change of coordination dynamics: Theory and experiment. *Journal of Motor Behavior, 24,* 29-48.

Treffner, P. J., & Turvey, M. T. (1995). Handedness and the asymmetric dynamics of bimanual rhythmic coordination. *Journal of Experimental Psychology: Human Perception and Performance, 21,* 318-333.

Zanone, P. G., & Kelso, J. A. S. (1992). Evolution of behavioral attractors with learning: Nonequilibrium phase transitions. *Journal of Experimental Psychology: Human Perception and Performance, 18,* 403-421.

Studies in Perception and Action IV
M. A. Schmuckler & J. M. Kennedy (Eds.)
© *1997 Lawrence Erlbaum Associates, Inc.*

Control Of Sucking In Term And Preterm Infants

Cathy M. Craig & David N. Lee

Department of Psychology, University of Edinburgh, Scotland.

Foetal sucking has been observed in utero as early as the fifteenth week of gestation (Ianniruberto & Tejani, 1981) and is classified as one of the most precocious and sophisticated motor skills evident in the new-born. Sucking is a vital part of successful feeding, and has to be coordinated with swallowing and breathing. A breakdown of this coordination, or dysfunction in any one of the three components, will result in a failure to thrive and may even provide an early indication of possible neurological damage (Ramsay et al., 1993).

The sucking action is dependent on the careful control and precise coordination of the lips, tongue, jaw and cheeks, the same muscles that are involved in speech production. The controlled movements of these different oro-motor muscles result in an intraoral environment of changing negative pressure, which regulates the flow of milk from the breast or bottle. The rate of milk flow is a direct function of the changing negative pressure created inside the mouth, along with the size of the aperture through which the milk is released and the viscosity of the milk being delivered.

Mechanics of a Suck

A suck essentially involves two distinct phases. However, before these phases can commence, the lips must first form an airtight seal around the nipple. Following this the jaw is lowered and the tongue is pushed down and forward inside the oral cavity, bringing about an increase in suction (negative intraoral pressure) (see Figure 1A). When the desired level of suction has been reached the second phase of the suck begins. The jaw starts to return to its starting position, as the tongue moves backwards in a peristaltic-like fashion, stripping the teat and moving the expelled milk to the back of the mouth, where it accumulates prior to being swallowed (see Figure 1B). In this phase, suction decreases and intraoral pressure returns to the resting value. The cycle then starts again. The time taken for a complete suck cycle varies from about 0.4 to

1 second. New-born infants are able to engage very proficiently in rhythmical
continuous sucking.

Pressure Traces

Intraoral pressure changes were measured using a 5 French catheter
protruding through the end of a standard teat into the oral cavity. This catheter
was in turn connected to a Hewlett Packard pressure sensor.   Pressure
recordings were taken from 5 healthy term bottle feeding infants during
standard feeding sessions. Two preterm infants were also tested (25 weeks
gestational age at birth). Figure 1C illustrates the smooth rhythmical nature of
the pressure changes that occur inside the mouth of a healthy term infant whilst
bottle feeding at 3 weeks of age.   Figure 1D shows the more disorganized
feeding pattern of a preterm infant at 35 weeks gestational age (also with 3
weeks feeding experience).

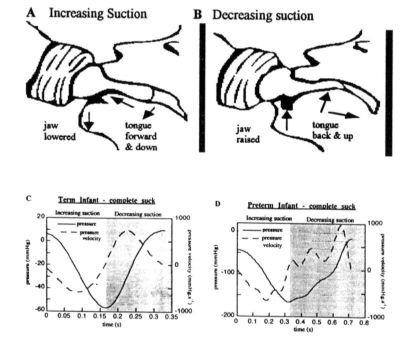

Figure 1. Illustrating the two distinct phases in a suck cycle, and the
corresponding intraoral pressure changes.

τ-Pacemaker

Control of sucking can be understood in terms of coupling the ts of gaps, i.e., keeping them in constant ratio (τ is the first order estimate of the time for a gap to close: it is a temporal measure of the width of a gap, as distance is a spatial measure). A central postulate of general τ theory is that movements are coordinated by τ-coupling (Lee et al., 1995). For example, hand movement to a destination can be synchronized to the motion of an object to a destination by coupling hand-destination τ and object-destination τ. Figure 2A illustrates drumming in time with a conductor. The motion of the baton acts as a τ-pacemaker.

In the self-paced action of sucking, τ-coupling to an intrinsic τ-pacemaker is assumed (Figure 2B). The virtual object in the pacemaker accelerates at a constant rate from rest at time t = 0 and reaches its destination at time t_{PM}. (Thus, at time t, the pacemaker τ is $\tau_{PM} = 0.5(t - t^2_{PM}/t)$, where t_{PM} = pacemaker period.) The infant controls its suction pressure to a desired level by keeping τ of the pressure gap, τ_P, coupled to pacemaker τ (i.e., $\tau_P = k\tau_{PM}$).

Results and Conclusions

The theory predicts that the plot of τ_P against τ_{PM} should be a straight line through the origin for a particular pacemaker period (Figure 2C). The degree of linearity was measured by r^2 of the linear regression of τ_P on τ_{PM}. k (in the equation $\tau_P = k\tau_{PM}$) was measured by the regression slope. Figure 2D summarizes the r^2 and slope (k) values for five term and two preterm infants during the increasing suction phase of the cycle, after the first week and third week of feeding experience. After three weeks of feeding experience all the subjects tested (except for preterm S7) tended towards a strong linear coupling of τ_P and τ_{PM}. The values of the slope (k) mainly reduced, which indicates a less abrupt approach to peak negative pressure. These findings applied to preterm S6 as well as the terms. However, preterm S7, who was the same gestational age as preterm S6, could only manage a mean r^2 of 0.87 and had lower mean slope (k) values. This difference between S6 (preterm) and S7 (preterm) was in agreement with the evaluations of feeding provided by the caregivers.

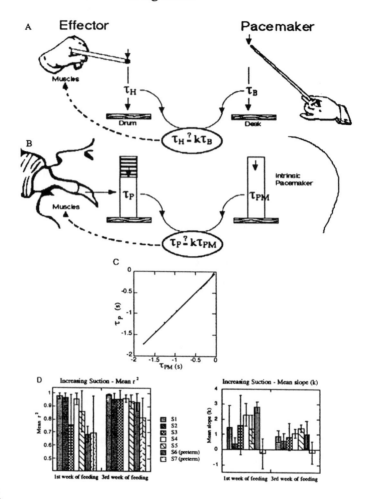

Figure 2.

References

Ianniruberto, A., & Tejani, E. (1981). Ultrasound study of foetal movements. *Seminars in Perinatology, 5,* 175-181.

Lee, D. N., Simmons, J. A., Saillant, P. A., & Bouffard, F. (1995). Steering by echolocation: A paradigm of ecological acoustics. *Journal of Comparative Physiology A, 176,* 347-354.

Ramsay, M., Gisel, E. G., & Boutry, M. (1993). Nonorganic failure-to-thrive - Growth failure secondary to feeding-skills disorder. *Developmental Medicine and Child Neurology, 25,* 4, 285-297.

Studies in Perception and Action IV
M. A. Schmuckler & J. M. Kennedy (Eds.)
© 1997 Lawrence Erlbaum Associates, Inc.

The Auditory Coordination Of Between-Person Rhythmic Movements

R. C. Schmidt and Keith McGregor

Department of Psychology, College of the Holy Cross, Worcester, MA, U.S.A.

Past research has demonstrated how the visual coordination of rhythmic movements between two people (e.g., two people coordinating handheld pendulums) exhibits patterns of coordination that can be explained by dynamical processes of self-organization. This research has shown that two patterns of coordination, inphase and antiphase (0° and 180° relative phase) can easily be maintained though visual coordination. If the difference in the inherent frequencies of the two effectors is increased (by making the handheld pendulums more different in their lengths), the relative phasing of the movements becomes more variable and exhibits a proportional lagging of the inherently slower (larger) effector. These coordinative properties have been modeled by a coupled oscillator dynamic that has steady-state attractors at 0° and 180° relative phase and whose stability can be manipulated by scaling the difference between inherent frequencies of the two oscillators (Schmidt & Turvey, 1994).

The present study will investigate whether this kind of dynamical organization is also established when auditory information links the two coordinating individuals. Although one can think of many cases in which we visually coordinate movements with another person, instances in which we use auditory information to do so are less common. Two individuals performing music together is perhaps one such instance where the hegemony of vision is suppressed and the auditory consequences of Person's A movements are used by Person B to coordinate his/her movements (and vice versa). The present study reproduces the structure of this natural occurrence in an adaptation of our between-person laboratory task. Of interest is (a) whether the two people will be able to coordinate the swinging of handheld pendulums using only a sound emitted from the bottom of the pendulums; (b) whether there is any evidence of relative phase attractors underlying this auditory coupling; and (c) how strong the auditory coupling is compared to other kinds of interlimb couplings previously observed.

Method

Pairs of subjects sat in chairs facing the same direction and oscillated hand-held pendulums in the sagittal plane using their outside hand. The pendulums consisted of an ash dowel with a bicycle hand grip attached to the top and a small rectangular metronome attached 3 cm from the bottom. Four pendulums of different lengths were used. Each of the five subject pairs was asked to oscillate isochronously five combinations of the pendulums during the experiment. These pendulum combinations had five different inherent frequency differences or $\Delta\omega$s. Angular excursions of the wrist were collected using electrogoniometers (Penny & Giles, Santa Monica, CA) attached to each subject's wrists and forearms.

For each trial, the subject pairs were instructed to look straight ahead so that they could not see one another, to swing their pendulums at a comfortable rate, to listen to the 440 Hz tone emitted from the metronome on the other person's pendulum and use it to coordinate the swinging of the pendulums either in an inphase or an antiphase pattern depending upon the trial. There were a total of ten conditions (2 phase modes x 5 pendulum combinations). Each condition was performed twice for a total of twenty 15 s trials.

Results and Discussion

In order to evaluate the auditory interlimb coordination, the continuous relative phase was calculated from the individual wrist angular excursions (Schmidt & Turvey, 1994). As can seen for a representative antiphase trial in Figure 1, the subjects found the task quite difficult. Phase locking was intermittent for most trials. Consequently, in order to evaluate the coordination, each trial was broken into three 5 s segments creating 300 such segments for the data set. Slightly more than half of the segments (55%) were phase locked. Of these 56% were correct inphase and 44% were correct antiphase phase locking. Interestingly, in a substantial number of the unlocked segments (16%), the coordination was captured momentarily in the alternative incorrect phase mode. These results suggest that auditory information can be used to establish the between-person coordination. However, the phase locking created is unstable and intermittent.

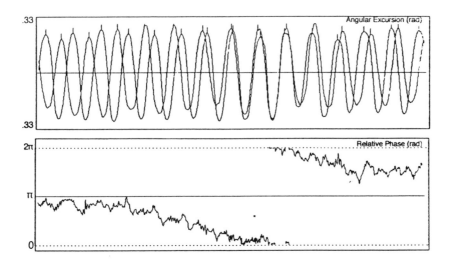

Figure 1. Between-person auditory coordination time series. Note intermittent 0° phase locking at *.

In order to determine whether the stable phase locking observed was produced by an coupled oscillatory strategy, the mean deviation from 0° and 180° (ϕ) and its standard deviation (ϕ SD) were calculated for each stable segment. A significant regression of ϕ on $\Delta\omega$ ($r^2(161)=.17$, $p < .001$) suggests a proportional lagging of the larger pendulum with the difference between the inherent frequencies of the two wrist-pendulums. A significant second order polynomial regression of ϕ SD on $\Delta\omega$ ($r^2(161)=.04$, $p < .05$) indicates a U-shaped relation between phase fluctuations and the inherent frequency difference of the two wrist-pendulums. These results demonstrate that as two pendulums differed more and more in their length, (a) the larger pendulum tended to follow the shorter one in its cycle and (b) the variability of relative phasing increased. Together they replicate the results found for visual between-person coordination and provide evidence that coupled oscillatory dynamics underlies the auditory between-person coordination.

How does the strength of the auditory coupling compare to that of the between-person visual coupling and the within-person 'neural' coupling of two wrists? Given that the number of unstable segments (55%) is much greater than the number of unstable segments observed in either of these kinds of coordination (4% and 0%, respectively), one expects that the auditory coupling should be much weaker. Assuming a simple coupled oscillator model, the strength of the coupling K can be estimated through a regression analysis (Schmidt & Turvey, 1995). For the present data, the auditory coupling K was estimated to be 0.13. For visual between-person and within-person coordination, K was estimated for comparable frequencies to be 0.40 and 0.83, respectively (Schmidt, Bienvenu, Fitzpatrick, & Amazeen, in press). Given the weakness of the coupling and the ensuing intermittency, methods developed for the analysis of relative coordination in addition to the steady state analyses performed here may be illuminating.

References

Schmidt, R. C., Bienvenu, M., Fitzpatrick, P. A., & Amazeen, P. G. (in press). A comparison of within- and between-person coordination: Coordination breakdowns and coupling strength. *Journal of Experimental Psychology: Human Perception and Performance.*

Schmidt, R. C., & Turvey, M. T. (1994). Phase-entrainment dynamics of visually coupled rhythmic movements. *Biological Cybernetics, 70,* 369-376.

Schmidt, R. C., & Turvey, M. T. (1995). Models of interlimb coordination: Equilibria, local analyses, and spectral patterning. *Journal of Experimental Psychology: Human Perception and Performance, 21,* 432-443.

Section III: *Action*

III.B: *Movement and Dynamics*

Studies in Perception and Action IV
M. A. Schmuckler & J. M. Kennedy (Eds.)
© *1997 Lawrence Erlbaum Associates, Inc.*

Effect Of Dynamic Constraints In Interceptive Actions

François-Xavier Li

University of Birmingham, School of Sport and Exercise Sciences,
Edgbaston, Birmingham, U.K.

In interceptive skills the importance of kinematic constraints, in particular the timing, has been frequently emphasized. However dynamic constraints should also play an important role. Little evidence has been given so far on the role of an object's dynamic such as its kinetic energy (Li & Laurent, 1995) and momentum (Stoffregen, Henderson & Sasaki, 1995). Therefore, the aim of this study was to investigate to what extent the variations of the momentum of an approaching object affect an interceptive action. To produce a performance independent from the object's momentum, e.g., knocking it out of the trajectory, actors could increase movement velocity. It is hypothesized that increasing the momentum of the object to hit would lead to an increase in the maximum velocity of the actor's movement.

Method

Thirteen right-handed male subjects volunteered to take part in the experiment. They were required to perform a backward-forward movement to hit an approaching ball with a bat (17.5 cm high by 3 cm wide). Three balls of the same diameter (6.5 cm) but with different weight (10, 20, & 200 gr.) were attached on a trolley. An electrical motor pulled this trolley along a linear track (6 m long) at three different velocities (1.5, 2.0 or 2.5 m/s). After the initial acceleration, the velocity of the trolley remained constant. Ball and bat movements were recorded using the movement analysis system Elite at 100 Hz with two markers located on the ball and on the bat.

The starting position at the future interception point was standardized. No constraints were imposed on when to initiate the movement nor on how hard to hit the ball. Before the experiment the three balls were presented to the subjects who manipulated them. Before each trial, the ball used was presented again and manipulated by the subjects to ensure that they were well informed on the type of ball they had to hit. Regarding the characteristics of the apparatus, the visual perception of ball mass during the approach can be ruled out. However, through the manipulation of each ball before performing the task, it is argued that ball mass could be perceived using dynamic touch (Turvey, 1996).

A two-way ANOVA with repeated measure on ball mass and ball velocity was performed separately for each dependent variable (time-to-contact (Tc) at movement initiation time, maximum linear velocity of the bat and amplitude of the bat's displacement).

Results

The analysis of variance on maximum movement velocity showed a significant main effect of both factors, ball mass and ball velocity [mass: $F(2,24) = 9.25$; $p < .001$; velocity: $F(2,24) = 13.76$; $p < .001$]. The maximum movement velocity increased with the increase of ball mass and ball velocity. The interaction between mass and velocity was found significant [$F(4,48) = 4.02$; $p < .01$], with movement velocity increasing with both ball mass and ball velocity.

The analysis of variance on movement amplitude showed that the main effects of mass and velocity were significant as well as their interaction [mass: $F(2,24) = 11.29$; $p < .0001$; velocity: $F(2,24) = 4.68$; $p < .05$; mass x velocity: $F(4,48) = 2.96$; $p < .05$]. Amplitude increased with the increase of mass and velocity.

Tc at initiation time showed different effects. Ball velocity had a significant main effect [$F(2,24) = 8.18$; $p < .01$]: Tc decreased with the increase of ball velocity. However, ball mass and the interaction mass x velocity were not found to have a significant effect on Tc.

Discussion

The results of movement velocity and movement amplitude showed that the mass of the oncoming object and its momentum are taken into account in the control of the interceptive action. However, the absence of effect of ball mass on Tc at initiation time suggests that the timing of the movement is not linked with this property of the object to intercept. The effect of ball velocity on Tc at initiation time reproduces the results already reported elsewhere (e.g., Li & Laurent, 1995). The perception of ball's mass before performing the action and the action parameters controlled to perform the action will be discussed successively.

In the experiment reported here, the mass and the momentum of the approaching ball could not be directly perceived by the subjects through an interaction phenomena such as a collision (Runeson & Frykholm, 1983). The present study didn't address the perception of such mass and momentum, but merely the effect of an anticipated mass on an interceptive behavior. However, the mass of the object could be perceived via a dynamic touch of the ball (see Turvey, 1996) before each trial and via the instructions given to the subject. The data showed that different balls have elicited different behaviors. This suggests that information specified the affordance for each different experimental condition. Further work, addressing in particular the use of multimodal information, i.e., visual and haptic, in a nested event is necessary.

Three main movement variables are available to the actor to perform successfully the interceptive action, i.e., amplitude, velocity and timing. Data presented here suggest that these three variables vary with approach velocity. This does not support the data reported by Li and Laurent (1995) who found that in a hitting and avoiding task amplitude was kept constant when Tc and movement velocity vary with approach velocity. These three parameters of the movements are linked, and only an adequate coordination of them in view of the characteristics of the approaching object can lead to successful behavior. The challenge is now to understand how these degrees of freedom are coordinated to perform a successful interceptive action when the dynamic of the task is modified.

Acknowledgments. This study was conducted while the author was at the Manchester Metropolitan University, UK. Some of these results have been presented at the fourth European Workshop on Ecological Psychology.

References

Li, F-X, & Laurent, M. (1995). Intensity coupling in interceptive tasks. In B. G. Bardy, R. J. Bootsma, & Y. Guiard (Eds.), *Studies in perception and action III* (pp. 191-194). Mahwah: Lawrence Erlbaum Associates.

Stoffregen, T. A., Henderson C. W., & Sasaki, M. (1995). Varying the tau-margin. In B. G. Bardy, R. J. Bootsma, & Y. Guiard (Eds.), *Studies in perception and action III* (pp. 199-202). Mahwah: Lawrence Erlbaum Associates.

Runeson, S., & Frykholm, G. (1983). Kinematic specification of dynamics as an informational basis for person-and-action perception: Expectation, gender recognition, and deceptive intention. *Journal of Experimental Psychology: General, 112,* 585-615.

Turvey, M. T. (1996). Dynamic touch. *American Psychologist, 51,* 1134-1152.

Studies in Perception and Action IV
M. A. Schmuckler & J. M. Kennedy (Eds.)
© *1997 Lawrence Erlbaum Associates, Inc.*

The Active Torque-Angle Relation During Arm Motion Shows Linearity Even With Changes In The External Load

Paola Cesari & Takako Shiratori

Department of Kinesiology, Pennsylvania State University,
State College, PA, U.S.A.

"Is it possible to have only one command from the brain in order to adjust a voluntary single joint movement in the presence of unexpected external perturbation?" Equilibrium Point Hypothesis (Feldman, 1980; Latash, 1993, 1994) proposes that this could be the case. According to this hypothesis, a linear relation between angle and torque is to be expected if a subject is asked to occupy a position against a load and "not to intervene voluntarily" when the load is changed. On the contrary, under the instruction "when you feel a perturbation, correct the motion" linearity was lost and the apparent joint stiffness increased by 50% to 250%.

The objective of this study was to analyze the relationship between active joint torque and angle during voluntary movement. Here we consider elbow extension in a sagital plane in a single joint targeted movement. The results indicate such a linear relation during voluntary motion.

Method

Two neurologically-healthy women volunteers participated in the study. Both the subjects were right-handed.

Five springs with different stiffness (0.037 Nm; 0.057 Nm; 0.127 Nm; 0.227 Nm; 0.393 Nm, same length) were used for this experiment. A bench with a rigid back support was used to seat the subjects. The subjects were asked to be seated comfortably with their back against the back support. Subject was then asked to grab on to a tennis ball which was attached to the spring with their right hand. The task was to reach with the tennis ball to a final position target which was placed at 80% of the upper-limb length at the shoulder height.

Kinematics data were collected from an optoelectric system (MacReflex). Reflective markers were attached to the right shoulder, elbow, and wrist joints. A trigger was implemented which was released at the instant of the initiation of the movement (time 0). The data was collected for 1.5 seconds for each trial at a sampling rate of 60 Hz.

Before collecting data, the subject was asked to perform 10 practice trials with only one spring (with stiffness 0.127 Nm) in order to achieve a consistent time profile in an attempt to fix a voluntary motor command. The instruction was given "at a comfortable speed, go from initial position to the final position without correcting your movement". After practice, data was collected using all springs. In order to give subjects an unexpected perturbation, the springs were changed in a random order for each trial. The instruction was as same as practice session. The task consisted of 4 blocks of 6 trials. After each block of trials, the subjects were asked to practice 4 times with the standard spring. Individual trials from the experiment were aligned in time to an origin (t_0). The method of alignment was kept the same within all trials. We consider data from the first frame to the 30th. Each frame correspond to a 0.016 (s) so that the time of the motion analyzed for each trials was from t = 0 to t = 400 ms. We decided to consider this specific range of time of the motion because we supposed that after 400 ms the subjects were not able to respect the instruction "do not intervene". We consider the torque as the sum of the "External Torque" (the "stiffness" of each spring) and the "Inertial Torque". By having the Angles and the Total Torque at each frame and for each trial we plotted the one against the other *by selecting each time a specific frame in time.*

Results and Conclusions

We found that between 300 ms and 400 ms after the initiation of the motion, there is a linear relationship between active torque and angles. This relationship is demonstrated for both subjects in each trial under all of the five different external perturbations. The linearity could be an indication of a general motor command from the brain, and the details of the motion (how to behave consistently in the presence of different external unexpected perturbation) are taken into account by the distal components, which may include the reflexes and the elastic components of the muscles.

References

Feldman, A. G. (1980) Superposition of motor programs. II. Rapid flexion of forearm in man. *Neuroscience, 5*, 91-95.

Latach, M. L. (1993). *Control of human movement.* Champaign, IL: Human Kinetics Publishers.

Latash, M. L. (1994). Reconstruction of equilibrium trajectories and joint stiffness patterns during single-joint voluntary movements under different instruction. *Biological Cybernetics, 71*, 441-450.

Studies in Perception and Action IV
M. A. Schmuckler & J. M. Kennedy (Eds.)
© *1997 Lawrence Erlbaum Associates, Inc.*

The Adiabatic Transformation Hypothesis In A Ball-Bouncing Task

B. Pavis[1], M. Broderick[1,2], & K. Newell[2]

[1] Cognitive and Behavioral Neuroscience Group, Poitiers University, France
[2] Department of Kinesiology, Pennsylvania State University, U.S.A.

Kugler and Turvey (1987; Kugler et al., 1990; Turvey et al., 1996) are concerned with establishing the lawful energy flow processes involved in assembling periodic behavior in a nonconservative biological system. They argue that the relation between an oscillating system's average kinetic energy and its frequency are addressed by Ehrenfest's general theorem, which "applies to all classes of conditionally periodic systems subject to changes that satisfy the criteria of adiabatic transformations" (1987, p. 311). An oscillating system that begins with a certain frequency whose parameters vary infinitely slowly, but settle at new levels at which they remain constant, will exhibit a new frequency. For such a system, Kugler and Turvey (1987, p. 311) render this statement of Ehrenfest's theorem: "The average kinetic energy of the system increases in the same proportion as the frequency under an adiabatic transformation." We offer a slightly different interpretation, more in line with Turvey et al. (1996) that Ehrenfest's theorem is concerned simply with the proportional relationship between kinetic energy and frequency; that is, the two need not be proportionally increasing. In any case, if the frequencies of such a system are f_0 and f_0', respectively, and the average kinetic energies of the first oscillation and the second are denoted E_0 and E_0', respectively, then

$$H = \frac{E_0}{f_0} = \frac{E_0'}{f_0'} \tag{1}$$

Now, the thermodynamic processes of an active biological system are generally not so slow. Kugler and Turvey's insight is that Ehrenfest's theorem can be extended to "non-rate-limited transformations and nonconservative systems" (p. 312). An example is an ice skater who begins a spin with arms extended and then brings them to the body, a case in which the skater increases the frequency of rotation while momentum is conserved. The amount of energy the skater derives internally from his body is directly proportional to his frequency of rotation. In this paper we investigate another non-conservative system, a person bouncing a ball, and examine the explanatory power of Ehrenfest's theorem with respect to this particular human behavior.

Method

Three adult subjects were analyzed. The subjects were instructed to bounce a regulation basketball in one place if possible, at their own preferred pace, and with their dominant hand. They stood on the floor and successively on the first five rungs of a step ladder with 22 cm height difference between each rung. The subjects were videotaped, and the videotapes were digitized with Video-Digit System. Four cycles of bouncing for each subject under each step condition were digitized.

Results and Discussion

The ball falling from a particular height will bounce up, but to a lesser height, because its coefficient of restitution is less than 1. The hand adds an escapement to keep the ball bouncing up to the same height, whose value can be derived from the kinetic energy theorem. Knowing the height of the subsequent bounce we could deduce the velocity of the ball just after its rebound. With the ball's mass of 0.5 kg and its coefficient of restitution at 0.66 ± 0.02 for the speeds measured, we could then deduce the maximum ball velocity and thus the energy added by the hand ($KE_{escapement}$) per cycle using

$$mgh_2 - \tfrac{1}{2}mv_{max}^2 = KE_{escapement} \qquad (2)$$

where h_2 = apex after rebound, and v_{max} = velocity of the ball just before striking the ground.

Figure 1A-C shows the relation between energy ($KE_{escapement}$) and frequency for the 3 subjects. The linear look of the graph suggests the proportional relationship that Kugler and Turvey propose for other systems, such as locomotion, and may satisfy the criteria for consideration as an adiabatic invariant (*H*). As in a locomotory system, where "the relevant quantities for expressing adiabatic invariance are hypothesized to be the summed changes in segmental kinetic energy $\Delta E_k s^{-1}$ and speed v " (Turvey et al., 1996), in the ball-bouncing system we have *KE* per cycle increasing with increase in ball velocity (Figure 1D-F), while the frequency of the global rebound decreases with increasing velocity of the ball.

Gravitational force and ball elasticity make a conservative engine using mechanical energy (E_m) that is susceptible to the nonconservative perturbation properties of the ball's contact with the floor and air resistance. These perturbations gradually dissipate the system's energy until the ball stops bouncing. Conservative potential energy, $m \bullet g \bullet (h_{apex} - h_{release})$, is not sufficient to compensate for the lost energy at the rebound from the floor. When the ball is bounced over and over to the same height, the inertial force of the hand is a nonconservative engine that generates kinetic energy (E_t) equal to that lost by the ball to nonconservative forces each cycle. The degradation process E_t is the energy produced during the contact between the ball and

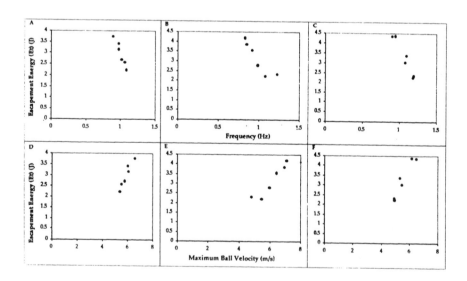

Figure 1. A-C. Relation between energy ($KE_{escapement}$) and frequency for individual subjects.   D-F. Relation between energy ($KE_{escapement}$) and maximum velocity for individual subjects.

hand from the ball's apex position H_{apex} and the ball release position $H_{release}$, where

$$E_t = E_m - (m \bullet g \bullet [H_{apex} - H_{release}]) \qquad (3)$$

The ball-hand system can be interpreted by the ratio of E_m to E_t, called $Q = \dfrac{E_m}{E_t}$. In the ball-hand system of the 3 subjects we studied, this ratio ranged from 1.2 to 1.9 (see Figure 2), indicating that the system is dominated by reversible (conservative) forces but that its limit-cycle stability depends heavily on the irreversible (nonconservative) forces introduced by the hand. This ratio of $Q > 1$, where the hand economizes the energy it must inject, has a price: the system is less stable to perturbations arising from any source. Under stress, say in a basketball game, we might expect to see the Q value diminish. Kugler and Turvey (1987) argue that in a biomechanical workspace the intersection of the $Q = 1$ trajectory and the adiabatic invariant H trajectory is a

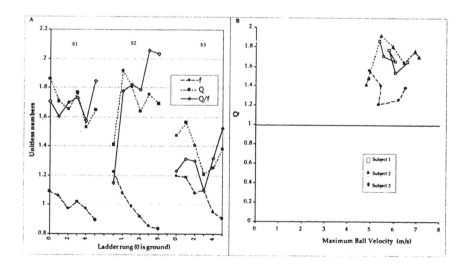

Figure 2. A. Frequency, Q value, and ratio of Q to frequency for each subject vs. ladder rung. Frequency decreases as step number increases. B. Maximum Ball Velocity vs. Q for each subject.

global attractor for oscillatory trajectories. Turvey et al. (1996) showed, for example, that the boundary between walking and running occurs at $Q = 1$. We present in Figure 2B a plot of maximum ball velocity (V_{max}) vs. Q. Our range of task conditions is not yet sufficiently rich to examine this relation properly.

Concluding Remarks

The primary motivation of this paper was the observation of the proportional relationship of kinetic energy and ball speed in ball bouncing which seemed parallel to the proportional relationship of metabolic cost and speed observed in walking and running (Turvey et al. 1996). From considerations that suggest a generalization of the notions of adiabatic transformability and adiabatic invariance in rhythmic movements, we hypothesized that adiabatic invariance describes functioning of the ball-bouncing control process. The results suggest an invariant relation that follows from Kugler and Turvey's insights regarding the nonconservative instantiation of Ehrenfest's adiabatic theorem. The coupled oscillations between ball and hand in our limited task range appear to be assembled in the domain $Q > 1$ like coupled oscillations in running. In this range, the relative constancy (except Subject 2) of the ratio $\dfrac{Q}{f}$ indicates that this invariant may be used to control the bouncing. On the other hand, Subject 2, the most skilled of the subjects, exhibits indications of increase in this ratio as velocity increases (frequency decreases). We are currently investigating further the $V_{max} \times Q$ coordinate space for a meaningful description of the task and the relation of skill level to it.

References

Kugler, P. N., & Turvey, M. T. (1987). *Information, natural law, and the self-assembly of rhythmic movement*. Hillsdale, NJ: Erlbaum.

Kugler, P. N., & Turvey, M. T., Schmidt, R. C., & Rosenblum, L. D. (1990). Investigating a nonconservative invariant of motion in coordinated rhythmic movements. *Ecological Psychology, 2*, 151-189.

Turvey, M. T., Holt, K., Obusek, J., Salo, A., & Kugler, P. N. (1996). Adiabatic transformability hypothesis of human locomotion. *Biological Cybernetics, 74*, 107-115.

Studies in Perception and Action IV
M. A. Schmuckler & J. M. Kennedy (Eds.)
© *1997 Lawrence Erlbaum Associates, Inc.*

Active Degrees Of Freedom Of Oscillatory Hand Movements

Michael A. Riley & Suvobrata Mitra

CESPA, University of Connecticut, Storrs, CT, U.S.A.

Recent developments in nonlinear time series analysis (Abarbanel, 1996) allow determination of the number of active degrees of freedom (ADFs), the number of first-order, autonomous, differential equations, associated with a time series. The number of ADFs is important in understanding the nature of the system producing the oscillations. Determination of the number of ADFs is also important in understanding how the high-dimensional complexity of the motor apparatus is rendered low-dimensional, and, therefore, controllable (Bernstein, 1967). It has been proposed that a reduction of dimensionality occurs by the formation of coordinative structures (Turvey, Shaw, & Mace, 1978). A coordinative structure is a group of muscles constrained to act as a single functional unit and whose components are internally regulated so as to change relatedly.

The present experiment was conducted to determine the number of ADFs for a simple rhythmic movement, namely, oscillation of the hand about the wrist. The limit-cycle, a popular model of rhythmic movement (e.g., Haken, Kelso, & Bunz, 1985; Kay, Kelso, Saltzman, & Schöner, 1987), is a second-order system (two ADFs); do observed movements have the same dynamical substructure as limit cycles? The wrist-pendulum paradigm (Kugler & Turvey, 1987) was used to address whether or not the number of ADFs changes if inertial properties of the oscillated unit differ. We used two pendulum systems differing in rotational inertia, one long and heavy and one short and light. Previous research (Beek, Schmidt, Morris, Sim, & Turvey, 1995) has revealed differences between the underlying dynamics (e.g., stiffness and friction terms) of such systems.

Method

Five RH students oscillated an aluminum pendulum (with a wood handle) about the wrist for 10 trials (5 with a 66 cm long pendulum with a 300 g added mass, 5 with a 36 cm pendulum with no added mass) lasting 90 s each. Data were collected with a sonic digitizer.

The analysis (Abarbanel, 1996) involves phase space reconstruction. Time-delayed copies of the original time series were added as independent coordinates of the reconstructed space; time delays were chosen using the average mutual information function. Dimensionality of the reconstructed phase space was determined using global false nearest neighbors (adding independent dimensions until "neighborliness" of two points [proximity in reconstructed phase space due to projection of a higher dimensional system onto the single axis of the measured variable] is removed). The number of ADFs are obtained using local false nearest neighbors analysis. Predictions by a local linear rule of the evolution of different-sized neighborhoods of points around the reconstructed attractor are made for different dimensions of the attractor. The number of ADFs is determined as the dimension at which quality of predictions becomes independent of neighborhood size and dimension. This was performed for each trial, and obtained values were averaged across trials. An ANOVA was conducted on percent bad predictions (% bad) of the linear rule with neighborhood size, dimension, and pendulum as independent factors. ADFs are obtained using simple effects analyses to determine when independence of % bad from neighborhood size and dimension occurs.

Results

All main effects were significant, as were pendulum by dimension and neighborhood size by dimension interactions ($p < .001$). The 3-way interaction was significant ($p < .05$). The number of ADFs was determined for each pendulum. Figure 1 (top) displays the significant neighborhood size by dimension interaction ($p < .001$) for the 36 cm pendulum. Statistical independence of neighborhood size and dimension was achieved by dimension 4 (4 ADFs). Figure 1 (bottom) displays the same interaction ($p < .001$) for the 66 cm system. For it, there are 3 ADFs.

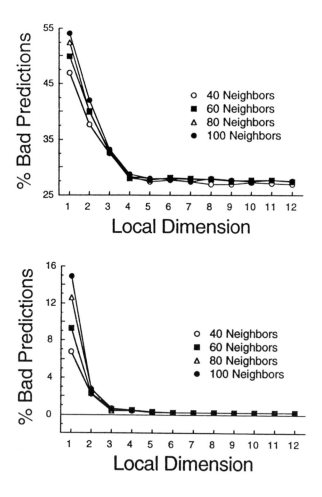

Figure 1. Number of ADFs is the local dimension at which the neighborhood size points cluster and the line slopes flatten. The 36 cm system has 4 ADFs (top). The 66 cm system has 3 ADFs (bottom).

Discussion

Results suggest that limit cycles (2 ADFs) may be too simple to account for rhythmic hand movements. The findings of Beek et al. (1995) of different dynamical compositions of systems which differ in rotational inertia were confirmed in the present context of ADFs. Results also highlight Bernstein's (1967) insight that the movement system must tailor force production to available external forces. There were fewer ADFs for the 66 cm pendulum than for the 36 cm pendulum. For the 66 cm pendulum, a stronger gravitational component is present; this may reduce the need for the injection of energy into the system by the organism.

Acknowledgments. This research was supported by NSF Grant SBR 94-22650. Thanks to Bruce Kay, Richard C. Schmidt, Elliot Saltzman, Henry Abarbanel, and Dave Collins.

References

Abarbanel, H. D. I. (1996). The analysis of observed chaotic data. New York: Springer.

Beek, P. J., Schmidt, R. C., Morris, A. W., Sim, M-Y., & Turvey, M. T. (1995). Linear and nonlinear stiffness and friction in biological rhythmic movements. *Biological Cybernetics, 73,* 499-507.

Bernstein, N. (1967). *Coordination and regulation of movements.* New York: Pergamon.

Haken, H., Kelso, J. A. S., & Bunz, H. (1985). A theoretical model of phase transitions in human hand movements. *Biological Cybernetics, 51,* 347-356.

Kay, B. A., Kelso, J. A. S., Saltzman, E. L., & Schöner, G. (1987). Space-time behavior of single and bimanual rhythmic movements: Data and limit cycle model. *Journal of Experimental Psychology: Human Perception and Performance, 13,* 178-192 .

Kugler, P. N., & Turvey, M. T. (1987). *Information, natural law, and the self-assembly of rhythmic movement.* Hillsdale, NJ: Erlbaum.

Turvey, M. T., Shaw, R. E., & Mace, W. (1978). Issues in the theory of action: Degrees of freedom, coordinative structures, and coalitions. In J. Requin (Ed.), *Attention and performance VII* (pp. 557-595). Hillsdale, NJ: Lawrence Erlbaum Associates.

Studies in Perception and Action IV
M. A. Schmuckler & J. M. Kennedy (Eds.)
© *1997 Lawrence Erlbaum Associates, Inc.*

Inertial Tensor Manipulations Of Length Perception
By Static Holding

Matthew Stroop[1] & Paula Fitzpatrick[2]

[1] CESPA, University of Connecticut, Storrs, CT, U.S.A.
[2] Department of Psychology, Assumption College, Worchester, MA, U.S.A.

Nonvisible perception of the lengths of freely wielded rods is a function of the inertia tensor. Both the major (I_1) and minor (I_3) eigenvalues tend to contribute (Fitzpatrick, Carello, & Turvey, 1994). An important question is whether the inertia tensor might similarly influence length perception under conditions of minimal movement—when a rod is simply held and the only movement is tremor. Recent research on static holding offered in support of a hypothesis that weight perception modulates length perception (Lederman, Ganeshan, & Ellis, 1996) can be interpreted in tensorial terms. Two experiments assessed the weight-percept and the inertia tensor hypotheses.

Experiment 1

Five pairs of rods with attached metal rings were used. The mass and position of the attachment equated the weight and static moment but distinguished rotational inertia within a pair. All quantities increased across rod pairs. Rods were held as still as possible; length was indicated by absolute magnitude production.

Mean perceived length varied systematically with actual length, $r^2(9) = .92$ ($p < .0001$), ranging from 38 to 78 cm for actual lengths from 38 to 107 cm (Figure 1). Mean perceived length increased as a function of pair, $F(4,32) = 126.34$, $MSE = 33.33$, $p < .0001$, and member within each pair, $F(1,8) = 13.17$, $MSE = 14.46$, $p < .01$. The interaction was not significant, $F(4,32) < 1$. Both effects indicate that perceived length increases with increases in I_1.

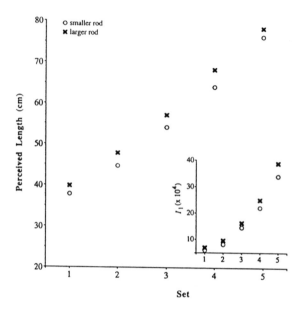

Figure 1. Mean perceived length as a function of static moment pair. Circles and Xs indicate smaller and larger values of I_1, respectively. Insert: I_1 (x 10^4) as a function of static moment pair.

The simple regression in logarithmic coordinates of mean perceived length on I_1 yielded $r^2(9) = .99$ ($p < .0001$). The contribution of I_3 was not significant in the multiple regression, perhaps due to the limited range of values possible with these rod-shaped objects (see Carello, Flascher, Fitzpatrick, & Turvey, in press).

A difference in rotational inertia between two rods that were otherwise identical in weight, static moment, gravitational torque, and diameter resulted in a corresponding difference in the perception of their lengths under conditions of minimal movement (static holding). This result contradicts the weight-percept model which predicted no difference in perceived length for members of a pair. Because the contribution of I_3 was not apparent, however, a second experiment increased the variation of that eigenvalue.

A   B

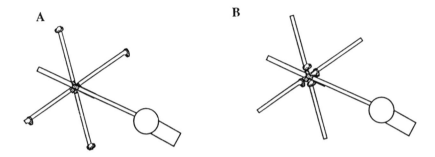

Figure 2. Tensor objects held in the hand. I_3 is larger for the left object than for the right object.

Experiment 2

So-called "tensor objects" (Figure 2) do not vary in length, width, diameter at the point of grasp, or mass. With these tubular constructions, the inertia tensor was controlled systematically through the manipulation of the mass and position of attached metal rings and the position of the crossbar along the central (grasped) tube.

Ten tensor objects were configured such that for two values of I_1 (approximately 17 and 59, both multiplied by 10^4 g cm^2), there were approximately five values of I_3 (17, 9, 5, 3, and 2, all multiplied by 10^4 g cm^2). Objects were held as still as possible; length was indicated by absolute magnitude production.

An $I_1 \times I_3$ ANOVA was conducted. There was a main effect of I_1, $F(1,14) = 71.34$, $MSE = 37.68$, $p < .0001$); the larger I_1 produced larger length reports than the smaller I_1. There was also a main effect of I_3, $F(4,56) = 8.54$, $MSE = 2.03$, $p < .0001$; perceived length decreased from the largest to the smallest I_3. Their interaction was also significant, $F(4,56) = 2.72$, $MSE = 2.11$, $p < .05$), with the rate of decline from the largest to the smallest I_3 greater for the smaller I_1 than for the larger I_1.

Conclusion

The major conclusion from the present research is the dependence of nonvisual length perception by static holding on the eigenvalues of the inertia tensor. That the inertia tensor constrains nonvisual length perception by static holding as well as by wielding suggests that bulk muscle requires relatively little deformation in order to register the invariant of rotational dynamics about a fixed point. There will always be some degree of motion of an object held in the manner of objects in the present experiments and that of Lederman et al. (1996), however small and, apparently, small (unintended) motions are sufficient to reveal the rotational invariant (Carello, Santana, & Burton, 1996).

Acknowledgments. The research reported here was supported by Grant SBR 93-09371 from the National Science Foundation.

References

Carello, C., Fitzpatrick, P., Flascher, I., & Turvey, M. T. (in press). Inertial eigenvalues, rod density, and rod diameter in length perception by dynamic touch. *Perception & Psychophysics.*

Carello, C., Santana, M-V., & Burton, G. (1996). Selective perception by dynamic touch. *Perception & Psychophysics, 58,* 1177-1190.

Fitzpatrick, P., Carello, C., & Turvey, M. T. (1994). Eigenvalues of the inertia tensor and exteroception by the "muscular sense." *Neuroscience, 60,* 551-568.

Lederman, S. J., Ganeshan, S. R., & Ellis, R. E. (1996). Effortful touch with minimal movement: Revisited. *Journal of Experimental Psychology: Human Perception and Performance, 4,* 851-868.

Studies in Perception and Action IV
M. A. Schmuckler & J. M. Kennedy (Eds.)
© *1997 Lawrence Erlbaum Associates, Inc.*

Minimal Movement And Selective Perception
By Dynamic Touch

Marie-Vee Santana

CESPA, University of Connecticut, Storrs, CT, U.S.A.

Under instructions to hold a rod as still as possible, experimental participants are able to selectively perceive the length of the whole rod or of the rod portion in front of the hand. This ability depends on the inertia tensor, I_{ij} (see Turvey & Carello, 1995, for a review). I_{ij} is a quantification of the rod's resistance to rotational acceleration in different directions. Had participants been completely successful in following the instructions to be immobile, the rotational components should not have been available. Complete immobility is unlikely because high-frequency impulses (or minimal movement) are needed in order to produce prolonged contractions. Under conditions typical for static holding experiments, minimal movement has been detected (Carello, Santana, & Burton, 1996). It has not yet been related systematically to intentional differences in perception. The present experiments explore the relationship of minimal movement to attentional differences in perception by dynamic touch. In particular, do systematic differences in minimal movement reflect differences apparent in selectively perceiving partial or whole length while holding rods as still as possible? In addition, is simply holding a rod (no perceptual intention involved) different from holding a rod with a purpose (attending to one or more of its parts)?

In two experiments, participants were instructed to hold rods as still as possible. The position of the rod's tip was tracked during each 30 s trial. There were three different rod lengths–30, 50, and 90 cm–and two positions of an attached weight–¼ L and ¾ L. All rods were held at the center of mass (CM). In Experiment 1, participants had to make two perceptual reports: whole and partial length (where partial length was defined as the length from the point of grasp to the forward tip of the rod). In Experiment 2, participants had three tasks: simply holding the rod still (no report), whole length report, and partial length report. In both experiments, the results of the perceptual data conformed to previous findings (e.g., Carello, Santana, & Burton, 1996).

Briefly, whole length was a function of I_{xx} while partial length was a function of both I_{xx} and I_{yz}.

In Experiment 1, time series data were averaged across haptic-perceptual conditions and analyzed using a 3 (length) x 2 (attachment position) x 2 (report) ANOVA. The slope of the Power-Frequency functions increased with actual length for all three perceived lengths showing greater power in the lower frequencies ($p < .0001$). Fluctuations tended to be greater for the ¼ L mass position than for the ¾ L mass position ($p < .08$). Of greater importance is the fact that tremor tended to be greater for the whole-length intention than for the partial-length intention ($p < .075$).

In Experiment 2, time series data were also averaged across haptic perceptual conditions and analyzed using a 3 (length) x 2 (attachment position) x 3 (report) ANOVA. The slope of the Power-Frequency functions increased with actual length for all three perceived lengths showing greater power in the lower frequencies ($p < .0001$) as shown on Figure 1A. Although no differences

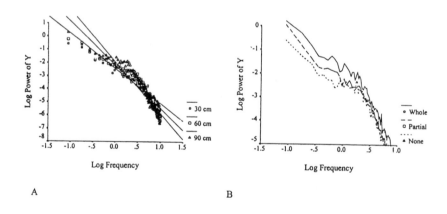

A   B

Figure 1. (a) Power-Frequency function shows slope increases with length. (b) Shows the Power-Frequency functions are qualitatively distinct for the three perceptual reports.

were found due to mass position, Figure 1B shows a highly significant main effect of report ($p < .001$). Apparently, differences in minimal movement depend on whether participants intend to simply hold the rods (no intention) or whether they intend to perceive something about them.

It has been argued that tremor-like movement is an important source of exploratory behavior (e.g., Riccio, 1993). The structure of tremor has been shown to reflect the fundamental rhythmic synergies of the body. For example, during an effort to maintain a constant posture of the finger, involuntary fluctuations reflect periodicities due to respiration, cardiac pulse, and extensor muscle activity (Padsha & Stein, 1973). The fluctuations that accompany holding rods verify this kind of reliable structure: As in the preliminary analysis reported in Carello et al. (1996) for one participant, the periodicity due to cardiac pulse is apparent for every rod. Despite the physical causes of this tremor-like behavior, its perceptual consequences are worth considering. The human organism's ability to selectively attend to different portions of a single object has been demonstrated over a variety of haptic tasks, as well as visual and acoustic ones. However, the question of how it is that the organism picks-up the relevant information about the held object is still unanswered. Tremor is offered here as a possibility.

Acknowledgments: This research was supported by NSF Grant SBR 93-09371 and SBR 94-22650. We gratefully thank Joy Mitra, Mike Riley, and Richard Schmidt for their invaluable help on the tremor analyses.

References

Carello, C., Santana, M-V., & Burton, G. (1996). Selective perception by dynamic touch. *Perception & Psychophysics, 58(8)*, 117-1190.

Padsha, J. M., & Stein, R. B. (1973). The bases of tremor during a maintained posture. In R. B. Stein Pearson, R. S., Smith, & J. B. Redford (Eds.), *Control of posture and locomotion* (pp. 415-419). New York: Plenum.

Riccio, G. E. (1993). Information in movement variability about the qualitative dynamics of posture and orientation. In K. M. Newell & D. M. Corcos (Eds.), *Variability and motor control*. Champaign, IL: Human Kinetics Publishers.

Turvey, M. T., & Carello, C. (1995). Dynamic touch. In W. Epstein & S. Rogers (Eds.), *Handbook of perception and cognition: V. Perception of space and motion* (pp. 401-490). San Diego, CA: Academic Press.

Section III: *Action*

III.C: *Posture and Locomotion*

Studies in Perception and Action IV
M. A. Schmuckler & J. M. Kennedy (Eds.)
© 1997 Lawrence Erlbaum Associates, Inc.

The Emergence Of Postural Coordination Modes

Benoît G. Bardy, Ludovic Marin, & Reinoud J. Bootsma

UMR Mouvement & Perception, University of the Mediterranean,
Faculty of Sport Sciences, Marseille, France

As for any other activity, the maintenance of human bi-pedal posture implies that the numerous degrees of freedom involved must be coordinated. According to the neuromuscular approach, advocated by Nashner and collaborators (e.g., Nashner & McCollum, 1985), the maintenance of stance relies on two preferred postural modes of coordination: In the *ankle mode*, the position of the center of mass (*Cm*) is adjusted through rotation of the body about the ankles without motion of the hips; In the *hip mode*, the *Cm* is maintained above the feet by rotating the trunk relative to the legs (i.e., by bending at the hips). In this approach, segmental coordination is thought to be a consequence of more basic patterns of coordination among muscles, which are, in turn, dependent upon neural computations. As an alternative, we propose a topological analysis of multi-segment postural coordination (Bardy et al., 1997; Marin, this volume). We suggest that stance is maintained through collective functional units of action that emerge in a self-organizing fashion from the interaction between task-based, body-based, and environment-based constraints (e.g., Riccio & Stoffregen, 1988). In two experiments, we manipulated body-based (the height of the center of mass, *Hc*; and the effective length of the feet, *FLe*) and task-based (the required amplitude of head movement, *Ah*) constraints and measured the relative phase between ankle and hip joints ($\phi h\text{-}a$) during a supra-postural head tracking task. Under the assumption that $\phi h\text{-}a$ is a collective variable suitable for describing hip-ankle coordination modes, we predicted that the coordination modes to be observed would reveal the presence of only a few attractive values of $\phi h\text{-}a$ (notably 0° in-phase and 180° anti-phase) and that the interaction between *Hc*, *Fle*, and *Ah* would determine the coordination mode adopted in each particular condition.

Experiment 1

Method

Participants ($N = 12$) stood barefooted on the ground, 1.50 m from a screen and were asked to intentionally follow with the head the oscillations of a simulated object (a 51 cm H x 56 cm V frontal square oscillating in depth). Displays were generated on a INDY 4600 XZ Silicon Graphics workstation and presented on a rear-projection screen (3.00 m H x 2.25 m V) using an ELECTROHOME 7500 video projector. Three *Hc* conditions (High, Medium, Low) were crossed with four *Ah* conditions (5, 14, 18, 35 cm). *Hc* was varied by attaching a 10 kg mass either at the neck or knee level, thus increasing or decreasing the height of *Cm*. For each trial, the display was presented for 80 s to allow the participant to achieve a steady-state and data were collected over the next 40 s (approximately 8 oscillation cycles). The hip-ankle relative phase $\phi h\text{-}a$ was obtained for each trial by subtracting the ankle phase from the hip phase.

Results

Two postural states emerged consistently from the data (Figure 1): 0° (in-phase coordination) and 180° (anti-phase coordination). In each condition, mean $\phi h\text{-}a$ was found to be significantly clustered around a mean (Raleigh test, $p < .05$), and the 95% confidence interval for $\phi h\text{-}a$ contained either the 0° or 180° phase. While $\phi h\text{-}a$ switched from in-phase to anti-phase with increasing *Ah*, the amplitude at which this occurred varied as a function of *Hc*: The higher the *Cm*, the earlier $\phi h\text{-}a$ changed from 0° to 180°.

Experiment 2

We next sought to extend this postural coordination analysis by investigating the combined effects of *Fle* and *Ah* on $\phi h\text{-}a$.

Method

The subjects and method employed were the same as in Experiment 1, except that the three *Cm* heights were replaced by three *Fle* conditions. The

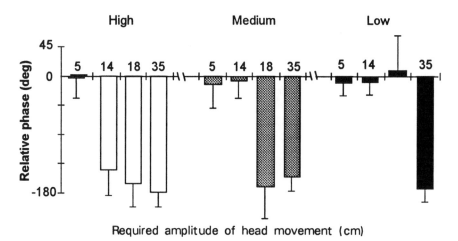

Figure 1. Hip-ankle relative phase in Experiment 1 as a function of *Ah* and *Hc* conditions.

Normal Feet condition (NF) was identical to the Medium *Cm* condition of Experiment 1. In the *Long Feet* (LF) condition, the participants' effective foot length was increased by having them wear a pair of shoes firmly attached to two wooden boards (84 cm long by 20 cm wide by 2 cm thick). In the *Short Feet* (SF) condition, these same shoes were attached to a beam (10 cm L by 40 W by 10 H) positioned parallel to the screen. These three *Fle* conditions were crossed with the four *Ah* of Experiment 1.

Results

Again, two states emerged from the data (Figure 2), reflecting in-phase and anti-phase coordination modes. In each condition, mean $\phi h\text{-}a$ was found to be significantly clustered around a mean (Raleigh test, $p < .05$), and the 95% confidence interval for $\phi h\text{-}a$ contained either the 0° or 180° phase. Relative to the NF condition, the long feet condition gave rise to a transition from in-phase to anti-phase coordination occurring for a smaller amplitude of head movement. For the small feet condition, subjects adopted the anti-phase mode already for the smallest amplitude of head movement condition.

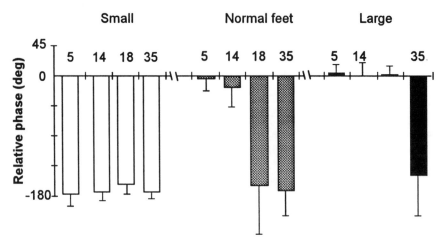

Figure 2. Hip-ankle relative phase in Experiment 2 as a function of *Ah* and *Fle* conditions.

Conclusion

In two experiments we examined the spontaneous emergence of multi-segment postural coordination under the influence of variations in body-based and task-based constraints. Despite a considerable range of variation of the parameters manipulated, we found that only two postural coordination patterns emerged, corresponding to in-phase and anti-phase motion between ankles and hips. These findings thus suggest that the persistent hypothesis that in the so-called ankle mode the human body would behave like an inverted pendulum with no (functional) movement around the hips (e.g., Nashner & McCollum, 1985) is not only ill-founded, but may also obscure the veritable nature of postural coordination. At the same time, they demonstrate the importance in analyzing the postural system (i) of investigating phase relations between joints, (ii) in sustained, periodic fore-aft body sway and (iii) during supra-postural tasks. Our results are consistent with a dynamical perspective on postural coordination, with a few stable states (0°, 180°) behaving as low-dimensional attractors in a high-dimensional postural space. Future research will analyze whether the observed postural state changes can be regarded as second-order phase transitions.

References

Nashner, L. M., & McCollum, G. (1985). The organization of human postural movements: A formal basis and experimental synthesis. *Behavioral and Brain Sciences, 8*, 135-172.

Bardy, B. G., Marin, L., Stoffregen, T. A., & Bootsma, R. J. (1997). *An emergent   approach of postural coordination modes.* Manuscript in preparation.

Marin, L. (1997). *Biomechanics as a (limited) constraint on postural coordination.* This volume.

Riccio, G. E., & Stoffregen, T. A. (1988). Affordances as constraints on the control of stance. *Human Movement Science, 7*, 265-300.

Studies in Perception and Action IV
M. A. Schmuckler & J. M. Kennedy (Eds.)
© *1997 Lawrence Erlbaum Associates, Inc.*

Biomechanics As A (Limited) Constraint On Postural Coordination

Ludovic Marin

UMR Mouvement & Perception, University of the Mediterranean,
Faculty of Sport Sciences, Marseille, France

Much of human behavior is dependent on the achievement and maintenance of bi-pedal posture. Due to the mechanical properties of the human body, the multiple degrees of freedom that compose the postural system need to be coordinated so as to promote functional control actions. Some analyses of the biomechanical factors that constrain postural modes of coordination (e.g., Horak & Nashner, 1986) have led to the conclusion of a direct correspondence between mechanical properties of the body or the supporting surface and postural modes of coordination (or *PCM*s, e.g., *ankle* and *hip* modes). Bardy, Marin and Bootsma (this volume) have proposed, however, that such a direct correspondence might not exist: The same PCM was observed when mechanical properties of the body were varied, and different PCMs were shown to emerge under mechanically constant conditions. Hence, how biomechanical factors constrain the emergence of specific PCMs remains an open question.

In this contribution, we propose a new way of investigating the biomechanical constraints on postural coordination, based on a topological analysis of the *stability region* for upright stance (cf. Riccio & Stoffregen, 1988). Traditionally, the feasible movements of body joints are described in a single dimensional space related to the (horizontal) position of the center of mass: The vertical projection of the *Cm* has to be kept within the base of support in order for the body to remain balanced. Here we examine in a two-dimensional state space the possible hip-ankle relationships that meet this criterion.

Figure 1 represents a simple biomechanical model of a two-linked inverted pendulum describing the configurations of the hips and the ankles during the achievement of stance.

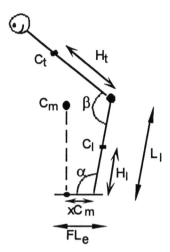

Figure 1. Biomechanics of hip-ankle configurations during stance (see text for details).

In the absence of external forces, (static) balance can be maintained if and only if xCm, i.e., the distance between the Cm projection and the ankle joint, is kept within the base of support (*Fle*). In static conditions, xCm only depends on the horizontal position of the center of mass Cm, and can be determined using the following equation:

$$xCm = (mtxCt + mlxCl) / (mt + ml) \tag{1}$$

where mt and ml are the trunk and leg masses, respectively, xCt the horizontal excursion of the center of mass of the trunk from the hip joint, xCl the horizontal excursion of the center of mass of the two legs from the ankle joint (see Figure 1). Centers of mass of the legs Cl and trunk Ct are:

$$xCt = - Htcos(\alpha+\beta) + Llcos\alpha \tag{2}$$

$$xCl = Hlcos\alpha \tag{3}$$

where α and β are ankle and hip angles, Ht the distance between the hip joint and xCt, Hl the distance between the ankle joint and xCl and Ll the length of the legs. Transforming Equation (1) using Equation (2) and Equation (3) yields, after simplification:

$$xCm = [(mlHl + mtLl)cos\alpha - mtHtcos(\alpha+\beta)] / (mt + ml) \qquad (4)$$

Equation 4 therefore describes the static location of the body center of mass for all combinations of ankle and hip angular positions. The stability region for upright stance can be obtained in the hip-ankle space by extracting the solutions of Equation (4) that meet with the criterion defined above. Figure 2 illustrates this stability region for a typical subject (*Ll* = 1 m; *Hl* = 0.55; *Ht* = 0.28 m; *ml* = 10.46 kg, *mt* = 44.07 kg; *FLe* = 0.27 m.

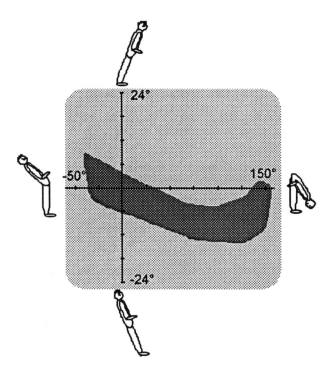

Figure 2. The calculated hip-ankle configuration space (in degrees) in the anterior-posterior plane for a typical subject (see text for details). Vertical and horizontal axles represent angular positions of the ankles and the hips, respectively. Angular positions have been arbitrary limited from -25° to +25° for the ankles, and from -50° to +150° for the hips. The dark area represents the stability region for upright stance.

Changing *Fle and Hc*

As indicated in Equation 4, the shape of the stability region is dependent on both the length of the feet, *Fle*, and the height of the body center of mass, *Hc*. Figure 3 illustrates the effects on the stability region of manipulating *Fle* (Figure 3A and 3B) and *Hc* (Figure 3C and 3D), consistent with the experimental manipulations of Bardy et al. (this volume). As evidenced, the width of the stability region and its orientation change sharply with changing body properties.

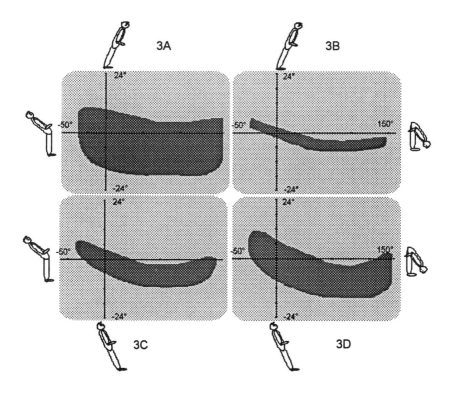

Figure 3. Effects of changing *Fle* and *Hc* on the stability region for stance. (3A): *Fle* = 84 cm; (3B): *Fle* = 10 cm; (3C): *Hc* = +5 cm (1.08 m); (3D): *Hc* = -9 cm (0.94 m).

Conclusion

The present analysis illustrates the role of biomechanical properties of the observer-environment system as a constraint on postural coordination. Biomechanical factors such as foot length or height of the center of mass can indeed shape the coordination dynamics (Beek, Peper, & Stegeman, 1995). However, within the stability region itself, an (in)finite number of hip-ankle coordination modes can still emerge, depending on non-biomechanical factors, such as intentional or informational constraints.

References

Bardy, B. G., Marin, L., & Bootsma, R. J. (1997). *The emergence of postural coordination modes*. This volume.

Beek, P. J., Peper, C. E., & Stegeman, D. F. (1995). Dynamical models of movement coordination. *Human Movement Science, 14*, 573-608.

Horak, F. B., & Nashner, L. M. (1986). Central programming of postural movements: Adaptation to altered support-surface surface configurations. *Journal of Neurophysiology, 55*, 1369-1381.

Riccio, G. E., & Stoffregen, T. A. (1988). Affordances as constraints on the control of stance. *Human Movement Science, 7*, 265-300.

Studies in Perception and Action IV
M. A. Schmuckler & J. M. Kennedy (Eds.)
© *1997 Lawrence Erlbaum Associates, Inc.*

Effects Of Postural Stability On Perception-Movement Coupling

Florent Fouque And Benoît G. Bardy

UMR Mouvement & Perception, University of the Mediterranean,
Faculty of Sport Sciences, Marseille, France

Over the last decade or so, it has been proposed that optical flow contains specific and non-equivocal information about the interaction between the observer and the environment. Moving rooms have been extensively used (e.g., Lishman & Lee, 1973) in this context. A typical result found in moving room experiments is that participants sway in phase with the room, a result showing the major role played by optical flow in the control of body sway.

The same optical flow pattern, however, can correspond to different physical realities. As a well-known example, a radial flow can specify that the observer is moving in his/her environment but also that the environment is moving around a (motionless) observer (as in a flight simulator). A theoretical consequence is that specificity between informational variables and physical reality only exists in intermodal relation between the senses (Stoffregen & Bardy, 1997). During stance, intermodal information about balance (as opposed to fall) is continuously specified by concordant optical, vestibular, and somato-sensory flows (Gibson, 1952). Hence, a working hypothesis is that postural control is more dependent on intermodal stimulation than on stimulation of individual perceptual systems. Thus, the aim of the two experiments reported below was to show that in moving rooms participants responded more to intermodal information than to optical patterns *per se*. In order to do this, we manipulated, independently of the room's motion, the postural stability of participants standing inside an oscillating room. We tested the effect of this manipulation on the coupling between body sway and room motion.

Experiment 1

Method

Subjects (N = 9) stood upright in the middle of a moving room, and were instructed to watch a map pasted on the back wall. The room had three sides (2.2 m) and a ceiling, was mounted on four wheels and was electronically moved with a sinusoidal motion (forward-backward, frequency = 0.2 Hz, amplitude = 2 cm). Data were recorded by a magnetic tracking system (Ascension Flock of Bird) with one bird attached to the room and the other to the subject's head. Two stability conditions were tested. In the *stable* condition, participants stood erect on a rigid horizontal surface. In the *unstable* condition, the same surface was tilted 20° and the participants were instructed to stand on the slope. Care was taken in placing the feet on the slope so that the subject's head was at the same location in space in both conditions. Ten trials of one minute were run in both conditions, in a random order counterbalanced between participants.

Results

As indicated in Figure 1, a reliable coupling (mean R = .40) was found between subject and room movements in the two conditions. However, this coupling was stronger in the unstable condition than in the stable condition: (Z-transformed) cross-correlations were higher in the unstable condition, $F(1,8)$ = 8.54, $p < .05$, as was the gain, $F(1,8)$ = 6.40, $p < .05$. No sign of adaptation was found during the experiment. These results thus indicated that postural instability increased the strength of the coupling between head and room.

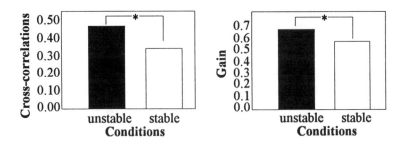

Figure 1. Cross-correlations (left) and gain (right) between head and room in Experiment 1.

Experiment 2

Results of Experiment 1 indicated that, for the amplitude tested (2 cm), postural instability increased the coupling between head and room. We next sought to extend these results with a larger range of room's amplitudes.

Method

Apparatus and data analysis were the same as in Experiment 1. Five amplitudes of room's motion were tested in both stability conditions: 2 cm, 7 cm, 12 cm, 17 cm and 22 cm (frequency = 0.2 Hz). Two 1-min. trials were performed in each condition, yielding a total of 20 trials per subject ($N = 10$).

Results

As evidenced in Figure 2, we observed a rapid decrease in cross-correlations as the room's amplitude increased, $F(4,36) = 2.60$, $p = .05$. For the gain, a significant effect was found for Amplitude, $F(4,36) = 65.16$, $p < .01$, for Stability, $F(1,9) = 10.77$, $p < .01$, as well as for the Amplitude x Stability interaction, $F(4,36) = 4.35$, $p < .01$. Post-hoc Newman-Keuls analyses indicated that stable and unstable conditions were significantly different from each other only for the smallest amplitude (2 cm). Hence, the difference between stable and unstable conditions observed in Experiment 1 disappeared as the amplitude of the room increased.

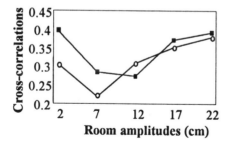 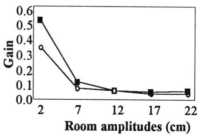

Figure 2. Cross-correlations (left) and gain (right) between head and room in Experiment 2 (squares are for unstable trials, open circles for stable trials).

Conclusion

Taken together, these results indicate that postural instability increases the strength of the coupling between perception and movement during natural sway (2 cm). Because the optical pattern resulting from the motion of the room was the same in the two stability conditions, this suggests that intermodal information about balance was used in the control of stance. Moreover, the necessity to keep the body erect led to a decrease in the coupling as the optical perturbation exceeded the postural capacities of the participants. Again, this suggests an intermodal specification of stance. Relations between visual, vestibular and somato-sensory systems seem therefore to change as a function of the stability of the postural system.

Acknowledgments.   Preparation of this article was supported by the Franco-American Commission for Educational Exchange. We would like to acknowledge Tom Stoffregen who is associated with this project.

References

Gibson, J. J. (1952). The relation between visual and postural determinants of the phenomenal vertical. *Psychological Review, 59*, 370-375.
Lishman, J. R., & Lee, D. N. (1973). The autonomy of visual kinaesthesis. *Perception, 2*, 287-294.
Stoffregen, T. A., & Bardy, B. G. (1997). *Perception across the senses.* Manuscript in preparation.

Studies in Perception and Action IV
M. A. Schmuckler & J. M. Kennedy (Eds.)
© *1997 Lawrence Erlbaum Associates, Inc.*

Postural Stabilization Of Visual Fixation

Thomas A. Stoffregen & L. J. Smart

Department of Psychology, University of Cincinnati, Cincinnati, OH, U.S.A.

Lee & Lishman (1975) reported that the influence of vision on posture was a function of the distance to the visible surroundings. When participants looked at a distant wall, postural motion had a relatively large amplitude. When they fixated a nearby object, postural motion decreased. Lee & Lishman (1975) argued that in the distant condition a larger postural motion was needed before the visual system would produce a compensatory postural response. In other words, Lee & Lishman interpreted the distance effect as a threshold effect; this interpretation has been accepted by later researchers (Dijkstra et. al., 1992; Paulus et al., 1989). One implication of this interpretation is that when there are both near and far objects, posture should always be controlled relative to the near object.

The threshold interpretation is consistent with widely held beliefs about posture and postural control. One is that posture is an autonomous system; that postural control is primary to or independent of other behavior. This is associated with the implicit belief that postural control is defined as the activity of maintaining the center of mass over the base of support, and that the goal of postural control is to minimize postural sway. Another is that when optical flow is present the "postural control system" will always seek to minimize it. We propose an alternate view. If the purpose of postural control is to facilitate supra-postural perception and action (Riccio & Stoffregen, 1988), then the definition of "acceptable" postural motion will vary with differences in supra-postural tasks. In this view, postural motion would not be keyed to the nearest object in sight. Rather it should be related to the object of regard: Rather then being controlled in a task-independent manner, postural sway would be adjusted to fit the needs of different fixation tasks. We evaluated this hypothesis by replicating the experiment of Lee & Lishman (1975), with the addition of a new condition.

Experiment 1

Method

Participants stood in a large room. Their postural motion was measured using a magnetic tracking system (Ascension Flock of Birds). In the Far Target condition, participants looked at a target attached to a wall 3.26 m distant, with no nearby objects. In the Near Target condition participants looked at an object 0.4 m distant. In the Near-Far condition participants ignored the nearby object and looked at the distant target. The nearby and far targets had the same visual angle (18.2° vertical by 11.6°), and were placed so that switching fixation from one to the other required no head movement and minimal ocular adjustment. Participants were instructed to "stare intently" at the designated target. Eight participants completed four 60 s trials in each condition.

Results

We measured the RMS (root mean square) deviation of Anterior-Posterior head position. The data are presented in Figure 1. A 1-within ANOVA revealed a significant effect of conditions. Post-hoc Newman-Keuls tests revealed that in the Near Target condition, participants swayed significantly less than in the other two conditions. The Far Target and Near-Far conditions did not differ from each other.

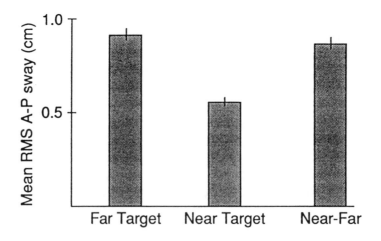

Figure 1. Results of Experiment 1.

Experiment 2

We next sought to extend the fixation effect to a situation having different constraints on visual stability. In experiment 1 greater vergence adjustments were required for the Near Target condition. With monocular viewing this fixation-specific constraint on visual stability would be removed.

Method

The method was the same as in Experiment I; the only difference being that viewing was monocular.

Results

Data are presented in Figure 2. An ANOVA revealed a significant effect of conditions, and post-hoc tests again revealed that participants swayed less in the Near Target condition than in the two other conditions. The Far Target and Near-Far conditions did not differ from each other.

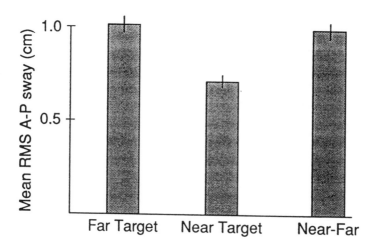

Figure 2. Results of Experiment 2.

Discussion

The Far Target and Near Target conditions replicate the findings of Lee and Lishman (1975) and Dijkstra et al. (1992). However, the results of the Near-Far condition cast these earlier data in a very different light. Our participants did not tune their postural control to the nearest available surface, as would be expected if posture were stabilized by optical flow in an automatic fashion. Rather, posture was controlled with respect to differences in fixation, independent of distance to the surround. This suggests that "postural stability" does not have a single definition. Instead, stability is defined in terms of specific supra-postural tasks (Riccio & Stoffregen, 1988).

References

Dijkstra, T. M. H., Gielen, C. C. A. M., & Melis, B. J. M. (1992). Postural responses to stationary and moving scenes as a function of distance to the scene. *Human Movement Science, 11,* 195-203.

Lee, D. N., & Lishman, J. R. (1975). Visual proprioceptive control of stance. *Journal of Human Movement Studies, 1,* 87-95.

Paulus, W., Straube, A., Krafszyk, S., & Brandt T. (1989). Differential effects of retinal target displacement, changing size and changing disparity in the control of anterior/posterior and lateral body sway. *Experimental Brain Research, 78,* 243-252.

Riccio, G. E., & Stoffregen, T. A. (1988). Affordances as constraints on the control of stance. *Human Movement Science, 7,* 265-300.

Studies in Perception and Action IV
M. A. Schmuckler & J. M. Kennedy (Eds.)
© *1997 Lawrence Erlbaum Associates, Inc.*

Interlimb Frequency Coupling Patterns During Locomotion

Richard E. A. van Emmerik[1], Robert C. Wagenaar[2], & Erwin E. H. van Wegen[1]

[1] Department of Exercise Science, University of Massachusetts, U.S.A.
[2] Department of Physical Therapy, Vrije Universiteit Hospital, Amsterdam, The Netherlands

Previous studies on the dynamics of interlimb coupling have investigated effects of physical asymmetries between oscillators through manipulation of natural frequency differences (Kugler & Turvey, 1987). With increasing asymmetry a more distinct tendency towards relative coordination with increasing phase fluctuations has been observed (e.g., Schmidt et al., 1991). These kind of changes could arise not only from imposed physical (e.g., mass and length) differences between oscillators, but also from different inherent spectroscopic components due to tremors. Iberall (1992) has stressed the importance of spectroscopic analysis at different time scales. In Parkinson's Disease (PD) patients, there is an increase in the power of the spectral range between 3-7 Hz due to tremor.

The present paper is an expansion of earlier work (Wagenaar & van Emmerik, 1994), and examines changes in arm-leg coupling with aging and PD, and the contribution of higher and lower spectral frequency components on this coupling. We address the following questions: 1) What are the predominant coupling frequencies between arms and legs? 2) What is the stability of the coupling under imposed velocity manipulations? and 3) How do tremor asymmetries affect the symmetry of the coupling between body sides?

Method

Three groups were examined, namely 1) a healthy young group (HY; N=7, mean age 25 years), 2) a healthy older group (HO; N=10, mean age 65.6), and 3) a Parkinson's Disease group (PD; N=14, mean age 66.2). Movements of arms and legs were recorded through accelerometry (Coulbourn T-45).

Walking velocity was continuously increased on a treadmill from 0.2 to 1.2 m/s in steps of 0.2 m/s (step duration 30 sec). From spectral analysis were obtained: a) the arm/leg frequency ratio based on the dominant frequencies in the 0-3 Hz range; b) the contribution of higher frequency tremor components based on the mean power in the 3-7 and 7-12 Hz ranges in the arm; and c) arm-leg coupling asymmetry between less affected and more affected body side based on the arm power in the 3-7 Hz range.

Results

Figure 1 depicts the percentage of occurrence of frequency couplings in the three groups. For the PD and HY groups, the dominant pattern at lower speeds is a 1:2 coupling of leg to arm. For the HO group both 1:2 and 1:1 couplings are equally prominent. Changes to a dominant 1:1 coupling occur at about 0.5-0.6 m/s in the PD and HO groups, whereas the HY group switches around 0.8-0.9 m/s. These data suggest that the arm-leg coupling in the younger subjects is more stable, as it switches at a higher walking velocity.

Figure 2 presents within-subject coupling ratio variability to further explore these stability differences. Frequency coupling stability was highest in

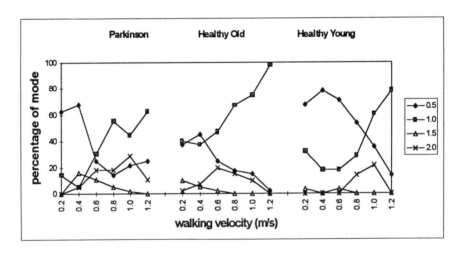

Figure 1. Changes in dominance of frequency coupling modes as a function of walking velocity. Results are from between-subjects comparisons. The frequency ratios plotted (0.5, 1.0, 1.5, 2.0, leg:arm ratio) account for close to 100% of all possible modes.

the HY and lowest in the PD group. For the PD group there was also a decrease in coupling ratio variability with walking velocity. Asymmetry between less and more affected side is largest in the PD group and smallest in the HY group (Table 1), although this asymmetry decreases with walking velocity (Figure 2).

Discussion

The present data show that higher frequency components (e.g., due to tremor) in the arm during locomotion can affect stability and symmetry of arm-leg coordination. The differences between healthy and Parkinsonian subjects show that the larger the pathological tremor, the less stable the coupling, and the larger the asymmetry between body sides. There were also systematic differences between the older and younger subjects. These were not due to larger contributions in the classical pathological tremor range, but to larger powers in the 7-12 Hz range (see Table 1). From the stability and symmetry data presented, it appears that the power increase in the 7-12 Hz range had a smaller effect on the coordination dynamics than the increase in the 3-7 Hz range.

In conclusion, the present experiment has shown that increased contribution of higher frequency components (both related to disease and aging) can reduce stability and increase asymmetry of interlimb coordination during locomotion. Scaling walking velocity as a control parameter, however, can reduce the effects of these higher frequency components in the individual oscillators.

Table 1

Power in 3-7 and 7-12 Hz Spectral Frequency Ranges (Arbitrary Units) and Asymmetry in Frequency Coupling, Averaged Across Velocity and Subjects.

| | Power 3-7 Hz | | Power 7-12 Hz | | Asymmetry in frequency coupling |
	More Affected	Less Affected	More Affected	Less Affected	
Parkinson	4.56	2.42	1.00	0.76	0.61
Healthy Old	2.10	1.43	0.68	0.65	0.34
Healthy Young	1.76	1.43	0.28	0.27	0.18

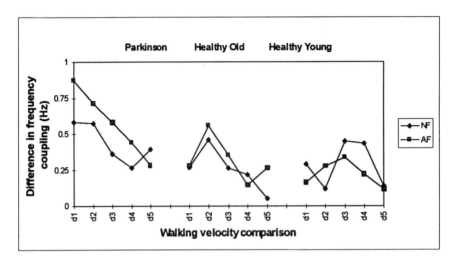

Figure 2. Average (across subjects) changes in between-velocity fluctuations in frequency coupling. d1-d5 identify speed comparisons, namely d1 = 0.2-0.4, d2 = 0.4-0.6, d3 = 0.6-0.8, d4 = 0.8-1.0, d5 = 1.0-1.2. NF = less affected side; AF = more affected side.

References

Iberall, A. S. (1992). Does intention have a fast characteristic time scale? *Ecological Psychology, 4,* 39-61.

Kugler, P. N., & Turvey, M. T. (1987). *Information, natural law, and the self-assembly of rhythmic movement.* Hillsdale, NJ: Erlbaum.

Schmidt, R. C, Beek, P. J.,Treffner, P. J., & Turvey, M. T. (1991). Dynamical substructure of coordinated rhythmic movements. *Journal of Experimental Psychology: Human Perception and Performance, 17,* 635-651.

Wagenaar, R. C., & van Emmerik, R. E. A. (1994). The dynamics of pathological gait: Stability and adaptability of movement coordination. *Human Movement Science, 13,* 441-471.

Studies in Perception and Action IV
M. A. Schmuckler & J. M. Kennedy (Eds.)
© 1997 Lawrence Erlbaum Associates, Inc.

The Intentional On-Line Control Of Walking Speed

F. Danion, M. Bonnard, & J. Pailhous

UMR Mouvement et Perception, CNRS, Université de la Méditerranée,
Faculté des Sciences du Sport, Marseille, France

It is well-known that human gait can adapt to very different dynamic contexts, such as walking on incline ground (Patla, 1986), with added masses (Bonnard & Pailhous, 1991), or against wind (Pugh, 1971). However very little is known about its on-line adaptive capabilities, that is, the capability to manage continuous variation in the external force field. As the external force field varies continuously, walking the same way poses a rather complex problem because, at each joint, on-line adaptation of the motor command is required to organize a generalized muscle torque capable of compensating for the continuous change in the external force. This capability to control and modulate intentionally the propulsive forces is fundamental for the adaptation of the body's progression, both in speed and direction. The purpose of this experiment was to determine how human beings can achieve such control on-line while facing with dynamic change in the environment.

Method

Four subjects walking steadily on a treadmill (torque controlled by a computer) were faced with a linear increase in resistance (impeding forward displacement) lasting three seconds, once per minute. The initial resistance corresponded to a normal external force (about 0.6 W kg^{-1} at 1.3 m s^{-1} according to Cavagna et al., 1976) whereas the final resistance was chosen to require a substantial increase in the traction power for walking at the same speed (about +50 %). At the end of the variation, the new resistance was maintained. The rate of change was designed such that on-line compensation was necessary within each cycle (otherwise significant alteration in kinematics would occur) without causing irreparable modification in the trajectory (as it is the case when using instantaneous perturbations). There were two tasks. As the resistance increased, subjects were either required to maintain their walking speed (compensation task) or to let the walking speed and amplitude adapt freely (no-intervention task). The latter provided an estimate of the effects of the perturbation alone. Throughout the experiment, the stride frequency (114 step min^{-1}) was fixed by a metronome.

Results

Subjects maintained their stride frequency on both tasks. As shown in Figure 1, in the no-intervention task, as the resistance began to increase, the subjects slowed down until 1.05 m s^{-1} (-22 %) whereas their effort remained relatively unchanged. In the compensation task, a similar decrease in walking speed was observed at the beginning of the perturbation, but it was slight (-2 %) and temporary. This slowing down stopped at cycle 3, and at cycle 4 the walking speed was back to its initial value. Figure 1B shows that this was achieved by an increase in traction power beginning suddenly at cycle 3. By contrast, during the following cycles, even at the end of the resistance increase, no such changes in speed were observed.

Discussion

The results observed in the compensation task show that the subjects are able to compensate for the effects of a continuous variation in the external force. This performance could never have been observed without a fine control of the propulsive forces within the stance phase. We suggest that the subjects used two different modes of control during steady states and transitional phases. In stable dynamic conditions, there appears to be an "intermittent control" mode, where propulsive forces are globally managed for the entire stance phase. As a result, no compensation occurred at the beginning of the perturbation. During the resistance increase, subjects appeared to switch from cycle 3 to an "on-line control" mode in order to continuously adapt the propulsive forces to the time course of the external force, so that no increase of walking speed was observed at the end of the perturbation.

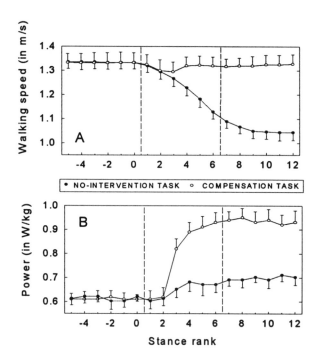

Figure 1. Time course of the mean walking speed (A) and traction power (B) of the group during the successive walking cycles observed as the resistance increased in the no-intervention and compensation tasks. The intervals between vertical lines correspond to the increase in resistance. All trials were aligned with the first stance performed entirely during the variation in resistance. For each parameter, and each cycle, between-subjects standard deviations are shown.

References

Bonnard, M., & Pailhous, J. (1991). Intentional compensation for selective loading affecting gait phases. *Journal of Motor Behavior, 23,* 4-12.

Cavagna, G. A., Thys, H., & Zamboni, A. (1976). The sources of external work in level walking and running. *Journal of Physiology, 262,* 639-657.

Patla, A. E. (1986). Effects of walking on various inclines on EMG pattern of lower limb muscles in humans. *Human Movement Science, 5,* 345-357.

Pugh, L. G. C. E. (1971). The influence of wind resistance in running and walking and the mechanical efficiency of work against horizontal or vertical forces. *Journal of Physiology, 213,* 255-276.

Studies in Perception and Action IV
M. A. Schmuckler & J. M. Kennedy (Eds.)
© 1997 Lawrence Erlbaum Associates, Inc.

The Visual Guidance Of Blind Walking: Information And Individual Differences

Richard A. Tyrrell[1], Melanie A. Pearson[1] & Jeffrey T. Andre[2]

[1] Department of Psychology, Clemson University, Clemson, SC, U.S.A.

[2] Department of Psychology, Franklin & Marshall College, Lancaster, PA, U.S.A.

Observation of mobile animals suggests that such animals' gaze need not be limited to their path. For example, predators are able to track their prey visually while navigating through their surroundings, and human drivers are able to look away from the roadway ahead while still maintaining their position within the proper lane. Some sort of spatial memory must be responsible for the ability to move through areas that were seen moments earlier. Tyrrell, Rudolph, Eggers, & Leibowitz (1993), among others, tested the hypothesis that the information that facilitates visual guidance persists and is useful for some time after the stimulus is removed. In that study, participants viewed a straight path (34 cm wide, 10 m long) for 10 seconds. They were then blindfolded and asked to stand still for a predetermined period. Immediately following this occlusion time, the blindfolded participants were asked to walk the path as best they could. Each participants' performance was defined as the distance he or she walked prior to first stepping outside the path. Performance gradually and significantly worsened with increasing occlusion times, suggesting that the information that supports visual guidance persists and gradually decays. The slow decay (i.e., a half-life of roughly 30 seconds) suggests that the visual guidance information persists long enough to be useful for supporting locomotion. Two experiments are now presented that further explore this effect.

Experiment 1

One explanation for the main effect of occlusion time on walking performance involves a progressive decline in the ability to remember the direction of straight ahead. That is, after long occlusion times, participants could be successfully walking in a misperceived direction. An alternative explanation is that while the ability to remember the direction of straight ahead remains intact, there is a decrease in the ability to walk in that direction. Experiment 1 tested these opposing explanations.

Method

Eighteen undergraduate and graduate students (mean age = 23.2) volunteered. During each trial, the participant aligned his or her feet with the path, viewed the path (10 m x .34 m) for 10 seconds, and was then blindfolded and instructed to stand still until he or she was told to "begin pointing," at which point he or she was instructed to point a laser straight down the path. A small laser had been mounted on the end of a rod that was positioned in the median plane at waist height. The rod pivoted at the participant's waist; the participant placed one hand on the pivot point and used their other hand to aim the laser. In a random order, each participant performed the task four times at each of seven occlusion times (ranging from 2 to 128 seconds). Each participant also performed the walking task (described earlier) four times at each of two occlusion times (5 and 60 seconds).

Results and Discussion

As expected, walking performance was significantly worse after the 60 second occlusion time than after the 5 second occlusion time ($p < .001$). However, neither pointing accuracy nor pointing precision was affected by occlusion time ($p > .10$): Performance after more than two minutes of occlusion was no worse than it was after just two seconds of occlusion (see Figure 1). Thus, although a time-sensitive mechanism mediates blind walking performance, this same mechanism does not mediate pointing performance. After a long period of occlusion, subjects are less able to walk straight ahead even though they are able to point in that direction. This suggests that walking performance is not limited by the ability to remember the direction of straight ahead, and the decay in performance appears to result from a gradual decrease in the ability to coordinate locomotion with perceptual memory.

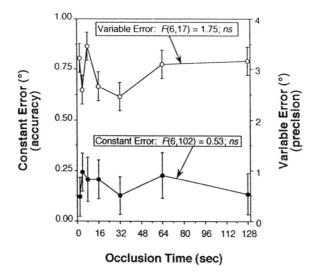

Figure 1. Precision and accuracy with which participants pointed a laser down a straight-ahead path as a function of the occlusion time experienced before pointing was initiated.

Experiment 2

To test whether visual guidance information remains useful for a longer period in some individuals than in others, we compared the performance of athletes and non-athletes on the walking task described above. As they are often required to move in one direction while looking in another, we chose to test soccer players.

Method

Eighteen players from a nationally ranked Division I-A women's soccer team were recruited, as were 18 female non-athletes from an Introductory Psychology class. In a random order, each participant performed the walking task described earlier five times at each of two occlusion times (2 seconds and 64 seconds).

Results

Consistent with earlier results, both groups performed worse after the longer occlusion time (for non-athletes, $t(17) = 3.65$, $p = .001$; for athletes, $t(17)$

Tyrrell, Pearson, & Andre

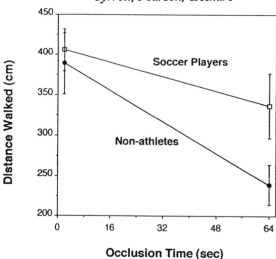

Figure 2. Mean distance (± 1 standard error) that soccer players and non-athletes successfully walked down a narrow straight-ahead path as a function of the occlusion time experienced before walking was initiated.

= 1.99, p = .031). After the short occlusion time, the performance of the athletes did not significantly differ from the non-athletes ($t(29)$ = 0.34, p > .10). However, after the long occlusion time the performance of the non-athletes was significantly worse than that of the athletes (see Figure 2, $t(29)$ = 2.13, p = .042).

Discussion

The fact that the athletes' performance was superior to the non-athletes only after the longer occlusion time suggests that the group difference cannot be explained simply by superior motor skills in athletes. Further, these results confirm earlier evidence (Tyrrell et al., 1993) that reliable individual differences exist in the degree to which visual guidance information remains useful following visual occlusion. Visual guidance information remains useful longer in soccer players than in non-athletes.

References

Tyrrell, R. A., Rudolph, K. K., Eggers, B. G., & Leibowitz, H. W. (1993). Evidence for the persistence of visual guidance information. *Perception & Psychophysics, 54,* 431-438.

Studies in Perception and Action IV
M. A. Schmuckler & J. M. Kennedy (Eds.)
© 1997 Lawrence Erlbaum Associates, Inc.

Motor Strategies In Landing From Jumps of Different Heights

Takeshi Sato & Masami Miyazaki

Department of Health Sciences, Waseda University, Tokyo, Japan

A motor performance which involves multijoint coordination and belongs to the natural repertoire of motor behavior has been studied. Before describing neuromuscular adaptations during the acquisition of muscle strength, power and motor tasks, a brief review of neuromuscular physiology will be provided. Human muscle studies have been performed under a variety of experimental conditions, and the electromyographic (EMG) signal has quite often been used as a means of assessment of muscle activity (Moritani, 1993). The control of movement in landing has been analyzed extensively in humans (Van Ingen Schenau et al., 1985) as well as in animals (Dietz et al., 1981). In landing performances, the leg extensor muscles are activated before ground contact of the feet.

It is known that surface EMG may be used to quantify the total activity of working muscles. Previous studies have reported that a progressive increase in integrated EMG (iEMG) occurs when dynamic muscle contractions are landed from higher jumps. Thus, the iEMG has been widely accepted as a means of assessing muscle activity and in some studies the rate of iEMG changes. The purpose of this study was to investigate the neuromuscular control of the leg muscles in landing from different heights. The modulation of pre-landing muscle activity was assessed by recording the superficial EMG.

Method

Subjects. Eleven physically active females volunteered for the study. Their age was 22.1 (SD 4.6) years, the mean height was 159 (SD 5) cm and mean body weight was 46.3 (SD 3.6) Kg. All of them were fully informed of the procedures and appraised of all possible risks involved in the study.

Experimental procedure. The measurements were done in an air-conditioned room. The subjects landed onto a force plate from three different heights, 30, 60, 85 cm, respectively.

EMG recordings. EMG activity from m. gastrocnemius cap. Medialis (GA), m. vastus lateralis (VL), m. tibialis anterior (TA), and m. soelus (SOL) of the right leg was recorded with a sampling frequency of 1500 Hz. Bipolar surface electrodes with a constant electrode distance of 20 mm were fixed longitudinally on each muscle belly and the electrode places were marked carefully. EMG activity was amplified and recorded telemetrically (RE2000, Nihon Kohden, Japan) simultaneously with landing force signals from the force plates on a DAT data recorder (PC118, Sonny, Japan). The EMG signal transmitter was fixed with a belt around the waist of each of the subjects. The total extra load for the subject was 0.5 kg.

Ground reaction forces. The subjects landed from 30, 60, and 85 cm height onto a 0.60 m × 1.00 m square-type force platform. The vertical components of the ground reaction force (GRF) were stored on a DAT tape recorder for future analysis by a computer.

Data analysis. The VXI device with a personal computer system was employed for analog-to-digital conversion and future treatment of the data. The sampling frequency of analog to digital conversion was 1500 Hz per channel. Nonsmoothed EMG signals were rectified, integrated, and averaged (AEMG) for each landing trial. The AEMG was calculated for each muscle separately and as an average of the four muscles recorded.

Statistics. Conventional methods were used to calculate means, standard deviations, and correlation coefficients.

Results

Ground reaction forces. The raw EMG of the four measured muscles and force curves of the landings from the three different heights are shown in Figure 1. Mean values for percent of relative GRF were 100 (30cm), 140.8 (60cm), and 213.6 (85cm), respectively.

EMG activities. EMG analysis of the four measured muscles revealed that that AEMG of the TA increased significantly (see Figure 2) from 30cm to 85cm in landing ($p < .05$) while no significant changes were found in the other three muscles. As a result of the changes in the GRF and the EMG activity of all the measured muscles, the AEMG/force ratio increased from 30cm to 60cm height. Pre-activation of EMG starting 150msec before landing impact had a tendency to increase as the jumping height increased.

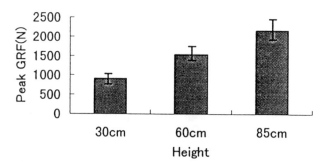

Figure 1. Change in peak ground reaction force for the three different heights.

Discussion

The present study was aimed at investigating landing performance in three different height conditions. The GRF depends on the body weight and jumping height.

According to previous studies (Sidaway et al., 1989) which have examined the inverse of an image across the retina, it was responsible for muscle pre-activation prior to landing impact. It has been shown that preparatory activity of the rectus femoris muscle occurred at an earlier phase to ground contact with increasing height of drop jump. Under 60cm landing requires a complex sequencing of lower-limb muscle activation. However all muscle activity was not increased as the landing force increased. Moreover pre-activation before landing was observed in all measured muscles, not achieving a statistically significant interaction. It was suggested that strategies for triggering pre-landing EMG were mutable and may depend on availability of sensory modalities.

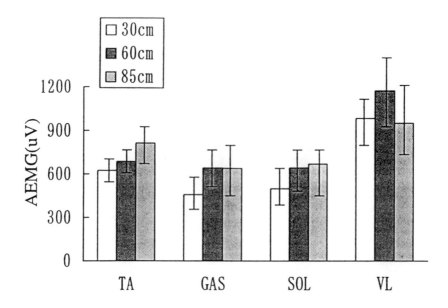

Figure 2. AEMG of each muscle during impact and push-off phase of landing.

References

Dietz, V., Noth, J., & Schmidtbleicher, D. (1981). Interaction between preactivity and stretch reflex in human triceps brachii during landing from forward falls. *Journal of Physiology, 311,* 113-125

Moritani, T. (1993). Neuromuscular adaptations during the acquisition of muscle strength, power and motor tasks. *Journal of Biomechanics, 26,* 95-107

Sidaway, B., McNitt, G. J., & Davis, G. (1989). Visual timing of muscle preactivation in preparation for landing. *Ecological Psychology, 1,* 253-264

Van Ingen Schenau, G. J., Bobbert, M. F., Huijing, P.A., & Woitiez, R. D. (1985). The instantaneous torque-angular velocity relation in plantar flexion during jumping. *Medicine Sciences and Sports Exercise, 17,* 422-426.

Studies in Perception and Action IV
M. A. Schmuckler & J. M. Kennedy (Eds.)
© *1997 Lawrence Erlbaum Associates, Inc.*

Temporal Stabilities Of The Bipedal Galloping Pattern

Andrew J. Peck

CESPA, University of Connecticut, Storrs, CT, U.S.A.

In the primary bipedal form of locomotion limbs move in an alternating fashion, as in walking and running, although other forms may be selected based on volition or constraints. In the bipedal gallop the legs are configured such that one leg, the *lead* leg, is in front of the other leg, the *back* leg, throughout the entire step cycle (Whitall, 1989). The interlimb phasing of the gallop, measured as the proportion of a limb cycle when the footstrike occurs on the contralateral limb, is approximately 66% compared to the 50% that characterizes the walk and the run.

The main goals of the present research are twofold: to determine (1) the stability of the gallop pattern relative to the stabilities of the putatively more basic walking/running and jumping patterns, and (2) the coordination dynamics that contains the gallop pattern as one of its stable modes.

Research of bipedal locomotory patterns at the level of synergies (Turvey & Carello, 1996) has yielded an equation of motion which accomodates characteristics of bipedal walking and jumping, but not galloping (Kelso, Delcolle, & Schöner, 1990):

$$\dot{\phi} = \Delta\omega - a \sin(\phi) - 2b \sin(2\phi) + \sqrt{Q}\xi_t, \tag{1}$$

where the rate of change of the relative phase (ϕ) between two oscillating limbs is a function of the frequency competition between the two individual oscillators, $\Delta\omega$, a 2π periodic coupling term with the coefficients b/a determining the relative strengths of the attractors in the equation at $\phi = 0$ and $\phi = \pi$, and a stochastic forcing term arising from the multiplicity of interactions among the underlying subsystems (Figure 1a). The repellor at $\pi/2$, corresponding to interlimb phasing of $\approx 100°$, in Equation (1) is transformed into an attractor, while preserving the archetypal attractors at $0°$ and $\pm 180°$, with the addition of the next two odd Fourier series terms (Figure 1b):

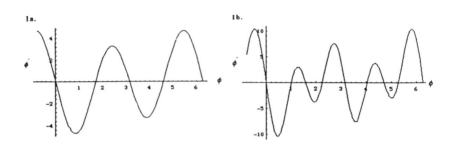

Figure 1. Characterization of motion in bipedal walking and jumping.

$$\dot{\phi} = \Delta\omega - a\ sin\ (\phi) - 2b\ sin\ (2\phi) - 3c\ sin\ (3\phi) - 4d\ sin(4\phi) + \sqrt{Q}\ \xi_t \quad (2)$$

In three experiments, the gallop pattern and the walk/run pattern are compared relative to expectations from Equation (2). Previous research has shown that fixed points of coupled pendular systems with $\Delta\omega \neq 0$ shift in relative phase when coordinated at either 0 or π relative phasing, with the direction and magnitude of the shift proportional to the magnitude and direction of $\Delta\omega$. Expectations of similar influences on the gallop, as predicted from manipulations of $\Delta\omega$ in Equation (3), were confirmed in Experiment 1 results, which yielded a significant fixed point shift of π and $\pi/2$ to 168.32° and -63.01° for $\Delta\omega = -2$ and to 190.45° and -98.65° for $\Delta\omega = 2$ ($\phi = 179.70°$ and -84.03° at $\Delta\omega = 0$ for π and $\pi/2$, respectively; Figure 2a).

Increases in movement frequency, modeled in Equation (1) as a decease in b/a, are associated with loss of stability at fixed points. In Equation (2), an increase in movement frequency, and the resulting loss of stability, is modeled through the decrease in the parameters d/c and actual scaling of movement frequency was expected to yield increases in SDϕ around all three fixed points. Metronome paced increases in movement frequency produced increases in SDϕ for the jump, walk, and gallop. Greatest SDϕ occurred around the gallop (Figure 2b).

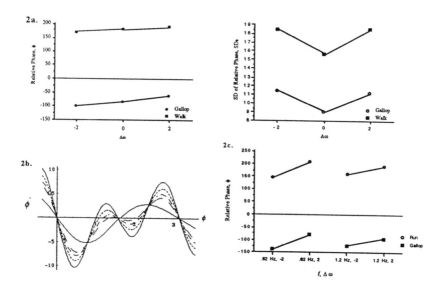

Figure 2. Experimental results.

Movement frequency has been shown to increase fixed point shift resulting from competition between coupled pendulums with different eigenfrequencies for $\phi = 0$ and $\phi = \pi$ (Schmidt & Turvey, 1995). Performance of walk and gallop patterns under conditions of increased movement frequencies and $\Delta\omega \neq 0$ resulted in greater fixed point shifts at higher movement frequencies than lower movement frequencies for both gaits (Figure 2c).

Utilizing a model-independent strategy, one which examines the temporal stability of bipedal gaits without regard for the specifics of limb oscillators and neural mechanisms which underlie actual locomotion, Experiments 1-3 suggest that the coordination dynamic underlying the gallop pattern is a relatively simple extension of the dynamical model underlying the familiar interlimb patterns of in-phase ($\phi = 0$) and anti-phase ($\phi = \pi$).

References

Kelso, J. A. S., Delcolle, J. D., & Schöner, G. (1990). Action-perception as a pattern formation process. In M. Jeannerod (Ed.), *Attention and performance XIII* (pp. 139-169). Hillsdale, NJ: Lawrence Erlbaum Associates.

Schmidt, R. C., & Turvey, M. T. (1995). Models of interlimb coordination—Equilibria, local analyses, and spectral patterning: Comment on Fuchs and Kelso (1994). *Journal of Experimental Psychology: Human Perception and Performance, 21,* 432-443.

Turvey, M. T., & Carello, C. (1996). Dynamics of Bernstein's level of synergies. In M. Latash & M. T. Turvey (Eds.), *Dexterity and its development* (pp. 339-376). Hillsdale, NJ: Lawrence Erlbaum Associates.

Whitall, J. (1989). A developmental study of the interlimb coordination in running and galloping. *Journal of Motor Behavior, 21,* 409-428.

Author Index

Keyword Index